MW00991300

Twinkle, Twinkle, Little Star

Twinkle, Twinkle, Little Star

but don't have sex or take the car

Dick Moore

HARPER & ROW, PUBLISHERS, New York

Cambridge, Philadelphia, San Francisco,
London, Mexico City, São Paulo, Sydney
1817

Permission is gratefully acknowledged for:

The lines from "Oh, How I Hate to Get Up in the Morning," by Irving Berlin. Copyright 1918 by Irving Berlin. Copyright renewed 1945 by Irving Berlin. Copyright assigned to Mrs. Ralph J. Bunche, Joe DiMaggio and Theodore R. Jackson and their successors as trustees of the God Bless America Fund. Reprinted by permission of Irving Berlin Music Corporation.

The lines from "In My Arms," by Frank Loesser and Ted Grouya. Copyright 1943 by Frank Music Corp. Copyright renewed 1971 by Frank Music Corp. International copyright secured. All rights reserved. Used by permission.

Photo credits follow the Index.

FIRST EDITION

Designer: Charlotte Staub

Library of Congress Cataloging in Publication Data

Moore, Dick, 1925–
Twinkle, twinkle, little star.

Includes index.
1. Moving-picture actors and actresses—United States—Biography. 2. Children as actors. 3. Moore, Dick, 1925– . I. Title.
PN1998.A2M554 1984 791.43'028'0922 84-47590
ISBN 0-06-015349-0

84 85 86 87 88 10 9 8 7 6 5 4 3 2 1

Contents

Acknowledgments vii
Foreword ix
1 Fade In 1
2 At Home with the Folks 27
3 "Lights! Camera! Action!" 51
4 "Sparkle, Shirley!" 79
5 Stay Young and Don't Get Sick 101
6 Time to Study, Time to Play 117
7 Grownups Run the Show 138
8 Standouts and Bugbears 167
9 Our Pay and What Happened to It 185
10 Sex Can Wait? 210
11 After Stardom, What? 230
12 Living in the Real World 254
13 Fade Out 279

Index 295

Acknowledgments

My thanks and love to those who allowed me to take them with me on this journey; who shared with me their memories, feelings, and opinions; who gave to me their time and creativity.

In the course of preparing this book, I saw, interviewed, and most especially thank Cora Sue Collins, Jackie Coogan, Jackie Cooper, Edith Fellows, Peggy Ann Garner, Lillian Gish, Bonita Granville (Wrather), Darryl Hickman, Sybil Jason, Gloria Jean, Marcia Mae Jones, Spanky McFarland, Sidney Miller, Kathleen Nolan, Margaret O'Brien, Donald O'Connor, Baby Peggy (Diana Cary), Juanita Quigley, Gene Reynolds, Mickey Rooney, Ann Rutherford, Dean Stockwell, Stymie (Matthew Beard), Shirley Temple (Black), Bobs Watson, Delmar Watson, Jane Withers, Natalie Wood.

Each of them is special in a very special way.

Joe Vergara deserves particular acknowledgment for his valuable help. My thanks, too, to David Peretz, Helaine Feldman,

Helene Besser, Dorothy Spears, Adele Greene, Lois Hicks, Eric Benson, Gene Feldman, Marvin Paige—and to those friends who gave encouragement and insight.

To Roddy McDowall I owe an extra measure of appreciation.

Finally, to my love, Jane Powell, I owe the most—more than I can ever put into words.

Foreword

At eleven months, I landed my first job. Most of my peers were three or four years old. Others were jobless until eight or ten.

Some of us were local kids. Others descended on Hollywood from Detroit or Cleveland or London or Atlanta. A number spent several years developing their talents before tackling Hollywood. Usually, they took their families with them.

In the main, we were Depression kids who supported our families, frequently our studios, occasionally the entire movie industry, and at least once—according to President Franklin Roosevelt—the nation. "As long as our country has Shirley Temple," FDR reportedly said, "we will be all right."

The 1930s and early 1940s in America were a throwback to the Dickensian era a century earlier, when children were perceived as little adults. Important to Hollywood's economy and to the public's need for escape, each of us was a representation, a cliché: Shirley

Temple and Mickey Rooney were irrepressible little adults who could accomplish more than real adults, and solve their problems. Jane Withers was the tough kid who broke the rules; Elizabeth Taylor, the symbol of beauty and serene perfection; Jackie Coogan, the little ragamuffin who broke your heart; Roddy McDowall and Freddie Bartholomew expressed intelligence and refinement; Stymie of "Our Gang" was the little "pickaninny," the only black among us; Spanky, the fat boy of the Gang, was intended to be laughed at. I was Dickie Moore, innocent and pure, who specialized in reconciling wayward parents and bringing enlightenment to folks like Marlene Dietrich.

Hollywood stars were the closest thing to royalty America produced. So as children we tasted a life immensely privileged, but laced with deprivation.

All of us were extraordinary people at a very early age. All of us shared common lives and times, huge responsibilities, and salaries that shriveled fathers' egos.

Do you recall your homeroom class? Roughly a score or so of children, right? All studying together, kids sorting out life's early clues; assembled briefly, then dispersed by differences in class assignments, neighborhoods, and fathers' jobs.

It was not that way for us. Homeroom was a clutch of tiny, sometimes solo classes strewn from Culver City to Burbank. Spelling and arithmetic spanned whole careers. Our lives touched each other's, drew apart, touched again, receded—waves hissing on a beach. From Lillian Gish to Margaret O'Brien, ours was a class of intimate strangers bound by the common experience of being child stars.

Baby Peggy (her real name was Diana Cary) was, in the early 1920s, Hollywood's first four-year-old self-made millionaire. Her parents probably hold the distinction of running through her money fastest. She was broke at six.

Then came Jackie Coogan, who shares with Shirley Temple the greatest, most enduring fame ever achieved by a child at any age at any time. He was the first child to be merchandised on a national scale. There were Jackie Coogan clothes, Jackie Coogan candy bars, toys—even a Jackie Coogan haircut, which, while copied around the world, could not command a royalty.

Shirley was the first child to carry the full weight of a talking, full-length, "A" picture on her small but willing shoulders. Her every motion picture was a "Shirley Temple picture." It wasn't just a film in which Shirley Temple starred.

When I bestowed her first screen kiss, just after the bombing of Pearl Harbor, the world was watching—literally. The event was recorded on the front page of every major newspaper. My timid peck on her cheek was the symbolic loss of the world's most beloved and famous child, the little girl whose energy, pluck, and irrepressible good cheer allowed folks to forget the Great Depression—at least for ninety minutes.

There will never be another Shirley Temple. Today, there are kids who make a splash, but they will never command the lifelong recognition we still have. Their films are not rerun on television. The continuity of product isn't there. And, in Jackie Coogan's words, "There's nothing charming about children anymore."

Our group is still around. Try today to track the people you shared first grade with. Most have evaporated, raindrops in a desert. Perennially visible, we have no place to hide.

The first scene in *Citizen Kane:* Orson Welles dies and knocks over a glass paperweight filled with swirling snowflakes. "Rosebud," he says, his last word on earth. Everett Sloane, as the newspaper reporter, spends the rest of the film trying to learn what "Rosebud" meant. We find out in the last scene, when they toss the accumulated baggage of Kane's lifetime into a vast incinerator; then we see the sled on which he played as a boy, its painted name, "Rosebud," peeling in the flames. "Rosebud" was a clue to Kane's lost childhood.

Recently, I felt impelled to find my "Rosebud" and those of my fellow child actors. How, I wondered, do their feelings about experiences we shared as children correspond to mine?

How do I approach somebody I may never have met, just

glimpsed across the parking lot, or in a casting office or a studio commissary? What do I write to the guy who desperately wanted the job I got when we were five? Or who beat me out of a juicy part when we were twelve?

Hell, the only way to know is to find out where they are. And tell them what I want to do and why.

Eventually, I interviewed thirty-one people who worked importantly as children in motion pictures. Sure, they said. They'd talk to me.

"The first time I met you, I knew why you were doing this," Jane Powell said later. "You're doing this as a catharsis, for yourself and possibly for the rest of us. Why not be honest and put that down on paper?"

I asked them the questions that had always troubled me. Was their story like mine?

We were two sets of kids, I learned. A few, like Mickey Rooney and Jackie Coogan, came from families of vaudevillians. Donald O'Connor's mother was a circus bareback rider. Performing was second nature to them.

The second set, including me and most of us, were strangers to the business. Our careers were products of what Natalie Wood called our parents' "unfulfilled dreams," and of their wish to have more money.

During the Great Depression, jobs were scarce for our dads. Reliance on our income became the central economic reality in our homes. No one watched the calendar. But careers withered as years passed.

Most parents were not really aware that they and the studios might be exploiting us. "Why, why did you put me in pictures when I was three years old?" Darryl Hickman confronted his mother when in his teens.

"But, dear, it's what you always wanted to do," Mrs. Hickman answered.

Most of us were told that our working would enable us to "afford an education." But formal study on any level was discouraged. Only a handful of us ever got to college. Jackie Coogan, always an original, educated himself by reading the *Encyclopaedia Britannica* six times.

What qualities did the Janes, Jackies, Mickeys, Peggys, and Stymies have in common?

Early intelligence, sharp memories. A shared fear that we would not be valued if we didn't earn a salary. A desperate need to win approval.

Natalie Wood described herself as "energetic," another common quality. But, said Natalie, "in my childhood I felt guilty and very isolated, very shy. There was no grownup I could in any way confide in." Another common theme.

Most of us have grappled with pervasive fears of loneliness and a feeling of responsibility for everyone around us. Walking into a room occupied by silent people, we start a conversation.

Most married at an early age, with no prior sexual experience. Almost invariably those marriages failed.

Whatever our present station, power, or eminence, however we may feel about our world, we are lifelong members of the same fraternity.

"Is there a single 'Rosebud,' Rod, a common denominator?" I asked at the conclusion of an interview.

"Yes, there is," Roddy McDowall said, "and that is a thing I do not wish to face."

"Why not? What is it?"

"It is that they were wrong. They were wrong to take us children and do that with our lives, to twist our environment in that way and then leave it for us to sort out."

We shall see. Our homeroom class still sorts the clues.

We are each a work in progress.

"When you are little,
things look very big."

Jane Powell

1. Fade In

Crisis gripped the set. The scene called for the actors to give the crying infant a bottle filled with wine.

Mother hadn't been aware of that. "You're not going to give my little Dickie wine," she said.

"Don't worry," the director said. "It's only Coca-Cola. We wouldn't give wine to a baby."

"You're not going to give him Coca-Cola, either. He's only eleven months old," said Mother.

So production stopped, one hundred people stood around on salary. Paralysis, Hollywood's most dread disease, suddenly quarantined the set because Mother was protecting my digestion.

John Barrymore, star of the film, who just happened to be on the set that day (he wasn't in this scene), came over to see what the commotion was about. He peered into the crib at me, the kid with the big brown eyes, then announced majestically, "Jesus Christ, it's an owl!"

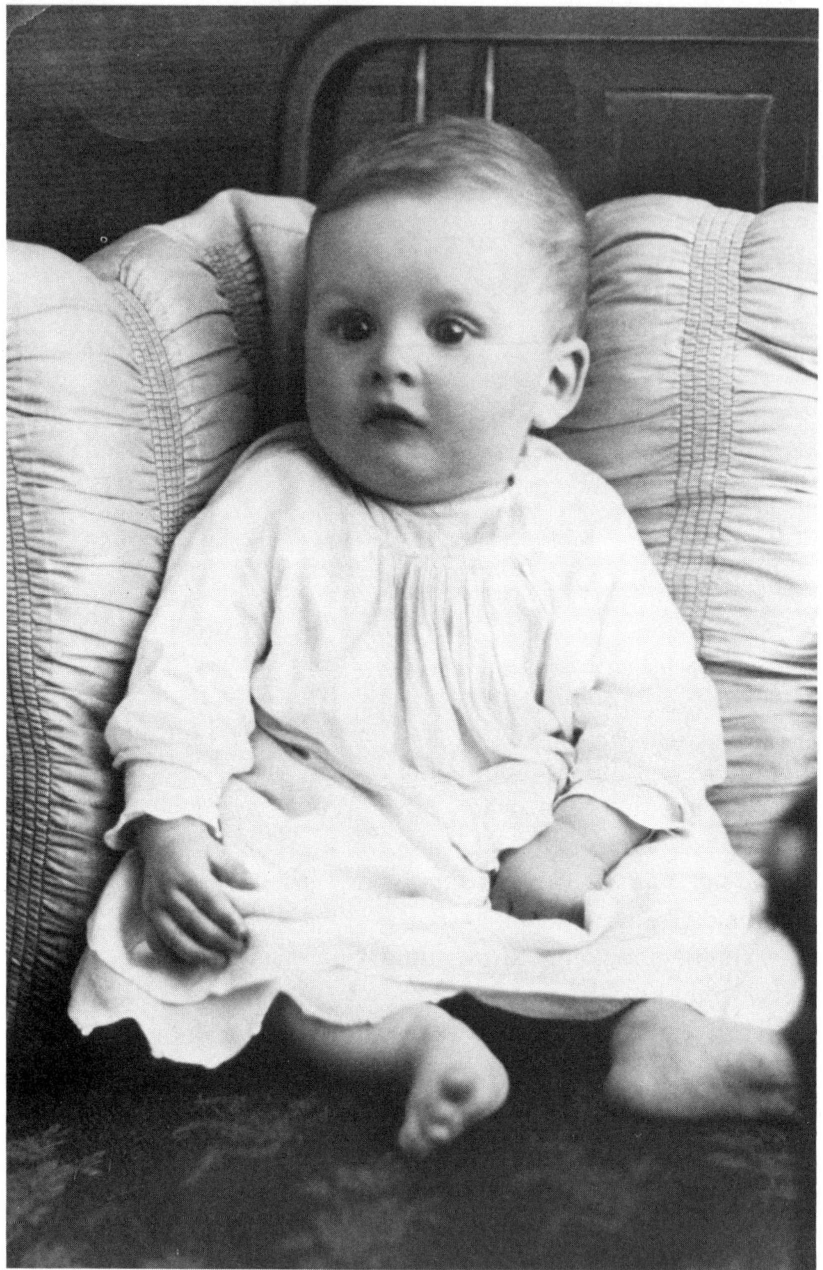

A few months after this photo was taken my career was launched.

The set broke up, but the crisis wasn't over. They were calling in another kid, whose mother wasn't so fussy about his drinking habits, when Mother remembered it was time for my prune juice.

Would you believe it! The cameraman told the director that prune juice photographed exactly like Coca-Cola, which photographed exactly like wine, and since I just happened to be crying anyway, they rolled the camera, the actors handed me the prune juice, and I sucked the bottle greedily.

"Print it," the director said.

I remember none of this, of course. But when you've heard an unremembered incident described repeatedly, you accept it as fact. Like when people haul out the family album: You don't recognize the baby on the bearskin rug, or remember sitting on Grandma's lap with a dozen friends and relatives lined up beside you. But your folks expect you to remember, and they're puzzled that you're not thrilled to relive experiences that have no meaning for you. You learn the family stories because everybody keeps repeating them, and there's nobody around to say they aren't true.

So that's how I became an actor at age eleven months, and everybody but me knew how it really happened.

Why me? How did it all begin?

Aunt Ruth was the catalyst. Not really a relation, but a pseudo aunt—Mother's best friend from when they worked together in a law office before I was born. Why she came to be called "Aunt" I don't know. But she was living with us, even though she had a fine job, especially for a woman in those days. Aunt Ruth was Joseph Schenck's secretary. Joe Schenck ran the "studio."

It rained hard one day and Aunt Ruth's yellow Packard convertible wasn't working, so this friend of hers, the casting director, stopped by the house on his way to work, to pick her up. Mother asked him in for coffee and there was I, in my playpen in the living room. He said, "My, what an adorable child. I think he's just what we're looking for. Have you ever considered letting him appear in pictures?" Mother said she never had, and the man said, "Too bad," and drove to work with Ruth.

He drove Ruth back that night and said he'd been talking to these people at the studio, and judging from his description, they agreed I might be just what they needed—a baby with big brown eyes to play John Barrymore as an infant in *The Beloved Rogue.*

"It's a wonderful opportunity," the casting director emphasized. "It should take only one day and it pays five dollars."

Mother was unmoved. Hollywood was not for me.

The studio, persisting, called the next day. Would Mother please just take me down so they could see if I really looked like John Barrymore as a baby? No commitment was involved. Anyway, the lights weren't hot, so what's to lose?

Aunt Ruth drove us to the studio next morning. They got so excited because I looked so much like John Barrymore must have looked when he was eleven months old—with the big brown eyes and all (his eyes were hazel)—that they offered $7.50 for the day. And all I had to do was lie in a crib and cry for thirty seconds, while the scene established the unfortunate surroundings that the character later played by Barrymore grew up in. Since I cried and slept anyway, why not get paid for it?

So I made my debut as a professional actor. A month later, I celebrated my first birthday.

My first memory is of the frog. And the mud. And the lights, and the camera. I'm wearing short pants and standing in a pit, waist deep in mud. Beside me is the frog. Looking down from the rim of the pit, a mile above, is a large glass eye. There are people milling about, but I can't see them distinctly because bright lights are shining down in my eyes. The bottom of the pit is slippery.

A man's voice, friendly, tells me to look up and then to hit the frog. Suddenly, I'm out of the pit, still covered with mud, talking to a man who calls me "son" and says that he's my father. There are lights and people all around, cables on the floor.

The friendly voice emerges from the maze. Its owner comes to me. "Dickie, can you say, 'Daddy, I'm dirty'? Say that for me, will you?" So I say it for him, and he says that's fine, and would I say it again when he tells me to. Another man spreads more mud on me, cold and wet. I shiver. I call the man Daddy and tell him I'm dirty, and he asks how I fell into the hole and why I was fighting with the frog. The friendly man sitting next to the camera leans forward. "Tell him the frog started it, Dickie." I tell him that the frog started it. "Print it," shouts the friendly man.

Later, I learn that I was three.

Another early scene recalled: Wetting the bed. Father, then unemployed in the Depression, hanging out the sheets to dry while Mother took me to the studio.

We're in an unfamiliar room. Wooden benches line the back. I hang behind my mother, holding her coat. Several other pairs like us, boys and mothers, all standing, face the man who walks toward us down the line, followed by another man, who writes things down.

"What is his salary?" The man points to a boy with bright-red hair.

"Five dollars a day," his mother says. "Stop sucking your thumb," she tells the red-haired boy.

The man moves closer. "How old is he?" he asks of the next boy.

"Six and three-quarters," this boy answers for himself, counting days until he is seven.

"But he just finished a picture where he played five. He's small for his age," his mother says.

My mother's coat is purple, warm and soft.

The man moves closer, pausing in front of the boy next to me. "What does he get by the day?" Five dollars. Everybody gets five dollars.

My turn; he can't see me there behind the coat. Mother brings me forward. The man's shoes are brown and rough. Each has a design shaped like the upper half of a heart, with holes set close together in the leather. Where the soles protrude, I see lots of little ridges, and large stitches in heavy, darker thread. The toes come to a point.

"How old is this child?" the man asks.

"Four." There is a strangeness in my mother's voice, discernible even in the unaccustomed brevity of her reply. The man's shoes have rubber heels.

"What's his salary?"

"Thirty dollars a day." She still sounds odd and tight, but there is a new and sudden flavor in the room. The shoes move backward a few steps, another pair moves toward them. Whispering across the room, silence where we are.

"What is this child's name?" the man asks, louder now.

"His name is Dickie Moore," my mother says, her voice a banner in the breeze. I move back behind her coat.

The men confer in whispers. Occasionally, a few words drift across the room and bend around my mother's coat.

". . . big black eyes . . ." "The age is right, but does he look like Barthelmess?" "Who does . . ." ". . . high cheekbones, too."

Papers rustle. "Our records show that the last time the child worked for us, he made seven dollars and fifty cents."

"It's thirty dollars now," my mother says.

The other kids go home.

One day, my name appeared in print. Mother saved the clipping. Far down in a review in the *Hollywood Reporter*—the local version of the Bible—a critic wrote that a "very cute kid, Dickie Moore, in a few feet delivered only a couple of lines, but had the audience ready to adopt him." The review went on to say that although only about half the picture had sound, the voices were "notably clear." There is promise for these talking pictures, the writer concluded.

"Upon completion of his present assignment at United Artists," *Variety* reported, "Dickie Moore will play a featured part in *The Devil Is Driving*. The young actor moves up to $250 per week on a three-week guarantee."

Soon another story: "Dickie Moore will appear in Bryan Foy's next all-dialogue film to start in June. Foy holds option for two more with the boy at $400 and $500 weekly. Dickie's career is really

With James Cagney and Marian Nixon in *Winner Take All.*

Margaret Sullavan and I quell a slave uprising on our family plantation in *So Red the Rose.*

zooming, and with Jackie Coogan nearly grown up, he is neck and neck with Shirley Temple and Baby LeRoy as one of the busiest children in Hollywood."

Each new part leaves one permanent impression, as though a single frame had been clipped from the nine thousand feet of film that were spliced to make each picture. I am listening to James Cagney tell me how he won the boxing championship of the world; I am crawling through a hole in a fence and tearing my clothes in a futile effort to escape the police; I am begging my grandfather not to kick out my starving mother; I am dying of rabies while Paul Muni desperately attempts to reassure me and effect a cure; climbing over a spiked wall before the Great Dane and the butler find out I am missing; or leading Pat O'Brien, the blind former big league ballplayer, to his Yankee Stadium box for the final game of a World Series (he gets hit on the head by a foul ball and sight returns). I am struggling with the knots in the rope that the gang of outlaws used to truss me up when they escaped; riding with my mother, Barbara Stanwyck, in our horse-drawn vegetable cart to sell our wares at dawn; zipping through the haystack in a runaway car with Stymie, Spanky, and other members of the Gang; sitting in a racing car on the lap of the driver who has just won the Indianapolis classic; falling off the stern of an ocean liner and swallowing half the Atlantic before they rescue me; telling the judge I don't want to live with either parent, I want to live with both; marching into President Walter Huston's office during a cabinet meeting and telling him the gardener said he had to give permission before I could sell lemonade on the White House lawn; rolling around in mountains of untoasted cornflakes which simulated snow and being rescued by a Saint Bernard; leaning out of the cab of a steam locomotive, talking to W. C. Fields, after shooting an arrow in Ben Turpin's ass; saying goodbye to my mother through the bars of an orphanage gate.

Those are the early memories of child star Dickie Moore. When

I see him now on late-night television, it's like watching someone else. I don't like him especially. He isn't entertaining, he can't sing or dance; he isn't funny. I don't think he's even cute. So what was all the fuss about? Who was that kid with big brown eyes? Was he adorable and shy, with a wistful face, as Barbara Stanwyck remembers him? Or was he the boy Ralph Bellamy recalls who, at five, on a set with Ralph and Spencer Tracy, deliberately stripped the leaves of a potted palm, thus delaying the next scene?

"I'll never forget that," Ralph says, laughing. "I said, 'Dickie, you're going to kill that plant,' and you said, 'If I possibly can.' "

For me, the early images go in and out of focus, a kaleidoscopic series of long shots, close-ups, medium shots, pans, dolly shots, wipes, montages, cuts, dissolves, fade-outs, and points of view.

Recently, I realized that I dream in exactly the same way: in visual frames that correspond to the way a film is cut.

To this day, people still ask how I got my start in pictures, how I learned my lines, and was it fun. Were the other child stars asked similar questions? What did they answer? This would be my first "Rosebud."

I phoned Jane Withers in Los Angeles. We arranged to meet for lunch at the Bel Air Hotel.

Compulsive about being on time, I arrived early. I waited at our table, wondering what Jane was like now. Of course, I'd seen her on TV as Josephine the Plumber, in her long-running commercial. I knew, too, that she had acted recently, that she was a successful real estate executive. But what had become of the saucy little brat in Shirley Temple's movie *Bright Eyes?* How had her experience as one of the top money-grossing stars in the thirties affected her attitudes, her life?

My reverie was interrupted by the maître d'. Jane was on the phone. She'd be late. She was at the hospital visiting her mother, who was nearly blind. Don't rush, I told her.

I remembered Mrs. Withers, whom I'd met at Jane's fifteenth-birthday party, as a gentle, quiet Southern lady who wore pretty hats, treated everyone with equal courtesy, and stayed mostly in the background.

Every Sunday was open house at the Withers place. Kids would come chauffeured by their parents, who often joined the party. Sometimes one hundred and fifty people ate the barbecue. I never went to these Sunday gatherings. Parties frightened me. I might be asked to perform, and I couldn't sing or dance or play the piano well. Without a script, I could do nothing.

I rose as Jane came bustling over, now mature, big-boned, radiating energy and warmth. Together we began to talk, then finally slowed the rush of words. "I want to apologize," Jane said. "I was upset because I was late, and I kissed you when I came in. I don't normally do that."

"Don't apologize. I loved it."

"But so many people in our business go 'Darling' and they give a hum to the air. Doesn't mean a thing. But I feel that I've known you all my life."

"We shared a kind of history, in a way. . . ."

"Yes, we did. But you were playing a different role in a different part of the arena. We really never got to know each other." Suddenly Jane cocked her head and listened. "Is Alex Haley sitting behind me?" she asked.

"I don't know," I answered. "There's a black man sitting at a table, but I'm not sure what Alex Haley looks like."

"I know it's Alex Haley. I saw him once on television. I'd give anything to meet him."

"What makes you sure it's Haley?"

"I started as a mimic on my radio show in Atlanta when I was three. I know voices."

At that moment, one of the men at the table rose, headed for the bar. I followed. "Pardon me, but is that Alex Haley at your table?" "Yes." "I'm sitting with Jane Withers and she would like to meet him. Do you think he'd mind?" "No."

After introductions, Haley said, "Often, people introduce themselves, and it's always nice. But this time I want to say 'Wow,' because I'm more impressed at meeting Jane Withers than you are at meeting me."

The third man at the table, elegant and slender, squeezed our hands. "Jane Withers and Dickie Moore! I grew up with both of you. My name is Norman Lear."

Back at our table, Jane told me how she got her start in films. Before she was born, her mother would study theater marquees and say to herself, "Let's see. Withers is a long name, so she will have to have a short first name to fit."

Jane always wanted to act. When she arrived in California, she did almost anything: voices for Looney Tunes, modeling. She laughed.

Imagine me a model! Catalina swimsuits needed a little girl to model swimsuits at the Coconut Grove and—miracle of miracles—they passed over a dozen bathing beauties and picked me to pose with Jackie Coogan. I heard someone say, "We always pose Jackie with beautiful girls. For a change, let's take that kid over there."

In my first movie job you could only see the back of my head, but after trying for eight months to crash the studios, I wasn't complaining. No agent would take me. Even Central Casting didn't want me.

As it happened, a nice neighbor asked me to go with her on an interview. Mother said, "We can't do that. Jane wasn't called." Our neighbor said it would be okay as long as we stood on the sidelines.

So we went to 20th Century–Fox on a "cattle call" for kids for *Handle with Care.* We were standing on the side and the director, David Butler, noticed me. "Hey, kid!" he said. "Yeah, you. Come over here."

I said, in my thick Southern drawl, "Yes, sir, what can I do for you?"

"Why aren't you in line with the others?"

"Oh, sir. I wasn't called on this interview."

"Where are you from?"

"Atlanta, Georgia," I said, and then I heard myself saying, "This is the first time I've ever been inside a studio. We've sure been trying, though."

"Well, just get over there with those other kids," he said.

After the interviews were over, he told his assistant director, "And, oh, yeah, take the kid from Georgia too."

Success at last! I wasn't quite six.

Like Jane Withers, a number of child stars were trained as musical performers. Shirley Temple and Donald O'Connor, among others.

Edith Fellows too. As singer, dancer, actress, she appeared in many films, including *Jane Eyre*, *Five Little Peppers*, *Huckleberry Finn*, and, with Bing Crosby, *Pennies from Heaven*.

As children, Edith and I never worked together. We met at Jane Withers's fifteenth-birthday party. No one knew Edith well because her grandmother, with whom she lived, permitted no unnecessary contact with other children. The Withers family prayed for Edith.

Edith was tiny. Her picture in the *Children's Casting Directory*, September 1930, had this caption: "Edythe Marilyn Fellows—Long Golden Brown Curls, Deep Blue Eyes, Age 5 years, Height 42 inches, Weight 36 pounds, Dramatic Readings, Comedies, Singing, Playing Uke, Dancing, Imitator, Impersonator of Characters, Different Types."

Pretty good for five. No question, Grandma's field was merchandising. Edith became a star at Columbia by the time she was eleven.

I wrote to Edith, telling her when I'd be in Hollywood. When I dialed her number, Edith lifted the receiver and, before I had a chance to identify myself, she blurted out, "If this isn't Dickie Moore, I'll die!"

As I walked toward Edith's bungalow, I recalled our last meeting, in the 1950s. We had done a play in stock together. We both had separated from our mates. Lonely, we clung together in her New York apartment. It was New Year's Eve. I wanted to make love. Edith concentrated on a telephone call from her hairdresser. His roommate had tossed him out of their apartment and changed the locks. I lay impatiently beside her as Edith reassured her lonely friend. Finally, she hung up and we held each other through the

Edith Fellows and practically her only friend.

night while the old year fell away. I left the next day and went to a movie alone. I don't know what she did.

Three decades later, I learned from Edith how she got into films:

When I was two, my father, grandmother, and I left Boston, where I was born. Daddy had landed a job as a mechanic in Charlotte, North Carolina. So we drove off in our touring car, that he had painted lavender.

I was so pigeon-toed that I stumbled all over myself. An orthopedic man suggested that dancing lessons might help. There was this wonderful dancing school in Charlotte, Henderson School of the Dance, where I started taking lessons.

I must have been good, because when I turned four, I did a "one-child" show. A man came backstage and said, "Goodness, that child should be in Hollywood." He said he was a talent scout, and Grandma got all excited. He gave us his card and said if we went to California he'd introduce me to Hal Roach.

The man said he needed fifty dollars up front for newspaper publicity, so that when I got to Hollywood they'd know who I was. Father dug up fifty dollars and gave it to him.

The problem was getting to California, because Daddy wasn't making that kind of money. But at dancing school they were so thrilled for me that they did a benefit performance to raise money for one-way tickets for Grandma and me.

It was terribly sad saying goodbye to my friends and dancing buddies. They all came to the railroad station to see us off. Nobody asked if I wanted to go. I don't know how I felt about it. I didn't know what Hollywood was. My grandmother did, and because she was excited and happy, I caught her excitement without understanding why.

When we got to California, I walked endlessly with my grandmother while she looked for the address on the talent scout's card. Finally, she asked a policeman for directions. He looked at the card, said, "Well, this should be the address right here," and pointed to a vacant lot.

The "talent scout" had been a con man. We had just enough money for a few days, but Grandma was too proud to let those back home know what happened. She was determined that we'd stay, so she got work doing housecleaning on a daily basis.

Sometimes she took me with her when she housecleaned. But often I wasn't allowed in the house, so she'd leave me with a neighbor lady, who had a small son who did extra work in pictures.

Once when I was with them, a call came from Central Casting for the boy to go to Hal Roach Studios for an interview for a Charlie Chase comedy. The neighbor couldn't leave me alone, so she took me.

When we got there, something got into me. I did any number of things to get attention. The part called for a little boy and they chose the neighbor kid.

Time to start shooting the movie, the little boy got chicken pox. His mother, shattered, called the studio. "Well, send the little girl," they said.

"But she doesn't work in pictures," said our neighbor.

"Send her anyway."

She did. I got the part.

Many of us with no special early training got our first jobs by accident. Bonita Granville (later nominated for an Academy Award for *These Three*) and her family moved into a Hollywood apartment building where a casting director lived. He saw Bonita; would her mother allow her to test for the part of Ann Harding's daughter in *Westward Passage?* Yes. Bonita got the job.

The child who played Greta Garbo as a baby in *Queen Christina* (and appeared in more than twenty films) was Cora Sue Collins.

"Have you ever thought of putting your little girl in pictures?" an agent asked Cora Sue's mother on the street.

"That's why I brought her to Hollywood," was the answer. A studio was looking for the smallest child who could remember lines. Cora Sue was three.

Juanita Quigley, youngest of three children, was born in Los Angeles in 1931 and began her career of more than a decade at age two and a half in *Imitation of Life.* We worked together in *In Love with Life,* and Juanita also appeared in more than twenty other films, including *The Great Ziegfeld* and *National Velvet.* The story she was told to tell people when she was growing up was that she, like Cora Sue, was walking on the street with her mother when a casting director approached. But Juanita is "not sure that's really accurate."

Stymie (Matthew Beard), the lovable black kid in "Our Gang"

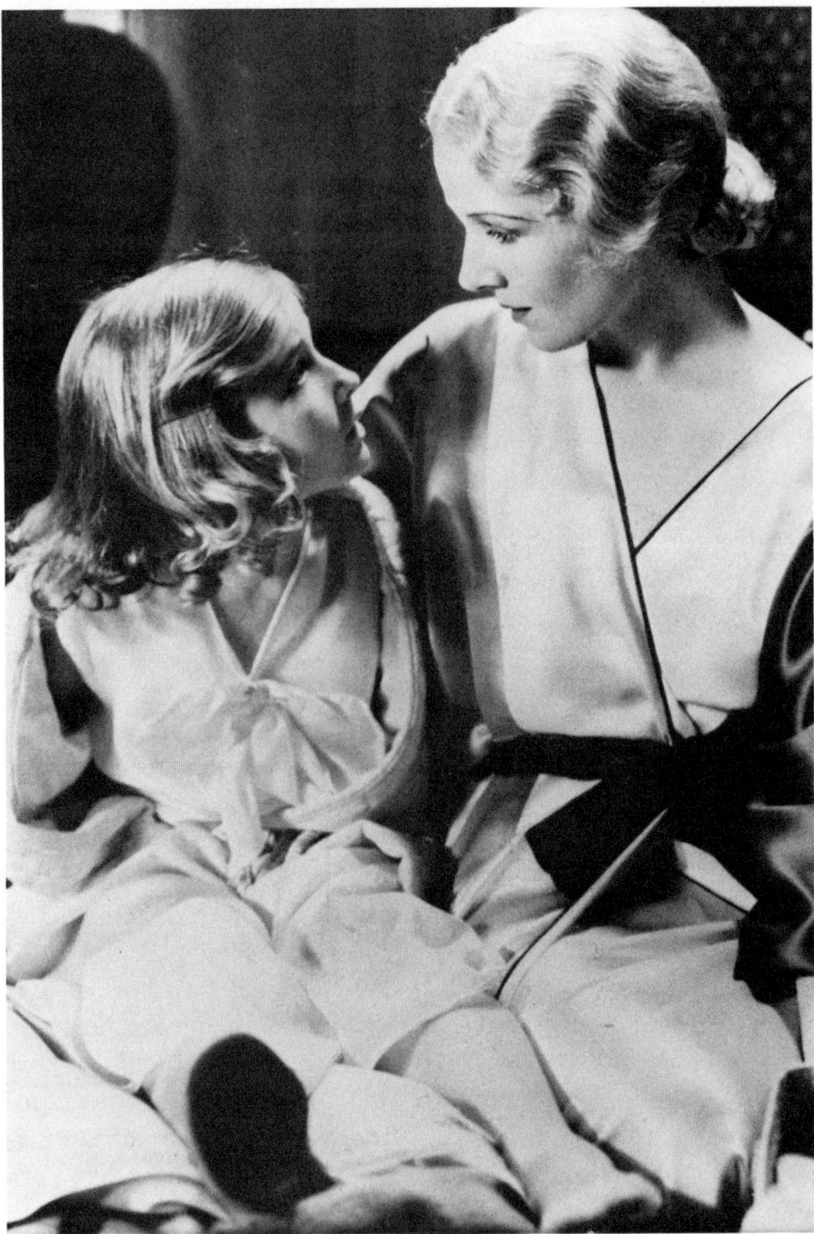

Bonita Granville's first movie role was as Ann Harding's daughter in *Westward Passage.* Bunny won the role because they looked so much alike.

comedies, started acting, literally, in his mother's arms. She was an extra and carried Stymie in a scene in *Hallelujah!* when he was seventeen months old. Later, his father heard of an opening at Roach. A nondenominational minister who ran a parking lot, Mr. Beard knew that movies were sinful, so he never set foot in a studio. Stymie's mother took him.

I spent a year and a half in the Gang. Once the Beards gave a party at their house, a two-story clapboard with peeling paint. We swung on a tire tied to a huge pepper tree, wore old clothes—long pants—and got dirty. Stymie's mother fried chicken, his dad showed us how to crank an ice cream maker. They had a dog. Nobody performed.

We lost touch when I left Roach at seven to work exclusively in feature films. As an adult, whenever I was asked about the Gang, I said Stymie was my favorite. He said the same of me. We sent each other messages, but never wrote. I was anxious to see Stymie.

We met in a chicken and waffle place in Hollywood, near Sunset. His picture was on the wall. He was thicker through the waist than I expected, immaculate in a beige suit, brown tie, white collar, and still the inevitable derby.

Stymie handed me a present—a picture of the two of us together, taken while we were at Roach. "I have to say it, man, you were my favorite when I was a child, Dickie Moore. You never called me 'nigger.' I remember staying the night at your house on Genesee Avenue. It was a good time."

Stymie's first memory was of a "huge" studio covered with ivy and of the big red bus that took the Gang to the studio ranch for outdoor locations. "Everyone would hang out of the bus, singing, 'Hail, hail, the Gang's all here!' " He smiled.

"What about the derby?" I asked. "When did you start wearing that?"

"Stan Laurel was responsible." (Laurel and Hardy also worked at Roach.) "Stan was my idol. Whenever I could, I'd rush over to watch him work. I'd reach up for his derby and put it on my head. Finally, Stan said, 'Get the kid a derby. Make him happy.' So I ended up wearing a derby in all my pictures. It's still my trademark."

My favorite film at Roach was *Free Wheeling,* released in 1932. I was the rich kid, with a stiff neck and strict parents. Stymie persuaded me to ride in the Gang's dilapidated taxi. It plowed through a giant haystack. My neck was cured!

"They built a hollow frame and covered it with hay. The driver hid under the floor of the car," Stymie said, smiling at the memory. "That was a lot of fun."

He loved the Gang. "We was doing child things." Also, with his thirteen or fourteen brothers and sisters—Stymie wasn't sure—his salary was important to the family. "Every Christmas, all the Little Rascals would get a present from the studio. They didn't give one to all the kids, but I'd get one and some of my brothers and sisters got presents too. That helped out some. There was resentment, though."

When he got too old for the Gang, he was fired. Other jobs were hard to find. Eventually, he went "looking for the bad guys" and found them. Stymie was arrested for sale and possession of heroin and spent nine years in jail. He then entered a drug rehabilitation center—"the ten years they taught me how to be a man"—and during that time, he met his former wife.

Stymie still sought acting roles. Carefully, he took a piece of paper from his wallet. "This is Hal Roach's phone number. I could call him right now if I wanted to. You know, it hurts to see yourself and the Little Rascals constantly on TV and you don't get any money out of it. Here I am with a couple of dollars in my pocket and the registration to my Chevy Nova, the only thing in my life I've ever owned. I wouldn't know how to live with my rent paid up."

Long pause while I fought tears. "Did you ever talk to Mr. Roach about it?"

"No. I wouldn't at his age. The man must be ninety-some years old. Maybe I should hate him for not sharing the TV money with us, but all the man has to do is smile at me and I'll forget the whole thing. He had a magic smile."

I spent two evenings with Stymie. As he left, he donned his derby, patted it, and said, "We ought to have a reunion or something. Get the kids together. I just hate the fact that you are my main man and I don't see you but every fifty years. Let's do it more often."

We vowed to see each other soon again. But we didn't. Three weeks later, Stymie had a stroke and died. "Oh, God," I thought, "he didn't sign our picture!"

Usually, our mothers sought careers for us. Shirley Temple's mother enrolled Shirley in the Meglin Kiddies, a local dancing school, where Shirley was discovered hiding under a piano and cast in "Baby Burlesk" short subjects.

Mickey Rooney, born to vaudeville, was taken to Monogram by his mother to audition for the "Mickey McGuire" series. The story goes that Mickey tested and his mother waited, and after five days she phoned the studio and said, "Look, have you made up your mind about my son as Mickey McGuire?" They said they hadn't, and she said, "Well, there isn't much time, because he's had five other offers since we saw you and you've got to make a decision." They called her right back in a panic. There had not been five other offers. She was working for the telephone company for $75 a month and Mickey got the job for $75 a week. So she quit.

Natasha Gurdin's mother was ambitious for her daughter. Natasha first appeared in *Happy Land*, starring Don Ameche and Frances Dee. Ann Rutherford played the ingenue, I was Ameche's son. We shot on location in Santa Rosa, California. World War II had just begun.

I don't remember Natasha, but Ann Rutherford's most "indelible memory" of the film is of this "delicious three-year-old" whose family owned a trailer which the studio rented to use as a dressing room outdoors. Ann hugged Natasha and showed her off to people between scenes. Natasha got a job as an extra.

Natasha Gurdin became Natalie Wood. I wanted to interview Natalie. She was one of the last children to grow up in the old Hollywood studio system, and the temperature of her fame rose every year of her life, from the moment her career began.

Although we had mutual friends, we had not yet met. In three successive trips to Hollywood I had tried to arrange a meeting. Natalie had agreed to see me, but her father was seriously ill and, as a consequence, her schedule wasn't certain. The day before our appointment, he died. The next time I was in Hollywood, we finally spent an afternoon together at her home.

A security gate had been installed in the front yard. Natalie and her husband, Robert (R.J.) Wagner, were both at the peak of their careers, and their children were young, friendly, and active.

From the outside, their house looked like other luxurious homes on a tree-lined street in Beverly Hills. Inside it was informal, uncluttered but lived in, with a compatible assortment of durable furniture that Natalie and R.J. each had when they decided to marry for the second time. She was delighted that I liked the house, and laughed when I told her, "You had to find each other again. Your furniture goes together."

Natalie, dressed in blue denims and a red gingham shirt, sipped iced tea with lemon. Through the window of the living room, two ducks quacked in the yard. She loved animals.

Roddy McDowall, a mutual friend, had told me that of all the people he knows, Natalie was most willing to accept responsibility for the consequences of her own actions. She spent many years in analysis.

Would she be willing to talk about that? "Of course," she said. She discussed James Dean; her love of boats; feelings about being an actress, a wife, and a mother; personal priorities; and memories of being three-year-old Natasha Gurdin, that little girl whom Ann Rutherford hugged in her first film.

I was in nursery school, but I do remember Santa Rosa vividly. It was a big event for a movie company to come to town, and everybody was interested in going down to watch the filming.

I remember Ann picking me up and holding me. I doubt that my father ever came on the set, because he was against movies. My mother, though, took me often. She asked herself, "How does this work? Which one's the director?"

When she figured out that Irving Pichel was the director, she said to me, "Natasha, go over there and sit on that man's lap and sing him your songs." I remember singing "In My Arms," with gestures: "Comes the dawn, I'll be gone. Ain't I never going to have a honey holding me tight . . ."

I remember, too, a parade with soldiers in that picture. My mother made me go march with the soldiers.

I really didn't want to do all this. I was kind of scared. But obviously I wasn't shy, because I did what I was told. Mother, of course, wanted me to attract attention.

After the film, Irving Pichel kept in touch. He used to send me books, dolls, and letters, and he would always say if he found the proper part he would think of me.

But he also tried to adopt me. He said to my mother, "Oh, your daughter is so adorable, I'd love to adopt her. What would you think of that?" My mother thought he was joking. She speaks still with a heavy Russian accent and sometimes she doesn't quite understand or make herself understood. So *she* thought that he was joking and *he* thought that she was serious.

The lawyers arrived at our house one day while the *Happy Land* filming was still going on. My father answered the door and when it became clear what the lawyers wanted, he was ready to kill Irving Pichel.

This is one of my earliest memories because there was such a big upheaval in the household. Obviously, it ended in a friendly way, because Pichel wrote us letters and my mother wrote to him. She read me his letters, and it was a big day when a doll or a book would arrive.

When I was five, Pichel wrote or called, saying that he had a part he wanted me to test for.

"Absolutely not," my father said. No daughter of his was going to lead a crazy Hollywood life.

But I, of course, loved the idea. My mother was a dancer, but she never danced professionally. She wanted a career for me. I think she felt unfulfilled and thought that I might have the opportunities she never had. Mother managed to convince my father that there wasn't the slightest chance of my getting the part. Also, the trip to Hollywood would be educational and interesting. Why not see the sights—at the studio's expense? Actually, I am sure she had every intention that I would get the part.

So I made the screen test and I remember proudly telling my mother afterward that I hadn't cried even though they asked me to. My mother got mad and said, "What do you mean, you didn't cry?" Then there was a great commotion. Finally, at my mother's urging, I called Mr. Pichel and asked for another chance. I hadn't understood that I was supposed to cry, I told him, and I would cry if that was what he really wanted.

From that time on, whenever I did a movie, I always counted the crying scenes. That was a barometer of how difficult the part was going to be for me.

I sent Natalie flowers as a token of appreciation for the time she spent with me, and when I returned to New York a few days later, a handwritten note was waiting in my office. It was mailed from Marina Del Rey, where they kept the boat. She thanked me for the lavender roses. "They are just magnificent, and my favorite. I so enjoyed the time we spent together and I certainly hope to see you again. Perhaps on your next trip out we could all have dinner—we would love it. Please call if you are free. R.J. sends fondest regards, too. Love, Natalie."

I saw Natalie once again, when she and her husband and Jane Powell and I visited Elizabeth Taylor backstage in New York. To the best of my knowledge, our interview was Natalie's last.

A few child stars were born to show people. They grew up in the family business, much as a young lawyer steps into his father's firm. Jackie Coogan, Donald O'Connor, Mickey Rooney, Kathleen Nolan grew up in this tradition.

"The only important place on God's earth is that stage," vaudevillian Jack Coogan, Sr., told his son long before *The Kid*, the movie with Charlie Chaplin which catapulted Jackie to world fame. Jackie's mother worked for Sid Grauman's father as Baby Lillian. It was unthinkable that Jackie would not perform.

I always wanted to meet Jackie Coogan. I'm grateful that I was able to spend time with him before his death from a heart attack on March 1, 1984. We hadn't known each other; he was eleven years older. I knew that he once knocked Sonny Tufts into a swimming pool, landed gliders behind enemy lines in World War II, yelled at Chiang Kai-shek to bring back his laundry by Tuesday, kicked Darryl F. Zanuck in the ass, and threatened to sue a TV director for "nonsupport" of his actors.

And he was one of the first and greatest child stars. At eight he was world famous, making $20,000 a week.

Jack invited me to spend a couple of days in Palm Springs, where I met his wife and teenage son, and visited their unpretentious stucco bungalow.

Nothing about Jack's appearance suggested the vulnerable youngster who captured the world's heart in *The Kid.* Jack was in his late sixties; age showed in his massive frame and lined features. He was trenchant, playful, reflective, and outrageous.

Jack's first memory was of a shimmy dance he did in a bathing suit in vaudeville. His dad called him on stage. After he stopped shimmying and the spotlights stopped shining in his eyes, he discovered that two thousand people were watching. "Then"—he laughed—"it was too late for me to run away and hide."

Jackie became part of his parents' act and took to imitations. In 1919, Sid Grauman, owner of Grauman's Chinese Theatre, saw Jackie. Knowing that Charlie Chaplin was looking for a young boy for *The Kid*, Grauman brought Chaplin to the vaudeville theater. Thus was launched one of Hollywood's great careers.

A rare photograph of Jackie Coogan and Charlie Chaplin during filming of *The Kid.*

Peggy Ann Garner won a special Oscar for her work in *A Tree Grows in Brooklyn.* For Peggy, the studio was a refuge from a difficult life at home.

Jackie spent one year and three days working with Charlie Chaplin on *The Kid.* Jack worshiped Chaplin.

During the shooting, he had to be close to me so it would reflect in our relationship on the screen. Even on Sundays—the one day we didn't work—he came over with his chauffeur in his Locomobile, to take me to the circus, auto races, everywhere; every Sunday.

We didn't have any script for *The Kid* and sometimes we'd sit on the set for ten days, wouldn't turn a camera. Chaplin was trying to get an idea, but when he got one, he'd have a whole sequence. Then when we would get up to do the scene, he would have it completely formulated in his mind, and he would say, "How would you like to . . ." That was the way he directed.

"Does that feel awkward?" he'd ask me. "Is it uncomfortable?" What Chaplin was trying to tell me was: "Don't try to force something that isn't part of your natural instinct. Don't be contrived." So Chaplin was an easy man to work for.

My dad was in the picture too. He was making more money than I was. He got a hundred and fifty a week and I got seventy-five. Chaplin saw how Dad could get all this emotion out of me because he knew me so well, so Chaplin asked him if he wanted a part in the picture, and my dad played a very elegant lounge lizard in one scene, and a drunk in a flophouse in another.

Chaplin was in practically every scene, so my dad also worked for him behind the camera, because he couldn't see himself. After we'd finish a scene, Chaplin would say to Dad, "All right?" and they would talk.

After the picture, I would drop by the studio occasionally to visit Chaplin, and it was like we'd take up a conversation where it had stopped maybe a year before. But I was no longer in regular contact with him after *The Kid* because he was one of the greatest womanizers of all time. His time was taken up with women.

Jack loved performing. He never felt used until after his father's death, in an automobile accident that only Jack survived. His mother married his business manager and Jack discovered that the $10 million he had earned was gone. He sued his mother and her new husband, and when he wouldn't drop the suit, he told me, L. B. Mayer had him blacklisted in Hollywood.

On leaving town, I called to thank Jack and to arrange to meet again.

"So long," he said as we hung up. "Stay away from mothers."

2. At Home with the Folks

One day, Dad lost his job. He was a bank teller by profession, and the Depression drafted him into the army of the unemployed. So his days were free. He could chauffeur me around.

We drove to MacArthur Park, where I posed for publicity pictures in a rented electric boat.

When the photos appeared in movie magazines, the caption said that six-year-old Dickie Moore was piloting his boat on his own private lake on the "spacious grounds of the Moore estate."

Dad answered my fan mail. When the story about my private lake appeared, the letters poured in. Some were from kids who begged me to help tide their fathers over until Roosevelt got them jobs.

Dad blew up. "I've been walking the streets like a goddamn whore, begging for work, and everybody thinks I'm a millionaire trying to steal the bread from starving families."

I ran to my room. A mockingbird was singing in the yard, but

I could hear Dad hollering. And I heard Mother hum her tune, the way she did when she wanted you to know you had no effect on her. "I'm sick of people thinking we own a lake and live in a mansion! From now on, if they want to take pictures they can do it in our house."

Mother stopped humming. "Even if this house was suitable, Jack, which it isn't, it would be very difficult for anyone to concentrate on taking pictures, with you following him with a broom and dustpan."

Mother resumed her humming. Dad said he had no intention of moving to another house; ours was good enough. And Ray Fargo, the architect, could take his plans and shove them. "And that damn Buick convertible you've got your eye on . . ." Dad raised his voice to pierce the barrier of Mother's humming. "It would take me half a day just to get the goddamn top down."

"You've nothing better to do."

Suddenly, it was quiet. I peered into the living room. Dad had shrunk. Calm now, he said, "Every time I go for a job, they tell me, 'You're a good man, John, a reliable man, but you don't need the work. You're Dickie Moore's father. The Depression hasn't touched you. Even if I could hire someone, I'd have to take a man with a family to support; they need the twenty bucks a week.' That's what they say to me."

"How do they know who you are?" Mother said. "Do you wear a sign? You don't walk in and say you're Dickie Moore's father, do you?"

"Everybody in banking knows. George Temple certainly knows." Dad had worked for two weeks as a temporary replacement at the branch where Shirley's father worked.

"What has George Temple got to do with it?" Mother gave Dad her full attention now.

Dad lit a cigarette. "He's not going to be able to last much longer, either. You should see the biddies who come into his bank with their daughters, bothering the man to death."

Mother had heard about these women. "Dance for Mr. Temple,"

they said to their little girls. Then, "Doesn't she dance better than Shirley, Mr. Temple?" and they demanded that he get their daughters into pictures.

(When I saw Shirley, she confirmed this story. "Banks had marble floors in those days, and with kids tap-dancing in the main lobby—well, it was a bad time for bankers and they didn't need that." Eventually, Mr. Temple had to quit.)

Dad acknowledged that Shirley was more famous than I was and that people hadn't brought their children in to interrupt his work. Still, he felt that the people who pestered George Temple at the bank kept John Moore from finding a job.

Dad, almost whispering: "There were five of us when I was Dickie's age. We had to walk five miles to school and six miles to church on Sunday."

"Through snowstorms?" Mother asked, trying to make Dad laugh. (She often tried; he never did.)

Mother knew perfectly well that it didn't snow in the British West Indies, where he grew up, Dad said. But often he had to walk through rainstorms, sometimes through hurricanes.

Dad was fond of telling us that he was born in Bordeaux, France, and had moved with his family at an early age to Guadeloupe, in the French West Indies. His father managed the local office of the West India and Panama Telegraph Company there. Dad's mother, who was French, was born in Guadeloupe.

Dad's father, an Englishman, didn't want his sons brought up in French schools, so Dad and his older brother were sent to Antigua, in the British West Indies, to live with their "Uncle Bleeblie" and his sisters while school was in session.

Uncle Bleeblie was a lawyer, a "big shot," who often had to order his older sisters to give Dad and his brother enough to eat. "Those aunts were so stingy they would let the bread rot rather than eat it. I was always hungry," Dad recalled.

When Dad was nine, he and his mother and brother moved to Toronto. Soon his sisters followed. His father stayed alone in Guadeloupe, where he died of spinal meningitis.

Dad enlisted in the "British Navy" (actually the Canadian Navy) and spent World War I as an ensign on a minesweeper patrolling out of Halifax. After the war, he and Mother met in Toronto at the Canadian Bank of Commerce, where Mother worked as a switchboard operator and Dad held down a job as the "French translator for the bank."

Mother did not discuss her childhood, and fidgeted evasively when questioned. "I really don't remember it." One thing Mother liked to talk about was being born in Belfast, Ireland—the "Black North," she boasted. She was proud that her father was an Orangeman, and that he had brought her and her mother to Toronto to find a better life. And she claimed that she'd kissed the Blarney Stone.

"There are only two kinds of people in this world," Mother often observed, "those who are Irish and those who wish they were."

She never mentioned her mother. Her dad, she told me grudgingly, worked for the government as the "man in charge of plants" at the botanical garden in Toronto.

Dad went west in 1921 and Mother followed. They were married in Los Angeles. Dad found work in a bank and Mother became a switchboard operator at Loeb & Loeb, a law firm representing clients in the motion picture industry.

After a short time on the job, Mother rushed into Mr. Loeb's office to resign. "I can't handle these phone calls anymore," she sobbed.

Waiting on the line to talk to Mr. Loeb was "Sessue Hayakawa, calling from Bujumbura in Burundi," and that was too much for Mother.

While we had no formal church affiliation, Mother and Dad felt that religion was important in bringing up children. They never went to church themselves, but insisted that I go, giving me a dime for the collection. They drove me to Sunday school and picked me up when it let out.

One morning, our Sunday school teacher lifted me onto a table in the middle of the room and told the class, "This young man is a movie star, boys and girls." He reeled off the titles of pictures I'd been in—he knew more of them than I did—and asked me to sign autographs. "Be sure to tell your parents that Dickie Moore attends your church and contributes generously."

I felt the room grow frigid, ice water cascading from the ceiling. The class became a firing squad. I felt obliged to speak, but couldn't. There was no script.

As if on cue, all eyes turned toward the door. Dad stood there motionless, staring. Suddenly, he crossed the room, swept me off the table, and carried me to the car. We drove home in silence. It was my last day as an Episcopalian.

Someone recommended Mary Baker Eddy. They said that nobody at her church paid any attention to actors. So I spent Sunday mornings as a Christian Scientist.

For me, important childhood memories were cars we had, the maids, houses that we lived in, and our dogs.

Mike was a gift. A doubtful Irish terrier, Mike went into a closet one night and had thirteen pups. "I guess Mike is a girl," Mother concluded.

Twelve puppies were strapping heavyweights; the thirteenth was the runt of the litter. Mother named her Tiny. Dad made a nest in the garage for Mike and helped feed the puppies with a baby bottle. "She can't nurse thirteen," he explained.

Mike didn't want to nurse thirteen even if she could have. She rejected Tiny from day one. Mike would drop Tiny in a patch of grass near the back fence, then return to the garage to nurse the others. Mother felt sorry for Tiny. Several times a day we rescued her. Finally, Mother brought Tiny into the house and fed her from the baby bottle. As the other pups grew up, we gave them away. Mother kept Tiny. For six months Tiny walked into walls, until Dad took her to the vet and had her put away. Eventually, Dad gave Mike away.

Big Boy was the largest dog we had. Fiercely protective of me and of the house, he easily hurdled the four-foot gate at the end of the driveway. When I wrestled with a friend in the front yard, Big

Boy would charge and hit my friend with his shoulder, then stand over him and growl until I took him indoors.

Once Big Boy growled at a man who came up our driveway, and the man told Dad that he was a deputy sheriff and would shoot Big Boy. "You shoot that dog and I'll shoot you!" Dad yelled. The man left angrily. I felt proud of Dad, glad that he was my father, one of the few times during childhood that I felt that way. I still dream about that scene.

Dad gave Big Boy to a man who owned an avocado ranch.

The folks did not entertain lavishly, but Mother insisted on having friends over and she was a jovial hostess. She considered herself a good plain cook. Her baked beans, often followed by lemon meringue pie, caused much comment. Mother found joy in serving second helpings of rabbit to new guests and listening modestly while they complimented her on the best chicken they ever ate. Then she would say, "I'm so glad you like it, because it's really rabbit."

Of Mother's many friends, few were in the movie business. An exception was Edie Lake, an ex-vaudevillian whose son, Arthur, became Dagwood Bumstead in radio and movies. After Arthur made a lot of money and married Marion Davies's niece, Edie often took Mother to Santa Anita racetrack and gave her sixteen dollars. Mother bet two dollars on each race. Edie took her to the Santa Monica Beach Club, to Trader Vic's, and to the Brown Derby for lunch. Mother didn't pay for anything.

During dinner at our house one night, someone mentioned Adolphe Menjou. I was working with him in a film.

"I hear he's a horse's ass," said Uncle George.

"He's a horse's ass, all right, that's what I think too," Dad said, glancing furtively in Mother's direction.

Mother didn't say she disliked Mr. Menjou. The corners of her mouth turned up, yet she seemed about to cry, a prevailing condition whenever anybody famous came in for criticism. "Actually, he's a very distinguished gentleman and he dresses beautifully," she said.

Alfred Fay, an insurance agent, turned the conversation to Dad's urgent need for additional insurance.

"What do I need more insurance for? We can't afford the premiums as it is," Dad answered. "Hell, I'll be worth more dead than alive."

"Lots of people are," said Mr. Fay. Uncle George changed the subject: How did we like the new Buick? Dad said the top was lousy, Mother said she loved the olive-green color. The maroon Essex we'd traded in had faded.

"This'll fade too," Dad warned. "We never should have bought the Buick." Alfred Fay agreed. We should have bought a Lincoln. His brother sold them; he could have saved us money. A Lincoln was too big, Dad said. Even the Buick's too big, because if I left Roach—and everybody seemed to think I should—there was no way of predicting our income. And our overhead might go higher. Why? Aunty Gladys wondered.

If I went to private school, it would be higher. Everybody said, nonsense, I'd be working all the time and going to school at the studios. The folks seemed relieved to hear it.

Now that I was a star, Mrs. Fay asked, would we be moving into a "more suitable" house? "What are your plans, Jack? Nora told me you've been looking at some lots."

"I saw one yesterday that looks like a pretty good deal. Seventy-five-foot frontage—wider than most."

"Oh, where is it?"

"Fifth Street, just off Fairfax."

"Just off Fairfax? Why, that's a rabbit pasture, right near the La Brea tar pits. You're not planning to build there . . . ?"

"That property is going up in value," Mother said.

"Gilmore plans to build a racetrack for midget cars across the street. You better check on that before you buy."

"We've bought the lot already, and Ray starts to build in January," Mother said, surprising everybody. "More baked beans, anyone?"

"Eat up," said Dad, "or we'll have to throw it out."

"Jack's such a gracious host," Mother sighed.

We built the house on Fifth Street and lived there when I was working, and had live-in maids. When I wasn't working, we rented it out and moved to a smaller house.

Our first maid, Marie, was hired to care for Pat, my newborn sister, so that Mother could spend her days with me at the studio.

Soon after Marie came, I was bitten by a dog. The folks were out, Marie was on the glider swing in the backyard, holding Pat. I told Marie about the dog, but she said to wait until the folks got home. She was paid to mind my baby sister.

Mother fired Marie. A succession of women then worked for us in the new house on Fifth Street.

There was a buzzer on the dining room floor at Mother's end of the table. With seeming nonchalance, Mother, who is short, would explore the floor with her foot, searching for the lump in the rug, almost sliding off her chair. Finding the button, she pushed firmly with her foot, a seraphic smile on her face, while the rasping buzzer in the kitchen told the maid in residence that her attention was needed in the dining room.

Once Mother called Martha with the buzzer. Martha was our current maid, a forerunner of Raquel Welch. She blowsed through the swinging door to answer the call.

"Martha, serve the pie," Mother instructed. Martha disappeared. Eventually, Mother buzzed again. "I said, Martha, serve the pie." More time elapsed, and again the swinging door opened and Martha's head protruded.

"Mrs. Moore," Martha said, in a whisper heard by all, "I dropped the pie on the floor." The guests all laughed. Mother went to the kitchen, scraped the pie off the floor, cut its remnants into pieces, and served them without apology.

When Mother and I left for a three-month personal appearance tour in 1936, Sally kept the house and cooked and cared for Pat, who was three.

Sally was immaculate, affectionate, cheerful, and attractive. She sang to Pat and played with her and bathed her every day.

The night after we returned from tour, Pat awakened screaming, her body covered with hives, which we both had periodically. Dad applied calamine lotion. Pat's rash persisted; a doctor was consulted. Pat had the "Spanish itch," the doctor said. The closest thing to Spanish in our house was Sally, who was Mexican. Sally was fired and Patricia cried for days.

Our last maid, Louise, a black woman, was liked by all of us until a friend gave Pat an angora sweater she had knitted for her. When Louise put it in our new washing machine, it fit Pat's Betsy Wetsy doll. Mother and I got home from the studio, and Pat—delighted—showed us the doll dressed in the angora sweater. After Louise left, Mother prepared our meals.

Mother made my lunch when I went to public school: sandwiches of peanut butter, cold lamb, sardines. I liked them all, but I disliked intensely my metal lunch box with the Thermos in the lid. Other kids took paper bags. "You must have milk," she said when I protested.

Mother was proud of having "pernicious anemia," which she advertised for forty years as a badge of failing health.

Dad told me on numerous occasions that Mother had "a terrible time" when I was born, and that things got worse "when Patricia came along." I was sure that "pernicious anemia" accounted for the fact that Mother never exercised, never got wet when we went to the beach. Each morning, I got a tablespoon of cod liver oil in a glass of orange juice to keep pernicious anemia from spreading. Mother took no medicine.

At Christmas time, Mother and I went to Bullock's Wilshire, an exclusive store in Beverly Hills where Gertrude Temple shopped.

A floorwalker recognized me. I wanted a Christmas present for my mother, I whispered. He led us to the lingerie department, where an elegant, perfumed lady modeled the latest fashions in silk negligees. Mother looked uncomfortable. "That's not what Dickie had in mind," she murmured. Sitting in my short pants and little cap, I was certain that the quarter I was squeezing in my pocket could not negotiate the purchase of the items on display. Nor was

My sister Pat and I promote a new portable radio.

Mother and Dad, Lake Arrowhead, California.

I sure they were appropriate. After we had seen everything in the lingerie department, we left without buying anything.

Next day, on a trip to the Thrifty Drug Store, I slipped away to find the largest gift selling for a quarter. The biggest bargain was a giant box of Kotex. But the salesman steered me toward a box of Kleenex, the second-largest thing within my budget. I bought that because he insisted, and I knew what it was for. Mother was delighted.

After dinner, if I was working in a picture, I learned my lines for the next day. Then I went to bed. If we were shooting on location next day, bedtime would be earlier than usual.

I was afraid of the dark. A small lamp was on the dresser, across from my bed. I waited for sleep, comforted by the round copper lamp with its ships sailing in an endless circle, propelled by the heat of the forty-watt bulb inside. Those ships moved by magic.

In the morning, Dad came in to wake me. It was dark out at 4 A.M., as it had been the night before, and the light of the copper lamp with its black schooners circling in silhouette still shone across the room.

Face buried in my pillow, I lay on my stomach, trying not to hear Dad enter, trying not to let him know I'd wet the bed again.

Maybe the car wouldn't come. Maybe the sun wouldn't rise and the day's shooting would be lost, maybe the car would break down on the way to the location, maybe somebody important would die. Maybe, maybe, maybe.

But the car came—a big black Chrysler or Lincoln or Buick, depending on which company the studio had a deal with to get cars in exchange for free publicity. The cars were always black, always looked as if they were built to carry coffins, always with jump seats in the back, always with a driver.

Lying in my bed, smelling my stale urine, I would hunker down beneath the sheets. In my mind I heard the song that I'd heard for as long as I remembered, a song I associated with the war Dad talked about. "Oh, how I hate to get up in the morning. Oh, how I'd love to remain in bed. . . . "

The shivering was not from lying in wet sheets that had turned cold by 4 A.M. The shivering was dread. Remembering the lines that Mother drilled me in the night before, I shouted them silently into the mattress. How terrible it would be to fail, to miss a cue, to say words wrong, to delay the shooting. Time cost so much money! I don't know who told me that. But I knew it.

"All ready?" Dad would shake me gently.

"All ready," I would answer, and smile. Dad would discover the wet sheets and curse softly through clenched teeth and help me dress, while Mother prepared herself for the arrival of the car to take us to location. It was still dark when we left home.

I was eight when Patricia was born. As she grew up, I seldom played with her, but she did not discourage easily. She knocked on my door and if I opened it, offered to clean my room. When she finished, I threw her out.

Still, we spent some time together. The "best times" of her life, Pat recalls, were when I took her, Big Boy, and a bow and arrow to an open field near the La Brea tar pits. We would tramp through clumps of grass, searching for jackrabbits. Occasionally, the Goodyear blimp landed nearby.

I wondered why Pat didn't have to work in films. She wondered why I did. "It isn't that I wouldn't do it, but that I couldn't," she recalls. Pat's failure to become a star was not for lack of Mother's trying.

At four, Pat auditioned for a show titled *Star Overnight.* Although she had taken dancing and piano lessons, stardom did not materialize. But a screen test followed, directed by none other than John Farrow, Maureen O'Sullivan's husband, a brilliant and tyrannical director, much feared by actors. Ordinarily, Mr. Farrow did not direct tests, but with Pat he was courteous and gentle.

Mr. Farrow indicated the man appearing with her in the scene. "Patricia, this nice man is supposed to be your daddy, but you're not really sure, so please ask him: 'You are my daddy, aren't you?' Will you say that for me?"

"No," Patricia answered. "He is not my daddy and I won't say it."

Pat did bits and extra work when Mother could arrange jobs that did not require payment of dues to the Screen Actors Guild.

Eventually, Pat got another screen test. She was supposed to play the piano, which she did. "While you're playing, dear, just whistle," Mother instructed her before the test began.

"I don't know how," Pat said.

"It doesn't matter," Mother reassured her. "Do the best you can."

Pat tried to whistle while she played. The studio called Mother. "We like Patricia very much, but the girl in the picture is supposed to be a Southern belle, and Patricia has a very dark complexion. Can you lighten her skin?"

Mother said she'd try. She rubbed bleaching cream into Pat's skin and took her to a dermatologist. "Don't you touch that girl's skin," the doctor said. "It won't do any good and you will ruin her. She has a lovely olive complexion. Leave it alone." The doctor wasn't friendly, Mother said.

Pat lost out on that film, but when she saw it at the local movie house she was glad, because the child who got the part had a scene in which she cried. "I knew I couldn't cry," Pat told me later.

When Pat appeared in a party scene in *Tea for Two,* with Doris Day and Gordon MacRae, her dark complexion was again an issue. As the camera was about to roll, David Butler, the director, yelled, "Wait! Who is that person? She looks like an Indian. Get the makeup man and powder her down."

"I could have died," Pat said.

Pat was not the first sibling to learn that having a child star in the family wasn't so great. Natalie Wood told me that her younger sister, Lana, "had a hard time of it because when she was growing up our mother's attention was focused on me, because I was the one who was working." Natalie also reported that when it was time for Elizabeth Taylor's brother to take his screen test, he shaved his head.

Roddy McDowall's sister, Virginia, shared the disadvantages of Roddy's fame but none of the rewards.

I met Virginia soon after I met Rod, with whom I shared the closest friendship I had with any child actor. As young adults, Roddy and I did two films together. He hated them both. Titled *Tuna Clipper* and *Killer Shark*, they were seafaring efforts in which Roddy starred. I played his best friend, swaggering, smirking, but redeemable. Roddy's character personified virtue, played with what he describes as his "prayerbook look."

Roddy thought I knew how to act, and that he did not. I felt the opposite. We quickly became friends.

Even when we outgrew adolescence, our mothers continued to be involved in our careers—indeed, in every aspect of our lives. Winifriede McDowall and Mother politely debated which of us had made the greatest contribution to the motion picture industry, and tried to impress each other by reciting titles of our old films and the names of stars we worked with. (Rod called it "picture dropping"; we laughed secretly.)

Rod (born Roderick Andrew Anthony Jude McDowall) went to Hollywood from London, where his mother had enrolled him and Virginia in a convent school that placed priority on elocution lessons. Infected with unfulfilled theatrical ambitions, Mrs. McDowall, an immense, outgoing woman, made the rounds in London to find work for her children. At six, Roddy won medals at the school. Soon he had an agent. Then came modeling work, jobs in films, and World War II. Roddy's father, Tom—a solid man who, Rod said, "puffed his pipe in quiet rage"—joined the British merchant fleet. Winifriede and the children came to New York. Two weeks later, Winifriede heard that MGM was looking for a child for *The Yearling.* Roddy was wrong for that part, but right for *Man Hunt.* A screen test in Hollywood, then a Fox contract. His second film, *How Green Was My Valley*, made him a star.

As the children grew up in Hollywood, the McDowall home

became a gathering place for teenagers and young adults in films. I was included whether I knew the other guests or not (I seldom did). As a hostess, Winifriede was tops. Her attitude was "The more the merrier."

"That's because she couldn't stand anything going on in somebody else's house, because she couldn't control it," Rod told me.

Now, with Roddy's parents dead and with my son—Rod's godson—a father himself, I looked forward to our reunion. It would be our first in a dozen years.

Rod invited me to his house in North Hollywood. Approaching the vine-covered California ranch home, I glanced at Roddy's red Alfa Romeo parked in the circular driveway. Something caught my eye. It was Rod's license plate: X MOPPET.

The house is furnished with pictures, books, sterling, that I remembered from another time and place. Old England still prevails. We spent the day discussing our lives before we met each other. I learned a lot about Roddy and his family that I hadn't known before.

"My childhood was totally isolated, really suffocating. As a child, I was always lied to about myself and about the world. My mother waited until I was seven before telling me there wasn't a Santa Claus. I was so guileless, such a Dopey Dwarf," Roddy said. I asked about Virginia.

Mother used to dress us the same way. She wanted to make dolls of both of us. Not that we weren't allowed to play. She was wonderful about joining in, about making a childhood. But always within a vacuum.

My parents kept Virginia under a tremendous psychological hold always. I don't think it was a malevolent drive. Mother was much brighter than her behavior. She spoiled the living bejesus out of us. Virginia had so many dresses and so many toys, which wasn't what Virginia was looking for. And so much love. We were drowning in love.

And there weren't any friends. There's only eleven months age difference between Virginia and myself. Mother was desperately afraid that we two children would be split. That's why she forced 20th Century–Fox to let Virginia go to school on the lot, which was a vicious thing to do because Virginia had no reason to be there. She spent all her school years on the lot, feeling totally excluded, and so shy and inhibited.

Mother was full of delusions of grandeur. She was not a pretty woman, so she romanced you intellectually. She'd bring pies to the studio and cook people into insanity. She'd gift them into adulation. But she never caused any trouble on the set.

What she did was to make all the decisions concerning our lives and pretend that my sister and I were making them. She had complete control over us. Ultimately, I was in despair over the hypocrisy in family behavior. For instance, she suddenly appeared to faint or die of apoplexy. But if the phone rang, she recovered and answered normally: "Oh, hello. How are you? I'm fine."

She was very clever, an entertaining woman. And she had a remarkable gift. She sensed instantly when people saw through her. She'd never go near them again.

My father was second officer in the British marine. His ship docked in Los Angeles from time to time. He had strong feelings about propriety and one's position in the community. He was one of those Englishmen who, on entering a room, always tells three stories.

"Who are you going to interview on this trip?" Roddy asked the next time I saw him in California. Jane Powell was on the list. We both knew Roddy well, but Jane and I had never met. "Let's all have dinner together before you do your interview," Rod offered. "It'll break the ice." Dinner was speedily arranged.

I picked Jane up at her Spanish-style home, high in the hills of Bel Air. The house commands a breathtaking view across the reservoir.

I rang the bell. The yapping of tiny dogs pierced the door, which opened promptly. Jane, at five feet one and a half and weighing ninety pounds, was smaller than I expected. Elegant, erect, superbly proportioned, with huge blue eyes and blond hair ("It's dyed," she tells anyone who's interested), she brought to mind a bouquet of daffodils. We met Rod at the restaurant, ate, talked, drank some wine.

At lunch the next day, alone with Jane, I asked my questions and wondered if she was free on Friday for lunch or dinner—maybe both?

"I'm free for lunch," Jane said. "I have plans for dinner."

On Friday, I took Jane, a gourmet cook, to the Central Market, a huge warehouse in downtown Los Angeles where everything from goat heads to dried bananas is sold to noisy throngs. She had never been there. We snacked in Chinatown. I tipped two dollars. She retrieved one and returned it to me.

I had to go to San Francisco for three days on business. Would she have an evening free when I got back? "We'll negotiate," Jane said.

It turned out she was free, and we've been together ever since.

Jane is an only child. Born Suzanne Burce in Portland, Oregon, she started dancing lessons at four, then singing lessons. Persuaded by a dancing school proprietor in Oakland, California, that his school offered certain stardom for their child, Jane's parents pulled up stakes and moved. Her dad quit his job at Wonder Bread. When Oakland did not deliver its promised wealth and fame, the Burces, funds exhausted, returned to Portland. Jane's dad sought his old job. "Just walk in backward and maybe they'll think you never left," Jane's Uncle Herb told her father. But the job was gone, and the Burce family had to scrounge.

Jane's dad sold cookware door to door and found a free apartment for his family on condition that he serve as superintendent. At six, Jane helped Daddy empty tenants' garbage pails and lined them with newspapers.

And Jane felt close to Mama.

My mother was my girlfriend, my confidante. She was always with me. Even after we came to Hollywood I wanted it that way, because she was not a typical stage mother.

But Mother was very shrewd. When I think of what she did to my father and to others, I'm amazed I didn't see through her as a child.

She treated Daddy like he was never good enough. She claimed he didn't have a sense of humor, but he had a great sense of humor. If he worked, he was wrong; if he didn't work, he was wrong. He could never do anything right, in her eyes. And he adored her. They were always arguing, but Daddy wasn't a fighter and that made her angry. She gave him the silent treatment.

My mother could never handle liquor. When she drank on Saturday night, I hated to see Sunday morning come. Daddy was not that way. He loved a good time, and till the day he died he was Santa Claus to everybody. I never heard him say a bad word about anybody. I wish I could be more like him.

Mama was a calculating person. I can't remember hearing her say anything nice about anybody. She would say, "Oh, yes. She is so pretty, but did you notice that . . ." "It was a lovely day, but . . ." There was always a "but." Looking back, I can't recall my mother ever giving time to anybody, going to the hospital to visit a sick friend or doing anything for anyone else.

Later, when my parents were divorced, Dad almost committed suicide because he loved my mother so. To this day I can't figure out why, because she really was not a nice lady. She married another man and bought a motel in Las Vegas. And then she bought a bar in Hollywood. I got a call one day because she had collapsed. I took her to the hospital, where they told me she had malnutrition.

Another only child, Peggy Ann Garner, won millions of fans and a special Oscar for her performance in *A Tree Grows in Brooklyn.*

Peggy began as a child model in New York, went with her mother to Hollywood at age seven, landed the role as Carole Lombard's daughter in *In Name Only.* Peggy's many other films include *Jane Eyre, The Keys of the Kingdom, Junior Miss.*

In our twenties, we got acquainted in New York through Roddy McDowall. We all had come east to broaden our horizons. Together with an ambitious, personable young singer named Merv Griffin, we hung out in Sardi's, nursing thirty-five-cent cups of coffee and comforting each other as we tried to negotiate the mine-strewn path from Hollywood Child to Serious Actor. Peggy and I worked together in summer stock. Peggy always appealed to me. A lot. But my feeling for her was never verbalized or reciprocated.

I stopped short when I saw her sitting on a couch in the lobby of the Bel Air Hotel. She was more fragile than I remembered. Her appearance as a child—even as a young adult—had been attractive enough, but hardly striking. Her average good looks, coupled with her trusting, forthright gaze and bashful honesty, contributed to her appeal. But now she looked genuinely pretty.

We talked until the restaurant closed, then moved outside. The sun dropped behind the hills and it got chilly. So we went our separate ways.

From the time I was a teenager, Mother whispered secretly that "poor Peggy" had no home life, and about the problems her mother caused. Her father worked for the government in some capacity related to the military and was away most of the time. When together, he and Peggy's mother quarreled bitterly, as far back as Peggy can remember:

Mother scared the daylights out of me. She never hit me, but she hurt more with words. She'd sit me down and convince me that I'd committed some cardinal sin. I didn't have to do anything wrong. Maybe something didn't go right at the studio. I was just paying for her inadequacies, her guilt.

Mother was aggressive. She destroyed everyone I can think of in one way or another—my grandmother, her sister, who committed suicide, my grandfather, her brother.

Many nights she left me alone and I didn't see her for days. Those were bad years. I'd come home and find her with someone or I'd be picked up in the middle of the night and taken to someone's apartment and put alone in a room. I realized something was wrong, but I didn't know exactly what. I couldn't put my finger on it because no one had ever told me what was right or wrong. I just knew that my mother shouldn't be doing those things.

I was taken to a lovely apartment one night and put into a room to sleep. All of a sudden, I jumped up like a rabbit. A strange woman was crawling into bed with me. It didn't seem right, so I ran out of the room and found Mother with someone in another room.

Despite all this, Mother did nice things, but I learned later that there was usually a hidden purpose, although at the time they were very nice.

I could tell marvelous stories about how she kept my grandfather going during the Depression when his steel business was staggering, how she got Rudy Vallee to play at their home in Canton, Ohio, how she turned the first floor of the house into a tearoom.

All her life she wanted to do something, to be somebody. She had the drive, the ambition, the aggressiveness, which I didn't have—and she was a beautiful woman. But she didn't have the talent. I did.

As young adults, Peggy and Jackie Cooper, another only child, worked together, fell in love, and played important roles in each other's lives for several years.

I wrote to Jackie. When he got my letter, he called me in New York. Three weeks later, I drove through the Universal gate in Hollywood to the trailer that served as an office for the television film Jack was directing.

We took his car to a nearby restaurant on Ventura, where he insisted on paying for lunch.

"Last week, someone noticed your name on my calendar and asked me if Dick Moore was Dickie Moore, and if so, what you were doing now," Jack said. "He was very interested, but I don't think our success as child actors is ever an advantage. It's actually against us."

I reminded Jack that he had been a star right from the start. He never had to test for parts after his first "Our Gang" comedy. His movies were immensely popular. *Skippy*, *The Champ*, *Treasure Island* became classics. "True," Jack said. "But then I grew up."

As a young adult, he read for the play *Death of a Salesman* in New York. The author, Arthur Miller, never left his seat, but director Elia Kazan walked down to the stage and told Jack he thought that casting a famous Hollywood actor would detract from the play.

"He didn't tell me the truth," Jack reminisced, "which is that I wasn't very good. Cameron Mitchell got the part."

Jack, lean and weathered, wears open shirts and blue jeans when he's working. A successful television director and still in demand as an actor, he doesn't like to work with children because "they ought to be out roughhousing; they should not be made to drain themselves."

Despite considerable success, he is disappointed that he is not in demand to direct feature films, which is what he wants to do. Jack was once in charge of production for Screen Gems, then the television arm of Columbia Pictures. He has since rejected offers to head up studios. The idea of being an executive behind a desk does not appeal to him. "It's funny," Jack mused. "If you don't want something in this town, they think you're negotiating."

As a child, Jackie was poor. His mother was a pianist for a singer of bawdy songs in vaudeville. Out of her fifty dollars a week earnings, she paid her train fare and expenses, and sent money home to Jack's grandmother, with whom he lived, for the $24-a-month rent on a house in Hollywood. Jack's mother was ill from the time he was born.

She had a hysterectomy before she was thirty-five. I knew I was losing her a couple of years before she died, and she knew it too. But she was my sister, my dearest friend, my mother, and one of the best people I've ever known in my life.

She suffered all the guilts, probably would have loved to say, "Chuck it! Go to school and play with the kids." But I think she had a premonition she wasn't going to live long. She knew I was a high-strung kid who would only read when I was forced to, would only *do* in school what I was forced to. I was spoiled and she knew I wasn't going to learn a trade. So she figured maybe I would grow into the movie business. I think she hoped beyond realism that I'd become a mature adult actor. Probably, deep in her heart she felt there'd be enough money to put me in some kind of a business or get me by somehow. And she was right.

She wanted me on my own. In those days you could get a driver's license at fourteen. I got mine on my fourteenth birthday and I drove to work the next day without her. She called the assistant director eight times a day, but she wanted me on my own.

We used to have long talks. A lot of guys have a mother till they're thirty, but I doubt that they fared as well as I did.

I never met my father. He walked out for a pack of cigarettes when

I was two and a half. He wasn't heard from again until I was thirteen, when he turned up crippled. I'd been making good money before then, so my mother had some respect for him for not coming around sooner.

He was selling patent medicines out of the back of his automobile when he got in an accident and couldn't work anymore. He went to a veterans hospital in Kansas City, and in his desperation he also went to a lawyer. The lawyer got in touch with my mother. Of course, if it was discovered that Jackie Cooper's father was crippled and that the family wouldn't take care of him, it would be a huge potential scandal. Also, he had been declared legally dead after seven years, and my mother had married again. So, how to keep it quiet?

Eventually, he signed some kind of contract never to enter the state of California, never to approach me or her. In return we would pay him a hundred dollars a week for life, and in 1935 that was a lot of money. It was ten percent of my annual income.

Then my mother died. I continued to send the money even after I went into the army. A year after the war I was home, not making any money and still sending the hundred dollars a week.

My accountant did a little investigating. My father was playing piano in a bar from a wheelchair, and he'd married his nurse.

So I stopped sending the hundred dollars a week. Two weeks later, my father sent me a letter. First time I'd ever heard from him in my life. I saw "John Cooper" and the address in Kansas City on the envelope, and I sent it back with a note that it was unopened and I didn't ever want to hear from him again. I never did hear from him again, so the man had some pride.

My first meeting with Donald O'Connor was at The Players, the New York actors' club founded by Edwin Booth.

I hadn't seen Donald since Jane Withers's fifteenth-birthday party. There, he had had an argument with his childhood sweetheart, Gwen (later his first wife), and appeared to throw away the diamond ring she had returned to him. This was calculated to impress her and it did, along with the rest of us. We did not know then that Donald had palmed a pebble during the argument with Gwen, and that's what he hurled out into the night, while keeping the ring safely nestled in his hand.

I always marveled at Donald's freedom before the cameras, especially his ability to dance. His musicals with Peggy Ryan and his dance numbers with Gene Kelly in *Singin' in the Rain* are classics.

The year before he entered the army, Donald and Peggy Ryan made twelve musicals together so that Universal could bank as many films as possible.

Donald does not like to dance. He doesn't know the choreographic shorthand. He learns by observation, and always felt he lagged behind the others. While Donald's dancing was putting Universal in the black, the studio—to conserve rehearsal time—sent him to a dancing teacher to learn the basic steps. "Two weeks later, the teacher sent a note back to the heads of Universal, saying I could never learn." Donald said, hinting at a smile.

Donald was the youngest child of circus people. His father was an acrobat and a strong man; his mother was a bareback rider, who joined the act at thirteen, bore the first of seven children at fourteen, and kept on riding. Three of Donald's siblings died soon after birth. When he was still an infant, Donald's older sister was killed by an automobile as she and Donald crossed a street. More children came along. The family turned to vaudeville.

Before Donald was born, his dad had dropped dead on stage in Brockton, Massachusetts. Still very young, Donald's mother was left to care for the family. The act survived. "She was with us almost every minute," Donald recalls. "I slept in the same bed with her until I was eleven."

Fueled by information about his father, obtained, "strangely enough, from people outside the family who knew him," Donald nurtures "the fantasy character that I grew up with: a very nice man, very quiet. He was a circus strong man, he was one of the greatest acrobats that ever lived, he was a trapeze artist, barrel jumper, clown, straight man, comic, legit actor. He could do everything." Donald said:

I found out he used to take on all comers in circuses with Peter Maher, an Irish middleweight champion. That's how they'd make an extra buck.

They'd bet five dollars that nobody in the audience could last one round with either of them. They'd back the challenger against a canvas drop and somebody behind it would hit him with a bat.

My mother found an old poster describing another stunt of Dad's. For twenty-five cents, he would hold back horses while they tried to pull his arms apart.

Recently, Jane Powell and I invited Donald and Gloria, his wife, to a party at Jane's home. Donald mistakenly assumed it was my birthday and brought a charming present, a papier-mâché clown. I appreciated the thought, but the gift's significance eluded me, until I remembered Donald's description of his childhood in the circus. Then I realized how powerful a force the circus was—and is—in shaping Donald's career and way of life.

3. "Lights! Camera! Action!"

The first talking version of *Oliver Twist* starred Dickie Moore. I was six and near the peak of my career. (Jackie Coogan had filmed a silent production of the Dickens classic several years before.)

When *Oliver* was released, I saw pictures of myself everywhere, holding an empty porridge bowl, looking up pathetically at an actor in a chef's hat, and pleading for more mush. In the film, the chef got furious and ordered me back to the table with the wooden benches. I didn't get an extra portion. The other orphans were astonished that I would even ask for one. But I was new in the orphanage and not up on the house rules. As punishment for my temerity, I had to scrub the wooden floors on my hands and knees.

I hadn't read *Oliver Twist* and had no clear concept of the novel's plot. I approached each scene without any understanding of its relationship to the overall story line. The filming, as it progressed, did little to clarify the story.

An early example of merchandising spin-offs from movies is this 1930s song. I got no money from it.

Even today, few films are shot in continuity. It's usual to shoot all the scenes that take place on a particular set before moving on to another set. *Where* an action occurred takes precedence over *when* it occurred. So for *Oliver* we could conceivably do the last scenes first, the opening scene last.

One set in *Oliver Twist* was the inside of the home of a wealthy family. My job as Oliver was to help rob the house. Fagin and his cohorts put me up to it. (Fagin was played by Irving Pichel, who was a noted actor of both stage and screen before he became a director.) They lifted me up to a tiny window that I barely could wriggle through. Once inside, I was to tiptoe to the front door and lift the latch so that they could sneak in and steal the owners blind.

But in this scene, the man who owns the house wakes up and shoots me as I'm coming through the window. When we did the scene, ashes from the gun went flying through the air, getting soot on everything. I hung from the window, following directions, and when the gun went off I dropped a foot or two and lay still, pretending to be wounded. To me, the most memorable things about the film were the old gun, the cloud of flying ash, and the explosion, which was the loudest sound I'd ever heard.

At one point in *Oliver Twist,* I had to cry. On this day, I found it hard to cry on cue. Finally, in desperation, the director, in a loud voice and in no uncertain terms, ordered Mother off the set.

"Mrs. Moore will leave the set," he yelled. Mother pretended to leave. I knew she hadn't gone. She hid behind a microphone boom in a darkened portion of the stage some distance away and peered anxiously toward the island of light where we were working.

I sensed that she was embarrassed. I felt uncomfortable for her. She wanted to obey the director, yet she didn't want to leave. I suspected that the director's order was a ruse to make me cry. I felt no panic at her supposed departure, only shame that my inability to cry on cue had brought on such an elaborate subterfuge.

Finally, I cried enough to get the shot and Mother rejoined us in the island of light.

When Chic Sale and I co-starred in *The Expert,* I had my first dental crisis. Mr. Sale, a star of note in that era, specialized in portraying a lovable old man—a sort of benevolent Mark Twain. When "Chic Sale" became the common name for privy, Mr. Sale achieved lasting immortality—far transcending that endowed by Hollywood. What better tribute to the rustic character he played!

I was astonished by how young he looked without his makeup. One day in the commissary, he said hello and I returned his greeting, not knowing until later who it was.

In the middle of *The Expert*, I lost one of my front teeth. I had been playing with it for days, despite Mother's repeated orders to keep my fingers out of my mouth. Finally, it just fell out. I had been told to save the tooth when the big moment arrived. The studio whisked me to a dentist, who constructed a miniature gold bridge to hold my tooth. For the rest of the filming, I had a good time with the bridge, putting it in and taking it out.

At about this time I signed a contract with Hal Roach to star in "Our Gang" comedies. Despite the fact that I was under contract, I never felt at home at Roach. I felt like a visitor—especially since I was the only boy whose mother dressed him in short pants.

The people I remember best, aside from the teacher, Mrs. Carter, were Stymie, Spanky, and our director, Mr. McGowan. I remember, too, a large concrete sunken pool with a miniature submarine parked on the bottom, which was being used in another picture. There was a scene where we went fishing in a creek—no fish, of course—and I wore knickers, which I liked better than short pants.

In one film, we baked a cake for my movie mother's birthday. We pretended to use too much baking powder. The cake was really made of rubber, a big rectangular balloon inflated through an unseen hose. It grew so large that Stymie couldn't remove it from the oven.

The plot of this comedy—each episode had its own complete and separate story—involved our trying to give my mother a new dress for her birthday because my father was so mean and cheap he wouldn't buy her one. So we kids got together and hustled up thirty-five cents and bought my mother the dress, which we presented to her at a party, where the cake was served.

All involved seemed to enjoy what they were doing, and they seemed to think the film was funny. It made me want to cry. I thought there must be something wrong with me for not understanding any of the jokes in the comedies we did. I never told anybody how I felt.

I usually played the rich kid in the Gang. In one comedy, *Free Wheeling,* my neck was in a brace, and my movie parents disapproved of my association with the ragamuffins who constituted the Gang. But all ended happily when Stymie twisted my neck and made me well.

In another, we prepared hot cereal and all sat down to breakfast. But we'd used plaster by mistake, and each portion hardened in its bowl. We bent our spoons trying to eat it.

We worked with animals a lot. Pete the dog, whose trademark was a ring around his eye, mystified me. One day, I noticed that Pete looked different. "Something's funny," I thought. "Yesterday, Pete's ring was around his other eye." Later, Stymie told me that Pete had five sons, all of whom worked. On his oldest son they painted the ring around the wrong eye. They got away with it at Roach, but MGM would not have let a mistake like that get by.

In one film, a chimpanzee played Stymie's alleged brother. One day, he seized a lighted cigarette from a member of the crew and put the wrong end in his mouth. He had always been temperamental, but after that he wasn't fit to work with.

Stymie, Spanky, and the other kids spent all their time at Roach, but I worked at other studios a good deal of the time. They made a lot of comedies without me, even while I was under contract, so they could "loan me out."

"Loanout" is when the studio holding your contract rents you out to another studio. Dad resented this practice. He said that Hal Roach had no right to pay me $500 a week and loan me out to Paramount for $1,500. Mother answered that being under contract was safer than free-lancing. The check came every week.

Eventually, Mother decided we should change agents. She acknowledged that Minna Wallis (whose brother, Hal Wallis, was

Heralding the new year was part of the job. Here, Pete the pup, Stymie, Dorothy DeBorba and I posed for a 1933 calendar.

In one of many "Our Gang" comedies, Spanky and I hawked papers on the back lot of Hal Roach Studios.

In Roach's *The Kid from Borneo,* the touring sideshow's Bumbo chased us, screaming, "Yum-yum! Eat 'em up!" We were afraid he would eat us alive, but he only wanted our candy. Racial stereotypes in some of the old "Our Gang" shorts were appalling by today's standards.

With Spanky *(center),* Stymie *(right),* and other members of the Gang. The monkey was mean and unpredictable. In one script he was supposed to be mistaken for Stymie's brother.

important at Warner Brothers studios) was a terrific agent. All the same, while Minna was in New York for a few weeks, tending to other clients' interests, Mother made a switch. When Minna came back, she was furious. There was a good deal of arguing in our house about it. What was going on? I asked. "Don't worry, dear, it doesn't concern you," Mother said. I didn't ask again.

One of the most difficult things about working in pictures was sitting around. Waiting. In costume and makeup. Nothing to do while they set up the shot you were in, or fiddled with the lights.

As a star, I had a stand-in, who replaced me while the lights and camera were focused. When everything was set, I resumed my position, rehearsed, and shot the scene. Child stars under contract often had the same stand-in for years, but since I free-lanced, I had different stand-ins. Sometimes they hired a midget because there wasn't any legal limit on a midget's working hours.

One Christmas, I was guest of honor at a banquet in Pasadena. People in Pasadena were very rich, Mother said. "Too rich for my blood," Dad said. We all went to the banquet—I in my short pants, patent-leather shoes, white shirt, and jacket. The banquet was for a motion picture charity, and the hundred people who were eating had paid $50 each, Mother said. (We hadn't, I was sure.)

I stood up and said hello, that I was glad to be there and I wished them all a Merry Christmas, and sat down. The banquet was notable in that there were fourteen pieces of silverware at every place. Dad fidgeted a lot. On the way home in the Buick, Mother said how proud she was of me because, throughout the endless meal, I always used the right utensil. She couldn't get over that. Actually, there was nothing to it. I just started on the outside and worked in, like everybody else.

That Christmas, I was grand marshal of the Hollywood Santa Claus Parade. I rode with Santa in his sleigh—the main float—as it moved slowly west down the center of Hollywood Boulevard behind an escort of motorcycle police. Santa didn't say much to me. He seemed not to know whether I believed in him or not. I wasn't sure, either, so we just ignored each other and waved and threw candy to the thousands of children and parents who lined the sidewalks. An occasional puff of untoasted cornflakes—which simulated snow—emanated from our float.

Riding with Santa Claus was okay, but my real ambition was to be a garbageman so I could wear white gloves.

Some folks in Hollywood confused reality with make-believe. People ask if we child actors did. I wonder too. Often, it seemed that I overdramatized a bit in real life, or tried to fake a feeling that I didn't really have because it seemed appropriate to the situation.

When I visited Natalie Wood at her home, I asked her whether she had had this kind of experience as a child. Natalie was pensive for a moment, then she said: "I found it very difficult to separate the reality of living from the fantasy of working, to figure out if I was just responding to a situation as though it were a scene or whether it was how I really felt about something. I think there are little remnants of that in any actor.

"As a very young child, acting was just like playing house or playing with dolls. I found it not to be a problem then, but I found it very difficult when I entered adolescence. I suddenly became self-conscious. I felt awkward. I guess I didn't look awkward, because I continued to work. I didn't go through the 'awkward age' professionally, but I certainly did emotionally. I was very withdrawn, very shy."

Donald O'Connor can't remember when he was not in show business. Even when he was a small child, the stage was his reality:

> Confusing fantasy with reality is a big hang-up with all actors, regardless of age. In my case, starting so young, I lived my fantasy. But later in life, when I started to develop, there came that question: "Am I the person I'm playing on the screen? Which one of us happens to be real? Or are they both real?"
>
> You go through a period where fantasy and reality become fused. I

Natalie Wood and Edmund Gwenn in *Miracle on 34th Street.* As a very young child, Natalie felt that acting "was just like playing house." Problems came with adolescence.

think a lot of actors live out the fantasy that they're playing. Their true identity is hidden, and whenever a question about it pops up, they suppress it. Of course, this confusion is fostered by the studios. As long as you're making a dollar for the studio, you're a valuable asset, so they build up your screen personality. They keep you out of trouble, keep you from growing and maturing. As long as they can keep you infantile, they can control and manipulate you. When an actor finds his own identity, he goes through a terrible time with his studio.

Marcia Mae Jones, too, confused the fantasy of her work with the reality of her childhood. A year older than I, Marcia Mae worked in more than forty films, making her debut as Dolores Costello as a baby in *Mannequin* in 1926. Her mother had been an extra. As Marcia Mae grew older, she became the people she portrayed. "It was my escape, " she said, "because I led such a strict life."

Edith Fellows, while not confused about reality, loved playing brats because "I was doing things I couldn't do at home." When she threw something at Claudette Colbert, she was really "throwing it at Grandma."

There was no doubt about reality for Sidney Miller, musician, comedian, actor. Sidney, born to an Orthodox Jewish family (his father was a tailor), often played Mickey Rooney's and Donald O'Connor's sidekick. "I felt totally out of it—that was my reality. I knew I was envious of the leading men or the kid who got the girl. I was the fellow with the big nose. When I wasn't the right type to play an office boy and I asked why, they said, 'Well, you're not American.' "

Jane Withers never confused the characters she played with her private life, but audiences did. After *Bright Eyes,* people stopped Jane on the street, twirled her around, and said, "You're the creepy little girl that was so awful to Shirley Temple."

"Yes, ma'am, I was, but it was only a movie," Jane tried to explain. "But they believed it so strongly, which floored me at first. I thought: 'Don't they know it's only a movie?' "

Many children under contract thought of their studio as home,

Shirley Temple in one of her first "Baby Burlesk" short subjects. When Shirley's parents took her to see her pictures, Shirley fell asleep.

In *The Great O'Malley*, Sybil Jason was billed over Humphrey Bogart. A young newcomer named Ann Sheridan was also in the cast. Sybil was advertised as "Warner Brothers' answer to Shirley Temple."

refuge, family. Mickey Rooney in his adolescence did nine Andy Hardy pictures in one year. "The people on the set became my second family. We were very close. They called it work, but I was always delighted with the fun of it."

Jackie Coogan agreed. "I loved it. I'm an extrovert, you know, complete."

Sybil Jason, billed at the age of six as "Warner Brothers' answer to Shirley Temple," was spotted by a studio talent scout in England and put under contract. Sybil lived to go to work each morning. "I'm an insomniac to this day because I couldn't wait to get there."

Gloria Jean "didn't enjoy it—I *loved* it. I wanted to do it." The singing star of many Universal films was groomed at eleven to follow in Deanna Durbin's footsteps.

For Peggy Ann Garner, the studio was home, safety, her life. During the filming of *A Tree Grows in Brooklyn*, she lived on the lot in Shirley Temple's former bungalow, "to keep me safe so I didn't come to work with bags under my eyes from crying all night, wondering, 'Is my mother coming home?'

"At the studio, I was protected. We had our own fire department, our own hospital, our own publicity department—and I never saw the bad things. If anybody was chased, it was my mother; and they probably caught her. But for me, it was safe."

How, I wondered, did the biggest star of us all, Shirley Temple, feel about the studio and about her responsibility as a child star?

Much as I wanted to see Shirley, I put off writing to her. I had heard she didn't give interviews about the past to anyone. Finally, I called. "Those days in films are gone," she told me on the phone. "I'm only interested in now." I waited several weeks, then tried again.

Our last sustained contact had been during the filming of *Miss Annie Rooney* ("It was a terrible picture," she later recalled), in which—at sixteen—I played her boyfriend and bestowed her first screen kiss. Photographers from every major wire service, newspaper, and magazine visited the set that day to record the event. My suit was soaked with sweat. Also, the script called for me to jitterbug with Shirley and her pals, including Peggy Ryan and some of the most accomplished dancers of that era. Shirley herself was a superb dancer—she had held her own with the legendary Bill Robinson, among others—while I stumbled over curbs.

In a last desperate bid to keep the film on schedule, the studio made a rubber mask of my face and put it on a real dancer, who doubled for me in the musical numbers. For me, *Miss Annie Rooney* —far from being the enjoyable and enviable experience my peers assumed it was—was mortifying and left me with traumas that took years to overcome.

So I had mixed feelings about seeing Shirley Temple Black after forty years, and it was all too clear that she would survive whether she saw me or not.

Still, I persisted and we gradually developed a telephone relationship. Eventually, Shirley invited me to visit her, so I flew to San Francisco and rented a car for the thirty-mile drive to her home.

"It's a two-story stucco house like the kind you used to draw in school," Shirley told me on the phone.

Shirley opened the door. Forty years! For her: two marriages, a new career in television, children, now a grandmother, politics as a candidate for Congress, former delegate to the United Nations, a traumatic but successful mastectomy, service as United States ambassador to Ghana, U.S. Chief of Protocol, now adviser to the State Department. Another life, another world. Today, one of Hollywood's all-time greatest stars never sees a movie unless she's "trapped on an airplane."

She stood in the doorway, wearing a bright print dress made from fabric she had bought ten years before in Ghana, when she was there as our ambassador. The impish gaze was still level and direct, the hazel eyes were even more knowing.

Silence.

Finally, she pointed to the left side of her face: "Kiss me here on the cheek, like last time."

Our interview was pleasant but restrained. After it was over, Shirley invited me to stay for lunch. She had made sandwiches and

In *Miss Annie Rooney*, Shirley teaches me how to jitterbug at my birthday party. In truth, I was so bad they had to put a rubber mask of my face on another actor to film the dancing scenes.

Early in 1942 this picture of Shirley Temple's first screen kiss appeared in thousands of newspapers throughout the world. The scene was traumatic for me because it was the first time I had ever kissed a girl.

salad. (She doesn't have a maid, and cooks and cleans the house herself.)

As I was leaving, she showed me her proudest possession: the flag of an ambassador. Obviously, that assignment is her favorite role, and one that even skeptics agree she performed with grace and skill.

Several weeks later, I phoned Shirley again. "I appreciate the fact that you're a very private person. But the transcript of our interview reads like a press release. Your personality does not come through. I'd like to see you again."

Long pause on the phone. "Oh, hell," I thought, "I blew it."

"When do you want to come?" she finally asked.

Standing again at her front door, surveying the circular driveway behind a screen of evergreens just off the road, I thought: "She needs this like a hole in the head."

Again it was Shirley who opened the door. Again she had made lunch; again we sat in the living room and talked. I wondered if the neighbors made a big deal about her living there. "After you move into a community you're a celebrity for about a year. Then you settle in," she replied. "We've lived here a long time." She led me to the piano and pointed to a large color photo in a silver frame. "This is our family." She identified each of the thirty-two people in the picture. Her husband's relatives, and hers: five generations of Temples and Blacks. Shirley is family oriented. She has always taken care of people. When her father died at ninety-three, he was suffering from Bell's palsy and couldn't swallow. Shirley personally cooked all his meals, pureed his food, spoon-fed him every bite.

How did Shirley, always so irrepressibly cheerful, feel about her career as a child? Protective of her privacy, she is careful with her words:

It was something I did during the day, along with school. Then I came home at a certain time and went to bed. I liked the work, especially the dancing, and I knew I was good at it.

Professionally, some of the dance numbers were my most memorable experiences, especially the "Toy Trumpet" with Bill Robinson in *Rebecca of Sunnybrook Farm.* It was a very complicated dance number, which he and I really enjoyed, and during the number I got a charley horse. They stopped production while a doctor came and massaged my leg. My mother put her arms around me and our picture was taken by *Time* magazine. It was the only *Time* cover I ever got, but you can't see my face because my mother's holding me. It's the only time, I think, I was upstaged. That was a great dance number.

The only thing I didn't enjoy too much was posing on the hottest day in August for the Christmas pictures, wearing a snowsuit. But I never rebelled. I'm the easygoing type.

To me it was work, but I liked it. I assumed that everybody did it.

So did Diana Cary (Baby Peggy), the first world-famous infant star, whose multimillion-dollar silent-film career coincided with Jackie Coogan's fame. Diana's father had been a movie cowboy and she, like others, was discovered while visiting the set of a silent film on which a neighbor's child was working.

At home one day, the tiny movie star stood on a box and peered over the fence at children playing in the next yard. "They were sliding down slides and riding merry-go-rounds. I asked my sister, 'What are they doing?' She said they were having a birthday party. 'How can they do that? Why aren't they working? What are their folks going to do if they don't work?' I asked. I had terrible contempt for those children."

We all knew we had a duty to perform, and we were trained to follow orders. "The studio said to me, 'Stay as sweet as you are. Never change,' and I never did," Jane Powell reports. "I just stayed blah! If they wanted me to wear a pink dress and I wanted yellow, I wore a pink dress. I did what I was told and I spent my life trying not to disappoint anybody."

Natalie Wood agreed with Jane: "We had an inordinate sense of being responsible and guilty. Guilt. That was the universal feeling.

"But I don't think I had any inflated sense of my own importance. I always felt I was part of the industry and that what I did was a job. I felt lucky that I happened to be working and doing something that I got a great deal of pleasure from."

Many of us shared Natalie's inordinate sense of responsibility, not just for ourselves but for the pictures we were in. When we saw ourselves on screen, we thought we could have improved our performances. "I had a sense of wanting to do better, but I didn't know what better was," Roddy McDowall remembers.

Mickey Rooney felt "responsible for the product after about thirteen." At fifteen, Mickey was helping to direct his films. He threw his arm over the shoulder of another actor and strolled with him to a corner of the set, instilling confidence and relaxation. At nine, Jackie Cooper lost respect for directors who didn't make him dig. Jane Withers, at seven, asked her writers to "let me change the lines so they'll sound more like a kid my age." The influence of her films on the children who saw them was a matter of concern to Jane.

Occasionally, when Mother read me the script and it didn't call for me to be punished for something I did, I'd say, "Mother, I can't do that." She knew what I was getting at, but she'd say, "Why?"

"Because if I do it and get away with it, some kid in Kansas City is going to try it and he's not going to have a happy ending. It may be a disaster."

Mother would say, "Jane, I appreciate your feeling. Are you going to talk to the writers about it?"

"Yes, ma'am, I am." That's when I first started talking to the writers. They were floored. A few of them tried to talk me out of it, but I said, "I will do it if you show me being punished, and I have to be assured that it's not going to be cut out of the picture." I knew all about cutting and camera angles.

Crying on cue was a source of both pride and anxiety. In almost every film kids did there was a crying scene. Occasionally, after a bout of emotional weeping, the director would yell, "Print!" and if the crew applauded, we had scaled the heights.

One publicity photo caption had Jane Withers "collaborating" with writer Lamar Trotti. Actually Jane did rewrite her lines to make them sound more like a little girl.

Margaret O'Brien, Charles Laughton, Robert Young in *The Canterville Ghost.* "All they had to do to get me to cry was to tell me that Charles Laughton was going to steal the scene," Margaret recalls.

Crying was harder for some than for others. All they had to do to get Margaret O'Brien to cry in *The Canterville Ghost* was to tell her that Charles Laughton was going to steal the scene.

During the filming of *These Three*, in which Marcia Mae Jones appeared with Bonita Granville, director William Wyler "sat very quietly and just stared at me, which meant that he was not pleased with my performance, and I would have to do it over and over again." Marcia Mae, now tall and slender, shifted in her chair as she thought back:

> But he would never tell me what he was displeased about. In one scene I was supposed to be screaming and hysterical, but I had been crying for weeks and I just couldn't cry anymore. He started screaming at me and he told me that of all the children he had interviewed, he'd picked me because he thought I was a good actress; and that I was a terrible actress and I had let him down. Of course, he got me crying to the point where I couldn't stop. Then he felt terrible and he kept apologizing and apologizing. I wasn't sure he really meant it. I was only eleven years old, but I've never forgotten it.

Bobs Watson was Hollywood's champion crier. " 'The crybaby of Hollywood,' they called me," Bobs said, smiling. We were talking in the living room of his Las Vegas home. Today, Bobs is a minister. On the wall is a treasured possession, a telegram from Spencer Tracy, sent on the night Tracy won his Oscar for *Boys Town*, in which Bobs was featured, and in which he cried his heart out. It says: "Dear Bobs, Part of this Oscar belongs to you. Uncle Spence."

Bobs was one of nine Watson children. All appeared in films; often there were several in one picture. They were managed by their father, Coy, who many of us felt would go to any length to advance his kids' careers, so it surprised me when Bobs told me that his dad would never permit Spencer Tracy's telegram to be publicized in any way. "It's a personal and private thing," Coy Watson said.

Bobs, best-known and youngest of the clan, appeared in 125

movies. It was strange to see Mr. Watson sitting with the movie mothers on the set.

Coy had got his start in movies renting horses for Westerns. Then he donned a cowboy outfit and galloped through a scene, changed clothes for the next scene, and played an Indian in hot pursuit. Mr. Watson had been a propman, an assistant director, a special effects artist. He knew the movie business.

The family lived near the old Mack Sennett studio, so when they needed a child for a film, they'd say, "What size do you want? Go down to the Watsons'."

Of the nine Watson children, I saw Bobs and Delmar most. Delmar, about my age, also was good at crying. But Bobs was champion.

Gene Reynolds worked with him in *In Old Chicago.* Gene, also my age and a veteran of over thirty films (his first was *Babes in Toyland*), always played a stoic child.

The location for *In Old Chicago* was Modesto, California, Gene recalled as he sipped a cup of tea. Gene talks quietly:

Two Watson boys were in that film. Bobs was one. We played the three O'Leary boys when they were young. We arrived at the hotel in Modesto and I ran up to see them in their room—they hadn't even unpacked—and the father had the two boys on the bed, with the script open. He looked at the oldest boy, whose face broke and he began to cry. Then he looked at the youngest kid—he was like a lion tamer—and, Jesus, the kid started to cry. And I thought: "Holy cow, these guys really are good!"

Then we did this scene where the covered wagon turns over and our father, O'Leary, is killed. And, Jesus, those two guys are crying like crazy and I couldn't shed a tear. I *felt* deeply and I was *in* the situation, but I did not have the facility to cry. I tried staring in the lights, but I think they finally blew some camphor in my eyes.

I realized that if I was going to survive in the business, I had to learn to cry. So as I walked home from Bancroft Junior High, I would think about it. I tried to think of something sad. In the beginning, it would take me about six blocks to cry. Then, finally, I could cry in half a block.

Once I was on a film called *Spirit of Culver,* with Jackie Cooper and

Frankie Thomas, Mickey Rooney, Sidney Miller, Bobs Watson, Gene Reynolds in *Boys Town.* Most of us believe that Mickey was the best actor of all of us.

Seven of the nine Watson children appeared in one film. Bobs *(right)* became most famous. The family lived near Mack Sennett's studio, so when they needed a child they'd say, "What size kid do you want, boy or girl? Go down to the Watsons'."

Freddie Bartholomew. We were in a military academy and I got a letter that my mother died. I cried like a trooper and then they called lunch, because God forbid they should pay an extra five dollars for the lunch penalty. So we go off and eat and play. Then we come back—they're going to do the close-up and I'm trying to cry, but nothing happens. Here's fifty people standing around waiting for this kid to cry. I felt: "Oh, my God, the time I'm wasting!" Deanna Durbin's first husband was the assistant director and he kept checking his watch. So finally Jackie Cooper says to me, "Why not let them blow that stuff in your eyes?" But I said, "No!" And Jackie says, "Why not? What does Uncle Norman [director Norman Taurog] say about it?" I said, "He says a good actor doesn't need it." And as I said those words, the tears just poured out of me and they got the shot.

"The reason they called me the crybaby of Hollywood was because my face got all screwed up," Bobs told me. "Yes, I cried a lot in *In Old Chicago* when our father was dragged to death by horses. After that, our mother, Mrs. O'Leary, took me and Billy and Gene Reynolds to Chicago and her cow kicked over the lantern." Now Bobs grew serious:

I don't know where all the crying came from, other than I had a very sensitive father that I loved very much, and he always explained to me what was happening in a scene. He'd say, "How would you feel if this were your real father?"

I can't explain it, but when tears were needed, I cried, and they were honest and real.

In *Boys Town,* when Mickey Rooney left, it really broke my heart. It was as simple as that. I used to see Rooney and Spencer Tracy in a very idealized way.

Rooney used to rock me on the set when I was just a baby and he would say to his mother, "Hey, Mom, why can't you get me a little brother like this?"

Natalie Wood, for all her talent, was "absolutely terrified" when called upon to cry. "But they didn't have to blow camphor in my eyes. Usually, my mother would tell me sad stories or she would remind me of how I felt when my dog got run over by a car. She really made me do emotion memories, the Method, but I didn't know it at the time. She would get me all worked up and say to the director, 'She's ready! Start shooting.'

"To this day, I admire anyone who can cry on cue. If they can do nothing else but that—they're great! You've seen me do it, but I find it very difficult."

A consistent characteristic of child actors is that we knew our lines and everybody else's. For me, memorizing them called for Mother's help. Each night, she read my next day's lines aloud to me. I repeated them. Then she played the other characters in the scene. When my cue came, I said the lines I'd just learned. Mother never said, "Read the line this way . . ." but she did my lines the way she felt I should, and I would imitate her.

Her lower lip protruded in a little pout, her mouth turned down, her eyes opened wide, mannerisms I transferred to the screen. As Mother played my roles, tears often welled up in her eyes, and she talked as though she were a child my age.

"I hear you have a remarkable memory," Adolphe Menjou said to me our first day on the set of a film in which we starred. In the scene we were filming, he was washing the middle of a dog, I was washing the tail, and a girl who played my older sister was washing the dog's front.

I told Mr. Menjou I didn't know whether I had a remarkable memory or not. "Well," he said, "I hear you are noted for your ability to remember lines. In three weeks of shooting on *The Expert*, I heard, you didn't fluff once. Is that true?" I said I guessed it was. Mr. Menjou said he hoped it was true, because he had just finished working with Shirley Temple, who was four, and she "blew her lines" in several scenes. "I can't understand why she's a star," Mr. Menjou said.

Shirley's method of learning lines was similar to mine: "My mother taught me my lines at night before I went to sleep. She read them to me before I could read and she did all the other parts. I

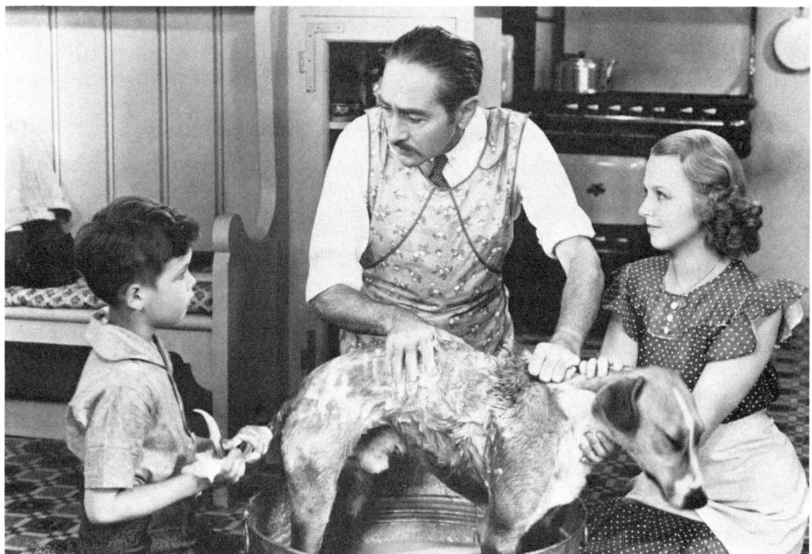

With Adolphe Menjou and Charlotte Henry in *The Human Side.* Menjou was critical of Shirley Temple because, he said, "she blew her lines."

Shirley Temple's *Bright Eyes* made Jane Withers a star. Jane was grateful but the girls never were close.

learned all of them that way." Margaret O'Brien's mother did the same. So did most others.

We understood that any direction given by our mothers would be superseded by whatever the director said. But there were many cases when parents tried to dictate interpretations of our roles, regardless of the directors' instructions.

For Marcia Mae Jones, having two directors—her mother and the one at the studio—was confusing. Bobs Watson felt that too:

> My dad was the one that really directed me, and I think some of the directors resented it a little bit. I remember one frustrating day on the set of *On Borrowed Time.* My dad wanted me to read the line in a specific manner. The director wanted me to do it a different way.
>
> I trusted my dad implicitly, so I read the dialogue the way he told me. After we had filmed it, the director said, "Bobby, this time I want you to read the line this way." I looked over at my dad and he shook his head no.
>
> During the few minutes when they touched up my makeup, my dad said, "You do it the way I told you to do it." So I went back in and I did it the way my dad told me, and the director said, very gently, "No, Bobby. I want you to do it this way." I looked over at my dad and he shook his head. I did it again the way my dad told me to do it.
>
> Then the director got very impatient. "No, I want you to do it *this* way." So, finally, I did it the director's way and he said, "Bobby, perfect!" I looked over at my dad and he shook his head and turned and walked away. That just broke my heart.

Even as a child, Bobs knew that his dad's approach to acting was old-fashioned and exaggerated, a holdover from the broad-brush strokes of silent films.

Jackie Cooper's mother, while reading him his lines, made little effort to influence his acting, only his manners on the set. She instructed him to be on time, to let the assistant director know when he had to go to the bathroom, to stand still when they were lighting him, to pay attention, and not to distract attention from the other actors.

Natalie Wood learned lines by reading them. "I realize now that I visualized the whole page. If it was a blue page [the first rewrite had blue pages, the second, pink, etc.], I would prefer to make corrections on the original white page, so that I could see the whole thing. I always felt I had to know my lines perfectly and not keep anybody waiting." Natalie asked me if that compulsion to be letter-perfect in our lines was a "common thread."

It was. Being letter-perfect in our lines was a universal point of pride. In *The Life of Emile Zola,* I appeared as Joseph Schildkraut's son. Schildkraut played Captain Dreyfus, and Paul Muni starred as Zola. Marcia Mae Jones was in *Emile Zola* too, and she was scared. Everybody warned her that Mr. Muni did not like to work with people who did not remember lines. So Marcia's mother drilled her, the dialogue director drilled her, the director drilled her. "They instilled such fear in me," said Marcia Mae, "that as I walked down the hall to take Mr. Muni his breakfast, they couldn't do the scene until I stopped shaking with the tray. Finally, when I got in to see Mr. Muni, he blew his lines and I didn't. That made me feel good."

During a scene with Lionel Barrymore in *On Borrowed Time,* Bobs Watson flubbed a line. "I ad-libbed my way out of it pretty well, but after it was over, I was almost ready to cry because I felt humiliated."

Barrymore hugged Bobs. "Okay, Bobby, don't feel bad, son. That's the first time you've missed in two weeks of shooting. Do you know that?"

The director said, "Bobby, we could print that, but we better go the way it's written."

"I felt very bad," Bobs said.

As with all children, many of our early habits and perceptions have remained throughout our lifetime. Remaining also, for a very few, is a palpable reminder of professional achievement: the ultimate in recognition not only by one's peers but by the giants of the motion picture industry, who both controlled and depended on us. That symbol of supreme achievement is Oscar, the Academy Award, crown jewel in the treasure trove of Hollywood.

Few children stayed up late enough to attend the presentation ceremonies (no television then to watch them on), much less to take one home. The first to take a special Oscar home was Shirley Temple. Margaret O'Brien, Peggy Ann Garner, Deanna Durbin and Mickey Rooney are among those who also won special Academy Awards. (They were not in competition with adults. Bonita Granville was nominated for *These Three*—based on Lillian Hellman's play *The Children's Hour*—against adult competition, but did not win.)

Peggy Ann's special award for *A Tree Grows in Brooklyn* was unexpected, at least by Peggy Ann, who wondered before she got her statue why they insisted that she sit in an aisle seat. When they announced her name, she thought it was a mistake, and had to be pushed on stage to claim her prize.

Shirley Temple's Oscar, like Margaret's and Peggy Ann's, is smaller than the ones America has come to know and love. "It hasn't grown," Shirley observed, as I scrutinized it on a bookshelf in her living room. "I've given it vitamins and lots of shots, but it's remained small. It also had a terrible case of chicken pox. It got so pockmarked because it wasn't gold that I had to get it dipped. It was kind of a greeny thing with black spots. Looks nicer now," said Shirley.

4. "Sparkle, Shirley!"

When we moved to the first house we owned, on Genesee Avenue, my best friend was Iris Herndon, the girl next door, who was my age.

Iris could build forts and would go with me to the vacant lot across the street to unearth bones, which we identified as human. We also broke off branches laden with caterpillars from the wild licorice plants that grew there. These we placed in jars. We supplied the caterpillars with fresh leaves until they spun cocoons. We stored the jars in our garage until butterflies appeared. We impaled the butterflies on pins.

Iris and I hid from Indians on the little elevated platform Dad had built in a fork of the giant apricot tree in our backyard. And we ate apricots.

Often, as Iris and I played in our backyard, we heard her mother dying. Mother thought that Mrs. Herndon suffered from a "nervous breakdown." Her groans and shrieks of pain poured through the open window of her bedroom, facing the yard where we played. Mrs. Herndon's screams followed us even to the vacant lot across the street. While Mrs. Herndon died, Iris and her eleven-year-old sister frequently had dinner at our house. Mother assigned all of us small duties and made sure we had enough to eat. I noticed for the first time Mother's lifelong habit of offering everyone food from her plate.

One afternoon, Mrs. Herndon stopped groaning. The ambulance came and Mother went next door and brought back Iris and her sister, and they spent the night with us.

Iris's sister helped Mother prepare breakfast next morning. "Use plenty of butter on the toast," Mother said. "It's good for you." Iris's sister offered to wash the dishes, but Mother told her to go outside and play.

The next day, I started working on a picture and for the few days we shot outdoors, Iris went with us. Soon the Herndons moved and I didn't see Iris again.

When we moved to Fifth Street, Alfred Rossi was a friend. Alfred lived across the street. Mr. Rossi was a buyer for the May Company. Alfred understood business. When the circus came to town, we parked cars in a vacant lot next door to our house and charged a quarter. If people wouldn't pay, I stood by helplessly, but Alfred pursued them, down the street if necessary, to demand the money. I was impressed by Alfred's assertiveness, especially since we didn't own the lot.

Seldom did I stay overnight with friends, nor did they spend the night at my house; I was ashamed of wetting the bed. When I joined the Boy Scouts, my ambition was to win a Merit Badge for camping. But I never went camping because I feared the embarrassment of rising in the morning unable to hide the soaked bedclothes or the odor of stale urine. A sleeping bag, I thought, would solve the problem, because one could slip easily out of it, but, understandably, Mother and Dad were unwilling to buy one for me. And always, the sheets flapping on the clothesline in our own backyard were signal flags announcing my deficiencies.

Stymie was my best friend in the Gang.

Stymie was the only child actor who spent the night at our house. Of all the kids in pictures, Stymie was my best friend. I felt safe with Stymie. (Today, I wonder if I really felt superior or was less afraid of Stymie because we could not compete for roles.)

When we got home from the studio that day, I put on old clothes, and Stymie and I climbed onto the platform in the apricot tree and went "plick, plick, plick" with cap guns, shooting imaginary outlaws. For dinner, Mother roasted leg of lamb with lots of garlic and that night I didn't wet the bed.

Next day, we went to the vacant lot to play (we missed Sunday school—oh, joy!) and late in the afternoon Mother called us in so that we'd be there when Stymie's parents came to pick him up.

Five o'clock passed. The Beards did not arrive. Dad peered out the window several times, then went outside to check. A block away, Mr. and Mrs. Beard sat in their parked car. Dad walked down the street with us in tow and leaned into their car. "Mrs. Beard, what's the big idea of parking way up here? We live down the block."

Stymie's mother smiled. "Oh, you know how it is, Mr. Moore," she said. "We didn't want your neighbors thinking you go around with colored folks."

Stymie's mother told him always to greet people with a big smile and always to be polite. Even so, he had few friends. His social life, or lack of it, was typical of most of us.

I had more friends than most because usually I wasn't under contract, and I went to public school. Also, Mother encouraged me to play with children in the neighborhood.

Others were more isolated.

When, at the height of Jackie Coogan's popularity, his mother —a former vaudevillian who could never resist a sale—took him downtown shopping, they were mobbed by three thousand people and had to be rescued by police. From then on, Jackie, who found the experience terrifying, ventured out only under controlled circumstances. His house, situated on Wilshire Boulevard near Western, where a movie theater now stands, had a ten-foot wall around it. Jackie had "a 140-yard golf hole and a 75-foot swimming pool, and everything in the world that I could want." He thought back on those years:

> Duke Kahanamoku came over from Hawaii to give me swimming lessons. My dog was the son of Rin Tin Tin. I had electric cars. But I was not allowed to go on the street.
>
> My father explained it to me. He said, "Look, Jackie, you're like an investment, like our Rolls-Royce. This car cost twenty-one thousand dollars." In those days that was a lot of money. Dad said, "I don't run it in jalopy races or let parking lot attendants park it for me. I park it myself. You're like that. If something goes wrong with you, I can't say, "Hey, send me out another Jackie Coogan. You're everything there is, the whole damn thing." My mother, on the other hand, always tried to minimize my importance.

While Jackie was allowed to have friends over, he was not allowed to leave the house.

Shirley Temple was the most isolated of all. Often, during our interviews, when I sought to compare her perceptions with those of her childhood colleagues, she did not remember the incidents or even the children. "I don't have many early memories of other children or their parents because I didn't socialize with my peer group at the studio," she told me. "A lot of them I didn't know at all. Zero. I had a lot of concentration to do. I just didn't have that experience and I didn't miss it, frankly. I was going back to the studies, back to the set, back and forth to lunch, to home.

"I had to have my lunch in my bungalow because I wasn't supposed to mix with adults. I was supposed to be kept a child. They figured that if I had lunch in the commissary I would learn jokes and would become a little adult, which they didn't want. So I ate alone."

Although Shirley was not told that she was number one at the box office, occasionally she noticed something that made her suspect her life was different. In a department store one Christmas, when she sat on Santa's lap, he asked for her autograph. Pressed for an explanation, Mrs. Temple came up with, "He's just a stand-in for the real Santa."

Toward the end of our first visit, I remarked, "You were really isolated, weren't you? Far more than any of us."

Shirley was silent for a minute, then the hazel eyes sparkled and the mouth turned upward in that familiar, mocking smile. "Yes," she said finally, "but I turned out all right."

One did not have to be a Coogan or a Temple to be cut off from other youngsters. Parents often discouraged their children from forming solid friendships because friends might tell each other about a part that was coming up and then, from the parents' point of view, the wrong child would get the job.

My awareness of this competition was heightened when I came down with scarlet fever. I overheard Mother tell Dad that Freddie Bartholomew, a stranger from England, had won the role of *David Copperfield.* He was now the hot new boy in town, under contract to MGM, and I was by then reduced to going out on interviews for parts.

I didn't know Freddie yet. But somehow I knew that his Aunt Cissie kept him isolated from virtually every other child. I heard, too, that Freddie's parents, who stayed in England when Aunt Cissie brought Freddie to America, sued after he became successful. I heard they wanted a hunk of the money he earned in Hollywood.

I knew this about Freddie without knowing how I knew and I was glad that he was isolated, and secretly elated that he and Aunt Cissie had trouble with his parents.

I also felt keenly competitive with Bobs Watson and Darryl Hickman, neither of whom I really knew. Both were younger than I, but as years went on, we seemed always to compete for roles.

Darryl started as an extra at three, played Henry Fonda's little brother in *The Grapes of Wrath,* was featured in *Leave Her to Heaven, Kiss and Tell* (with Shirley), and, later, with Tracy and Hepburn in *Keeper of the Flame.* In all, Darryl played good parts in more than fifty films.

As an adolescent, I was filled with fear at the prospect of going out on interviews, and when I went, it seemed that Darryl Hickman was always there.

"I knew then you were afraid," Darryl recounted after lunch in his living room in Pacific Palisades. We were sipping white wine. "But I didn't know you were as afraid as I was. Still, we weren't any more afraid than anyone you're going to talk to on this entire fucking trip you're taking to find 'Rosebuds.' They were all as afraid as we were."

"Mickey Rooney says he was never afraid of anything," I mused. "But then again, Jackie Cooper says, 'Whatever Mickey feels is the right thing to say, right after he says it he believes it.' "

Darryl nodded. "We were all afraid—afraid of being what we were. We all played a role. You played a role, I played a role, Roddy played a role. Roddy's still doing what he thinks he's supposed to do. I'm still trying to deal with what I think I'm supposed to do. We all are—Jane Powell, Jane Withers, Dean Stockwell. Dean wasn't doing what he *was.* Dean was doing something he needed to because he thought he was supposed to."

Dean Stockwell? No! I had seen Dean a few days earlier. He seemed angry, but in touch with his feelings. He revealed to me that despite his huge success in many films, including *Kim, The Boy with Green Hair, Gentleman's Agreement,* people had always told him, "You look like Dickie Moore."

"It used to piss me off," Dean confessed. I reported this to Darryl, who told me that this happened to him too.

"When I went to MGM in 1941 and did *Men of Boys Town,* people called me Dickie constantly. I was terribly aware of you and I was compared to you, because you were a star and I was just coming along. You were an enormous presence in those days, but I also knew that your career was on the decline in some way. I was very aware of Dickie Moore."

The catalyst for my career's decline was scarlet fever. Stymie meanwhile sensed he was in trouble at Hal Roach, for a different reason. They let his hair grow out, which gave Stymie a "kind of funny feeling" that he couldn't explain at the time.

"I wasn't going to the barbershop regular anymore, getting my head shaved. You could see it in some of the later comedies. And I was getting pretty tall. I outgrew the other kids and that didn't work." Stymie spoke dispassionately. "That's why Spanky stayed in for ten years; he stayed short."

When Stymie was dropped in 1935, it was "a heck of a transition. It felt very bad, 'cause nobody explained to me what happened. They'd brought Buckwheat in when I started getting too large, just as they had brought me in when Farina started getting too large; and I knew that Farina had had the same feeling when I took his place."

Edith Fellows's career also went into decline. She fought back tears at our last meeting as she recalled:

While I was under contract to Columbia, they bought a property for me, *Her First Beau,* and I persuaded the people at the studio to let my girlfriend Millie Lou play my friend in the film. But I never got to do the picture because the next time my option came up, the studio dropped me. If they'd kept me on, my salary would have gone to twelve hundred a week.

Now, Charlie Barton directed me in many films. I loved Charlie. He called one day after I had been let go by Columbia. Grandma had just died. Charlie said, "We're finally going to film *Her First Beau.*" I got all excited. But he said, "No, Jane Withers is the star. But you know that little part you wanted your girlfriend Millie Lou to do? We'd like you to play that."

I knew Jane, and I liked her, but I was hurt that Charlie could ask me to play a bit part. I almost said no. But instead I said, "Okay, Charlie, I'll do the part, but I want the money I would have got if my option had been taken up. You tell them that." I couldn't believe it was me talking. It was the first time I ever got tough. I never was that materialistic, actually. But I was so hurt that I had to hit back with something. I was sure they would turn me down, because the part did not call for that kind of money. But they said they'd pay me what I wanted. I guess they figured I had some name value left.

So I went back to Columbia, to my family. But I had to swallow a lot to go back and play that part.

My old teacher, Lillian Bartley, was still at the studio. We were shooting on Valentine's Day and Lillian came to me and said, "The guys in the proproom are making a huge round heart of wood and they've painted it pink, with 'To Our Valentine' written on it. I'm just telling you so that it won't be a shock and you won't cry."

I said, "Thank you. I appreciate that."

Well. Lunchtime came and I see the prop guys, my buddies, lugging this huge Valentine onto the set. And I'm saying to myself, "Don't cry, Edith, don't get sentimental. Be tough. Grow up!"

They walked right past me and gave the Valentine to Jane.

Lillian took me into the dressing room, shut the door, and said, "For God's sake, Edith, cry!" And I did. I'm crying now.

When I told Jane Withers Edith's story, she jumped as though I had plugged her into an electric socket. "Oh, dear God, I didn't know that," Jane exclaimed. "I remember the Valentine. I still have it. I treasure it."

Jane grew pensive, her mind tunneling back through memories of fifty years to the time when she appeared in *Bright Eyes* with Shirley Temple, the film that made Jane a star. Finally, Jane spoke, with unusual deliberation. "That story about Edith and me and the Valentine reminds me so much of something that happened on *Bright Eyes.* Naturally, Shirley was the star of the picture, but we were the only two children in the film. When the shooting ended, they had a little party. I wasn't even invited to it. But when an actress [Lois Wilson] finished her part in the film, she brought this beautiful doll to Shirley. I'm sure she didn't realize what it would do to another child, but we were both there, you know."

I asked Jane about her relationship with Shirley. I had been told that after *Bright Eyes,* Jane was not permitted to enter the main Fox lot on Pico Boulevard. All of her films were shot at a little studio on Western Avenue which Fox owned. The story went that Mrs. Temple was a factor in Jane's exile. A sunny, outgoing child, Shirley knew nothing about such matters. She did later affirm that she and Jane "were on different lots. We weren't friends as children. We did one film together and that's all. We didn't socialize at all."

Jane had also heard the story of her banishment to Western

Avenue. "I don't know if it was true or not. But on *Bright Eyes,* I was not permitted even to associate with Shirley when we weren't in a scene together." Jane elaborated:

I couldn't even talk to her. Later, our director, David Butler, said he always felt his hands were tied and he had a gag in his mouth through that whole movie. He told me, "You stole the picture. When we were working with you, we knew it would happen and we knew it was going to be absolute misery for all of us."

I was not permitted to talk to Shirley at all. I even was told to go and wash my hands before I went into a scene with her. That upset Mother a lot. She wanted to go and talk with Mrs. Temple.

She told the studio people, "Jane is a very clean child. And don't worry, I'll make very sure that her hands are washed before she goes into a scene with Shirley." And she did. But they wouldn't let Mother talk directly to Mrs. Temple.

The only time we even saw Mrs. Temple was after *Bright Eyes* was released and we were getting telegrams and wonderful letters congratulating me. We were thrilled and we thought she would be too, because if it hadn't been for Shirley, I might have ended up selling hats in Bullock's.

We saw Shirley and Mrs. Temple on the lot and Mother said, "Oh, we must go thank her and tell her how much this means to us."

She saw us coming and she crossed the street and started down the other way with Shirley. Shirley kept looking back and smiling and waving. I was saying "Hi" to her, and Mother was bound and determined to say thank you. So she crossed over and we ran and got in front of her, so she had to stop. I remember this as though it were yesterday.

My mother said, "Hello, Mrs. Temple." She replied, "Hello," and was very curt. Mother said, "I have been trying to talk to you all through the film, which was not possible. I just wanted to thank you for the great opportunity that Shirley's picture afforded Jane."

I said, "It just meant the world to me to work with you."

Mother said, "Look at these marvelous telegrams and these letters that people are sending, saying congratulations. I felt you'd be happy about it."

Mrs. Temple said, "Come, Shirley, we must be going." Then she grabbed Shirley. Shirley looked a little bewildered and she started to say something. Her mother literally jerked her away. I never saw her again, until we were adults. I always wanted desperately to know her. I didn't know if she was afraid because of what her mother had said, or what, but even later she was not anxious to make friends.

By the time I worked with Shirley in *Miss Annie Rooney,* both of us were teenagers. Shirley had left Fox. Mrs. Temple, a tall, angular woman, wore expensive tailored suits and alligator shoes. (Mother was impressed by those.)

Before each of Shirley's scenes, Mrs. Temple positioned herself behind the camera just before the action started, and called softly, "Sparkle, Shirley!" to help focus her daughter's concentration. She had done this since Shirley was a tot.

I liked Gertrude Temple. I wondered why she was so nice to me when, I knew, I was so terrible in her daughter's picture. Mrs. Temple made no effort to keep me away from Shirley, who by then was attending Westlake School for Girls. She treated Mother and me cordially and invited us one day to their home.

There, after lunch, we toured the grounds and inspected the Doll House, a bright, farmhouse-style poolside bungalow, larger than our home. Entirely separate from the main house, it held Shirley's vast doll collection, which reposed inside glass cases. During that visit, Mrs. Temple spoke of a meeting she'd had with studio boss Darryl F. Zanuck after *The Blue Bird* was released. The film, the last that Shirley did for Fox, was not successful, and rumors circulated that Zanuck would not stand in the way if Mrs. Temple wanted Shirley to leave the studio. Although Shirley was no longer Hollywood's number one box office attraction, Zanuck's studio, under the terms of her contract, continued to pay her salary—and Mrs. Temple's too.

"Zanuck didn't look at me once during our meeting in his office," Mrs. Temple told us. "He carried on the entire conversation with a golf club in his hand and never looked up from the ball he was putting on the carpet. I told him if he wanted to get rid of us, he would have to pay off every penny that was called for in our contract." Mrs. Temple smiled tightly. She didn't like Darryl Zanuck, and he didn't like her because she was as tough as he was. Yes, Gertrude Temple was fiercely protective of Shirley. She knew that no one else would be.

Before Shirley hit it big, Fox was going down the tubes. A visible symbol of the studio's resurgence was its new Main Administration Building, built with money that Shirley's pictures earned. Everyone called it the Temple Building, except when Mr. Zanuck was within earshot. Zanuck did not like to believe that anyone but Darryl F. Zanuck had a hand in the studio's newfound success, so when he was near, the new edifice was called "The Main Administration Building."

Shirley didn't know this until I told her recently. She suddenly became an ambassador (her favorite role) again: "It's just like the Persian Gulf or the Arabian Gulf. What you call it depends on which side you're on."

After *The Little Princess,* starring Shirley Temple, was released, Hedda Hopper and Louella Parsons, the preeminent Hollywood columnists of the day, raved about Sybil Jason's work in the film. Hopper reported a "rumor" that Sybil "will never work with Shirley Temple again."

Then Sybil was signed for *The Blue Bird.* "In preproduction tests, they made me read Shirley's lines while they tested for the other players," Sybil remembered. "Even at that age, I knew it wasn't right for me to do that." But, Sybil said, she did what she was told.

I had some damn good sequences. In one scene, Shirley brings the blue bird to me and suddenly I discover I can walk. It was a hell of a sequence.

About two weeks before the premiere, Walter Lang, the director of both *Little Princess* and *Blue Bird,* called my sister and me to his office and said, "I don't know how to say this. It's the best damned sequence in the whole movie, but Mrs. Temple said if it's not cut out, Shirley and she will walk out of the studio." He said, "My hands are tied. I want to explain to you. It's cut out of the movie. I had to do it."

When the film was shown, the sequence didn't make sense. Suddenly I'm in the bed and suddenly I'm outside with Shirley.

Mrs. Temple had the right to say who was in the movie, how it was cast, to choose the director, the cameraman.

Shirley never realized any of this. I knew something was happening, but it didn't faze me at the time because Shirley was so damned sweet.

When Delmar Watson was in *Heidi*, another Shirley Temple film, they would not give him his lines to study in advance. Delmar remembers that he was mystified by this. "They said they wanted my character to be kind of dumb, but it was the only time I was in a picture of that length where they would not give me my lines until the night before I was supposed to do a scene."

"They're not being fair to the boy," Coy Watson complained to his family around the dinner table. "They're changing his dialogue right on the set. It's almost like they're making him stumble over his lines to make Shirley look better."

Mr. Watson blamed the studio. Later, when they wanted Delmar's brother Bobs to appear with Shirley in *The Blue Bird*, Mr. Watson named the price and then said, "And I want a completed script that won't be changed." The deal fell through.

Coy Watson was a taskmaster. Bobs and Delmar recall him as loving and attentive. To me he seemed aloof, interested only in his boys and their performance. "You had to watch your ribs when you were in a scene with them," Jackie Coogan told me. "They'd poke you out of the way with an elbow."

One day, Mother came home from the studio after a group of us had tested for a part. The test called for us to cry. She told Dad that Mr. Watson had said to Bobs, "You cry now or you'll cry when you get home." Mother was horrified.

So was Bobs when I asked him about it forty-five years later. "That never happened. Not once, not ever," he said emphatically. Then Bobs talked lovingly about his father and the joy of being able, because his dad was always with him on the set, to spend so much time with him. Bobs told me how much he still misses his dad. And Bobs cried.

Among Bobs's many films was *Wyoming*, starring Wallace Beery and Ann Rutherford. Ann remembers Coy Watson as "the Mrs. Temple of the troupe":

There was one scene where some member of little Bobs's family was supposed to have died and he was supposed to go into hysterics. Actually, he was a very happy little boy. He was having a perfectly lovely time that morning and the director was having a bit of a problem with him. I saw Coy, his father, call him aside and check his watch and then whisper something in Bobs's ear. Little Bobs recoiled in horror and went rushing back onto the set, weeping. I've never seen a scene played as brilliantly in my life. The only thing that threw me was that all during the scene, Wallace Beery was quietly inspecting his head and killing fleas with his fingernails; picked his nose a little, scratched his navel. He did all those terrible things to steal attention while little Bobs was playing this brilliantly emotional scene.

Afterward, we were all comforting Bobs, and his father came over and said, "It's all right. You did it within the time."

And I said, "Did what?"

He said, "Well, I told him his dog would have to be sent to the pound unless he did this scene within the next ten minutes."

He was really a very loving father, but that was his method.

Parents used many methods to advance their children's careers. When Diana Cary's stardom waned, she competed for small parts like everybody else and learned firsthand what movie mothers (she calls them "the saber-tooth tigers of the Hollywood jungle") could be like.

Diana shook her head:

The first real exposure I had was for a film called *The Good Fairy*, with Margaret Sullavan, which required lots of children for background shots. There was no chance to do anything, but the mothers were all hoping. "Doesn't she look good? She's right behind the star." "She said a line." "I'll bet she'll have a line with Margaret Sullavan, and you know what *that* means."

These mothers made so much out of so little. They were so desperate. They had no real identity of their own. Everything was tied up in the child. The main thing that surprised me about them was that they were so vicious.

When I had been under contract, I'd never had a feeling of competing. Later, when I got an interview, I'd be in a small waiting room with six or eight other girls—Anita Louise, Rochelle Hudson, and myself—and their mothers, and the air was electric; and the man who interviewed us would take us in one at a time and they would come back out, and they all tried to look like they had it in their pocket. It was a very strange feeling.

By this time I was in my late teens and it seemed strange that these women had to go with their daughters, who were seventeen- or eighteen-year-old girls. But the mothers were very concerned about moral aspects. They'd had these daughters on the road for quite a while. That was what impressed me: how long these girls had been earning a living.

I would see mothers go up to directors in the commissary, but the stories about mothers throwing their feminine charms at directors to try to get their child a job were exaggerated, because most directors had a horror of stage mothers. They didn't come pretty enough to risk the consequences of being asked to practically take over the child's career. Most of the mothers were rather dumpy, unattractive women who were either overweight or showed the effects of a hard life. The children were beautiful. You'd wonder how this child could be the daughter of this rather unattractive mother. They were hardscrabble people, who came to Hollywood primarily for the money.

Margaret O'Brien's mother was one good-looking woman who played the Hollywood game well. She got to be on extremely friendly terms with Louis B. Mayer, the boss of MGM. This enabled her to march into his office at option time and demand (and get) more money. And she had firmly held opinions about scripts.

"Mother was a very smart businesswoman," Margaret affirmed. "For example, everyone thought that Lillian Burns was just the drama coach at MGM, but Mother knew that Lillian had a lot to say about who got roles and who didn't."

Most of Metro's contract children shared a special table at the far end of the MGM commissary, where they ate lunch. Margaret made an indelible impression on Darryl Hickman:

> Margaret would come into the commissary with her mother and sometimes her aunt and they would have lunch at that table. But Margaret used to stop and sit on a number of laps in the commissary before she got to the table. Or if she got to the table and somebody came in whose lap needed sitting on, she would go and sit on it. It was lap hopping. It was like a ritual. I always remember her doing this in a way that seemed very dutiful, but I'm not sure she had any sense of why she was sitting on all those laps—a lot of Santa Clauses, I guess, giving her whatever prize she was hoping to get. But I think her mother directed this little commissary scene.

Parents who played an obviously active, manipulating role in their children's careers were generally intimidating people. Yet, ironically, I (and others, I discovered) envied kids who had them. Even at five, I felt in some vague way that neither Mother nor Dad was in control of what was happening to me. We seemed forever to be pawns in someone else's game. I wished that Mrs. Temple were my mother. She was the queen.

Mickey Rooney, for many years the king, was, as usual, a law unto himself. Once his career was launched, Mickey ran the show himself, starting at age six.

By a substantial majority, our peers consider Mickey to be the best actor of us all—then as well as now. But off the screen, they found him harder to take.

"He was one of the biggest talents ever in any business," Jane Withers said positively. Jane worked with Mickey when he was still Mickey McGuire, in a show called the *Marco Juvenile Review*, which paid $6 a performance. "I was much younger than Mickey, but even as a child I was always upset with Mickey's arrogance. I wanted to go up and shake him and say, 'Look, fella, aren't you aware of how terribly lucky you are? Sure, you're very talented, but so are a lot of other people. Do you realize the situation you're in and how many young people's lives you influence?' "

Jackie Cooper also worked with Mickey, but they were not friends. "Even if he'd wanted to be friendly with me, my mother wouldn't have tolerated it because she believed he touched peepees with girls, and she didn't want any of that when I was thirteen."

Jackie Coogan never minced words: "Mickey around guys is a pain in the ass. He's got a great sense of humor and he loves to put on the paper hats and lampshades. He's the life of the party. He's doing his father, Joe Yule, but who the hell knows anything about Joe Yule?"

Boys Town was the vehicle that brought many Hollywood youngsters into daily contact with Rooney. Bobs Watson, who played Pee Wee, idolized Mickey on and off the screen. Even at seven, Bobs was struck by the older boy's brilliance as an actor:

> There was a scene where I get hit by a car and Mickey runs over and picks me up and he cries. I never felt so much emotion coming out of anybody. He was absolutely fantastic.
>
> Years later, Norman Taurog, who directed *Boys Town*, lived near where I was working and he invited me to visit. Of course, we got to reminiscing, and Taurog told me what really happened when we shot that scene.
>
> Mickey had been acting like a "spoiled brat," Taurog told me. "He had been giving us a lot of trouble and he said, 'Well, I don't know whether I'm going to do this scene your way or not.' "
>
> Taurog said, "Mickey, you can do the scene any way you want, if you want that little kid Bobs to steal it from you. He's giving you a run for your money. Just watch what he's doing. See if you can match it. I don't think you can, but you do whatever you want to."
>
> Mickey came through like Gangbusters.

Our work seldom brought us into contact with children who were not in pictures. Even when it did, such relationships were, for the most part, fleeting.

Most of us felt different, shy. Rare attempts to socialize with children outside the business, when permitted, were usually unsuccessful. Roddy McDowall knows exactly when he started feeling different. It was right after *How Green Was My Valley* was released.

Before that, he never thought that being in films made him special as a kid. "But when I went out into the street after the film came out, the kids on the block wouldn't play with me." More than forty years later, Roddy still seemed bewildered. "They wouldn't even talk to me. They were afraid of me. Double jeopardy because I was English and I talked funny, and also because I didn't go to school."

Ann Rutherford, Jackie Cooper, Mickey Rooney, Margaret O'-Brien, Jane Powell, Darryl Hickman, Elizabeth Taylor, Dean Stockwell, Freddie Bartholomew, and Judy Garland were some of the youngsters under contract to MGM. A common misperception is that they all were close friends. Not true. Margaret O'Brien's experience was typical. "I really didn't know anybody when I came to the studio, because they were teenagers when I was little. Elizabeth Taylor was older and dating and Jane Powell was already engaged. Natalie Wood was in another studio, so I didn't know her until we were teenagers. Roddy was older. Dean Stockwell and I were the same age and we would play on the set of *Secret Garden.* I really liked Dean, but he didn't want to play with girls. Darryl Hickman was a little older, so he didn't want to bother with me."

I told Darryl what Margaret said. Was his experience the same? I asked. "My problem was they always seemed to put girls under contract, and the only one who would play football with me was Elizabeth Taylor. She would get out on the lawn in front of the schoolhouse and we would tackle each other. She was the tomboy, the one most willing to punch and tackle and block and shove and hit." Darryl laughed. "If only I knew then what I know now."

It wasn't always thus. Early in their careers, Gloria Jean and Elizabeth went to school at Universal. Gloria laughed, as she remembered that "Elizabeth was very, very shy, and when people would come into the schoolhouse she'd hide under the table. The teacher would say, 'Elizabeth, you've got to get over this shyness.' "

Jane Powell, too, was shy. And lonely. She met Roddy McDowall during her third picture, *Holiday in Mexico,* and he began invit-

Jane Powell and Roddy McDowall met during the filming of *Holiday in Mexico.* Both shy, they became and remain close friends. Jane says, "Roddy saw the loneliness in me."

ing her over to his house on Sunday afternoons. That's the only place she ever went, Jane says.

For the first two years in Hollywood, I was really miserable. If it hadn't been for the Sundays at Roddy's, I don't know what I'd have done. I think he saw the loneliness in me. I wanted to go to a public school so bad, because at least there I could meet people. But I never met anybody. I was always in between. Elizabeth was younger than I was and of course she was very sophisticated. She never went anyplace either, but she had her horses. I sang, so I was always taking lessons when I wasn't going to school or working. That's all I knew. There was no place for me to meet people. I tried going to church, but then when events came up I would be working and I'd miss the hayride or whatever.

And then letters would come from Portland telling me about the wonderful times they were having, the proms and parties, which I never had.

Among the most painfully shy of a shy group was Deanna (Edna Mae) Durbin, queen of the Universal lot. But most other children liked her.

Juanita Quigley, ten years younger than Deanna, idolized the older girl "because she was so sincere." Under contract to Universal at seven, Juanita appeared with Deanna in *That Certain Age.* The second assistant director on that picture was Vaughn Paul, whom Deanna married in 1941 when she was nineteen. Just prior to the wedding, Juanita rang Deanna's doorbell.

I arrived in the midst of all the confusion and excitement with her family and many other people there. I walked up to the door just to hand my wedding present in, but Deanna insisted that I come in and sit down and she talked to me and spent a lot of time showing her concern for me. She didn't have to do that, but that was her nature.

At the peak of her immense popularity, Deanna—together with Donald O'Connor—ensured Universal's status as a major studio. Universal knew that Deanna couldn't last forever, though they probably didn't know she would flee town. At any rate, they found and signed young Gloria Jean Schoonover to follow in her footsteps.

"One of the thrills of my life was meeting Deanna Durbin when I signed my contract," Gloria recounted to me. "She was very formal and nice. She shook my hand and said, 'I'm glad someone is following in my footsteps.' People thought we were close. They took pictures of us together and Deanna put her arm around me. I don't think she spoke two words. From what I understand, she didn't care for me."

All of Gloria Jean's Universal pictures were shot in black and white. Technicolor was an exciting new development, and Gloria desperately wanted to do a film in color. She was told she could not because Deanna owned stock in the studio. "I met her mother once and she told me that she was disappointed that Deanna acted above her after becoming famous," Gloria said sadly. "She said, 'I don't know whatever happened to my daughter.' "

What happened to Mrs. Durbin's daughter was that "she felt she was a stock issue and never grew up as a person," Donald O'Connor said with quiet conviction when our conversation turned to Deanna. Donald knew Deanna well:

> You hear a lot of stories about how she was stuck-up, temperamental, hard to get along with. It wasn't that at all. It got to a point where she could no longer perform. She could no longer work if there were any strangers around.
>
> The first picture I made after I got out of the service was with Deanna, *Something in the Wind.* We were in the isolation booth of the recording stage and the orchestra was outside. We were getting along just fine, singing and telling jokes, when a couple of tourists walked onto the set. Deanna started to shake and sweat. It had nothing to do with temperament. She was going through a traumatic situation. Personally and professionally, she couldn't cope with it.
>
> She got to a point where she had to make a decision: to keep on like that or quit. She chose not to work anymore.

Everyone who touched Jane Withers's life envied Jane her parents. "Both of them were nice country folks," Edith Fellows recalls. "They never changed." Jane agrees emphatically, yet for all the positive things she has to say about her childhood, I was told that when somebody suggested putting Jane's daughter in films, her immediate response was: "Oh, no, not that."

5. Stay Young and Don't Get Sick

Mother couldn't get over the birthday card I gave her when I was eight. It was so cute, she said.

"Look at what Dickie wrote on my card," she said to Aunty Ruth. " 'Happy Birthday to Mother, from your friend, Dickie Moore.' "

"It's adorable," Aunty Ruth said.

"Let me see," said Aunty Jo, reaching for the card. Aunty Jo, like Aunty Ruth, was not related to us. She had been the nurse at my birth and had become a family friend. Aunty Jo examined the card and commented that my handwriting had become legible. She could actually read it, she said.

I'd had plenty of practice writing that year—1933—because I had signed hundreds of autographs. From 1931 to that point, no fewer than twenty-five major films starred or featured Dickie Moore. My picture appeared often in magazines, along with articles and interviews. Every photo I sent out bore the legend: "from your friend, Dickie Moore." So Mother's card got the same treatment.

Besides acting in movies, I modeled a line of clothes named after me. Big Little Books appeared about my life and about some of the characters I played. Once I bought a paper cup of vanilla ice cream and looked to see which movie star's picture was on the inside of the lid (a forerunner of bubble gum cards). It was mine, inscribed, as always, "Best wishes, from your friend, Dickie Moore."

During this period, Mother decided that I should take swimming lessons. So for several Saturdays we turned up at Bimini Plunge, a complex with several pools. The experience was terrifying: the acrid smell of chlorine, the inflatable water wings, which I was sure would not support me. The teacher descended with me into the pool and retreated backward toward deep water, instructing me to follow. I cheated as much as possible, keeping my feet on the bottom of the pool until the water got too deep.

I hated Saturdays. My instructor, a burly man with thick black hair, exhorted me to greater daring. Since I was a "natural swimmer, with nothing to fear," I should submerge my head, he said. Instead, I continued desperately to dog paddle in a futile effort to catch up, but always he stayed just beyond reach. Finally, at the end of the pool, I grabbed the edge and hung on. As each lesson ended, my instructor tossed me off the deep end. I paddled frantically and grabbed the side for dear life.

When my swimming lessons ended, I did a film, *Gallant Lady*, with Ann Harding and Otto Kruger. I played Ann Harding's son, who in one scene fell off a dock into a lake. I was supposed to swim inexpertly and to cough and splutter upon reaching safety. It was perfect casting.

On weekends, Mother dressed me in short pants, and she and Dad and I would go for Sunday dinner, most often to the Carolina Pines. There for $1.95 they served what Dad described as "a full-course meal." Deluxe dinners were $2.95. We didn't order those.

Sometimes, when Dad prevailed, we went to Ptomaine Tommy's, a tiled emporium with a long counter along one side and sawdust on the floor. Tommy was a friend of Frank Moorhouse, for whom Dad worked briefly, until Frank's battery factory failed. At Tommy's, for twenty-five cents, we had hamburgers with onions.

Tommy had become locally famous by winning a lawsuit brought by a customer who claimed to have ingested, along with Tommy's hamburgers, a case of ptomaine poisoning. Tommy expanded the name of his restaurant to celebrate the verdict.

When I wasn't occupied with swimming or piano lessons, school or Sunday school, acting, or the Carolina Pines, I played with children in the neighborhood.

Those were busy days. Mother talked about our going to London to star in a film, if British Equity consented. (Then, as now, the British actors' union decided which foreigners could or couldn't work in England.) They ruled me out. But I heard Mother say that I was up for a film to be called *David Copperfield.* It would, she said, be a Very Important Picture. I didn't get it.

Still, I went from one film to another. Changes were taking place at home: the novelty of the Buick was wearing off; a new house was being built for us, in a different neighborhood; Mother got fat and one day she went to the hospital and later returned home with my sister Patricia.

In the midst of this excitement, I got scarlet fever. My temperature soared and my chest was covered with a rash. Then I developed an earache. The doctor who had delivered Pat came to check on me as well. "He'll be okay," he said. My room was quarantined. The doctor lanced my ear, but still I slept most of the time. Dad and Mother worried. The doctor said my ear was draining and that these things took time; don't worry.

Aunty Jo thought otherwise. "That boy is really sick," she said. "I'm calling Dr. Godshall." Leon Godshall was in charge of eyes, ears, noses, and throats at Cedars of Lebanon Hospital. She called him. "He's waiting for you, Jack," she said to Dad, "and I want you to get Dickie over there right now."

Dad bundled me up and we went to see Dr. Godshall. He took an x-ray and put me in the hospital. That afternoon they shaved my head. That night he operated.

The ether was like cold liquid being poured right through my body. I wanted to throw up.

Next day, I awakened with a nurse in my room and asked for

waffles. The nurse jumped up and said, "Let's call your folks. They'll be so happy."

"Where are they?" I asked. "Why aren't they here?" The nurse explained that Mother wasn't well and that my new sister, Pat, was home. She phoned them. Mother and Dad arrived at the hospital laughing, touching me, and saying what a miracle it was I wanted waffles.

Dr. Godshall came also. He smiled. After he left, Aunty Jo, Mother, and Dad compared notes on what Dr. Godshall had told them the night before, after he operated. He had said that the mastoid bone was practically eaten away, that this operation should have been done weeks ago, and that "if he lives through the night, he will be okay."

I spent Saturday mornings in Dr. Godshall's office with Argyrol packs stuffed up my nose. Somewhere along the way, I'd picked up sinus trouble. Dad usually took me to Dr. Godshall. I shared his embarrassment as he asked, "How much is this visit, Doctor? Dickie is not working so much anymore and nobody wants bookkeepers."

"Don't worry about it," Dr. Godshall said. "A visit is two dollars." Dad would shift his weight and cough and glance backward over his shoulder. "Thanks, Doctor," he would say. "That's mighty decent of you."

After my operation, I wasn't strong enough to work for several months. Besides, I had no hair. When I started getting jobs again, I noticed that the parts were smaller. Sometimes I did not have a private dressing room on the set. We were not always able to drive our car through the front gate of the studio. On location, we didn't always get the big box lunch with cold chicken. Occasionally, we got the smaller size, for people less important.

Sometimes I didn't have a stand-in.

Before the scarlet fever, we just showed up for work, but now I had to go on interviews and meet directors—sometimes even casting directors—to see if I was right for parts.

"Dickie's been out of the public eye for some time." Dad would explain my diminished status to friends. "You just can't take a vacation in this business." How did he know that scarlet fever seemed like a vacation?

Before getting sick, I had played in the fish pond in front of Fairfax High School, collecting polliwogs in mayonnaise jars and watching them become frogs. Playing in the fish pond was the reason I had "contracted" scarlet fever, Dad said accusingly. I wondered what a contract had to do with scarlet fever.

Slowly, my strength returned. One sunny day, Mother, Dad, and I drove over to Fifth Street to look at the skeleton of our new house. The foundations still smelled of fresh concrete, the frame was up, the floor was down. Scraps of lumber, nails, little metal slugs—like nickels punched from holes in the electric switchboxes—lay everywhere. I took some slugs home.

We toured the building site. Dad pointed to a future bedroom here, a bathroom there. Mother stood where the patio would be. Now we would have to get a mortgage, she told Dad. Money was tight, Dad said. My ears began to ring and I felt dizzy. Instead of visiting our house as conquerors, we were there as beggars, victims. Our life suddenly was dark and wrong because of something I had done.

We had lost a year, possibly a future. Could we get it back before time passed me by? How do you kill the clock?

We lied about my age. At eight, we said that I was seven; at nine, we said I was eight; at ten, I pretended to be nine. When I turned eleven, we finally told the truth.

Many children lied about their ages, and the studios lied for them. It fostered the idea that we were precocious. Knocking years off our ages, it was hoped, would stretch our acting careers. Studios and parents with investments to protect wanted us to stay the productive kids we were.

As Baby Peggy, Diana Cary started in the business at twenty months. They lied about her age, Diana said, because "our only value lay in our youth, like a bonsai tree which is only valuable because it looks like a mighty oak, but is only three inches tall. We were all bonsai. The entire 'Our Gang' was nothing but a bonsai forest."

At four and a half, Diana knew she was aging. "I was picking up on the vibes from my folks that I was nearly at the end of my rope. Things were not going well. My career was in danger. I was getting old."

At first, Universal wanted Gloria Jean to be older so she could play romantic leads. Gloria noticed a change later. When she started to develop, "They got frightened. 'Wait a minute,' they said. 'This girl's starting to look pretty old.' They took me to the wardrobe department and the wardrobe lady strapped gauze around me to flatten me. They did that with Judy Garland too. Judy developed at an early age, so they bound her up for *The Wizard of Oz* and flattened her out. Judy hated that."

Fox was not enthused about Jane Withers's physical development, which came very quickly. They still had her in pigtails, and kids would write and ask her, "Hey, how come you're still in pigtails and we're wearing party dresses?"

Jane told the people at the studio, "I'm really embarrassed, gentlemen. You're not letting me grow up. I can hardly breathe in this dress." She was almost fifteen, and was so disgusted at the attempts to keep her a little girl that she wrote herself a film called *Small Town Deb.* She grew up in that.

Ann Rutherford, who broke in a bit older than the rest of us, bucked the trend by trying to be as womanly as possible. "I told them I was eighteen, otherwise they wouldn't have used me," Ann said, laughing. "I did about fifteen pictures for Mascot within ten months, until my mother took one good look at me in daylight and broke my contract. I had circles under my circles. In those days, you shot a six-day week, and if you were on location, you shot a seven-day week; and most of those pictures were made in eleven days. If it was a big feature, they made it in fourteen days. And if you were shooting in town, they could work you until midnight every night.

"I didn't even drive. A car picked me up at home in the morning

Ann Rutherford (here with Walter Huston and James Stewart) was a leading lady in Westerns at sixteen. "What did I know," Ann recalled. "I just stuffed Kleenex in my bra and went out and said, 'I'm a leading lady.' "

Mickey Rooney as Mickey McGuire.

and took me home at midnight, and I'd just sleep faster. I went from one picture right to another. But I loved it."

Ann was a leading lady in all those films. "What did I know?" she asked rhetorically. "I stuffed a lot of Kleenex in my bra and went out and said, 'I'm a leading lady.' "

Metro wanted to make Jackie Cooper younger. He was ten when his mother talked to him about it. "I was against it, she was against it, that was that," said Jackie. "I had to live with the kids in the neighborhood. And, God knows, when you're ten you don't want to go around saying you're nine."

Delmar Watson felt that the studios didn't lie about his age because he wasn't under contract. But, he said during our talk, "Shirley Temple went from two years younger than I was to four years younger."

Mickey Rooney can't recall that anyone ever lied about his age, but he knew the practice was prevalent and understood why. "When the studio realized they were losing that baby-doll quality of Shirley, they tried to disguise it, but they couldn't hide her puberty," Mickey observed. "And all of a sudden little Elizabeth Taylor began to sprout. They couldn't do anything about that, either, the way she was going."

Even the dog Brownie—Baby Peggy's first on-screen leading man—was preoccupied with age. Diana remembers Brownie as "a very clever dog and very well known, but after about six months of our working together, he died in his sleep. He was much older than he ever admitted."

Age, teeth, diet, and health are not matters of great concern for most children. For us they were. So were hair, clothes, and names. Boys wore their hair long: We could always cut it, but couldn't grow it overnight. For free-lance actors, another consideration was "dressing for the part."

When they needed a kid for a New York scene or for a Western, Mr. Watson dressed his boys in tough-kid clothes with knickers or cowboy outfits, and "we'd go out in the streets in these dumb clothes," Delmar Watson said. "It wasn't bad when we were on the set, but I hated to be out in public, where people would say, 'What the hell is that kid doing in those funny clothes?' "

Names were changed like wardrobes. Mickey Rooney was born Joe Yule, Jr. According to Mickey, "They changed my name to Mickey McGuire at five, Mickey Rooney at twelve. I knew that it was a theatrical move, and it didn't bother me because I have always been nothing but Joe Yule."

Jackie Cooper's family name is Bigelow; Natalie Wood was Natasha Gurdin; Judy Garland, Frances Gumm. John Richard Moore, Jr., became Dickie at the moment of birth. Spanky is George McFarland, Stymie was Matthew Beard. Gloria Jean Schoonover lost her last name, of course. Jane Powell is Suzanne Burce. She wanted to be Cheryl, but learned her new name was Jane Powell when they phoned her from the studio.

"Hello, is Jane Powell there?"

"Sorry, wrong number." Suzanne started to hang up.

"No, that's your name, Jane Powell. It's the name of the girl you will play in your first picture."

"Oh, well, if you're going to change my name, could you maybe call her Cheryl? Cheryl *anything!* Cheryl Powell would be fine."

"No, your name is Jane Powell."

Like Jane, Margaret O'Brien was named after her character in her first film, *Journey for Margaret.*

Some children watched their weight. Judy Garland dieted for at least two years before *The Wizard of Oz.* During that time, Sybil Jason rode with Judy in the Hollywood Christmas parade:

> Santa sat in the middle and Judy and I sat on each side of him. Judy waved to everybody on her side while I waved to everybody on my side. Santa had his sack full of candy and he was throwing it out to the people lining Hollywood Boulevard.
>
> Judy had an obsession with food. The poor child must have been starving even then, because the first thing she asked me was, "Did you eat?" I said, "Well, I had a little snack before we came, but I understand they're going to feed us at the end of the parade."

While we were waving, I noticed Judy digging her hand into Santa's sack and eating all the candy she could get. I mean, she was hungry.

After the parade, there was a wonderful buffet and Judy started to fill her plate and some man from MGM came along and took it from her. She didn't have anything to eat all night. She sat at the table with a glass of water in front of her.

In the early days of movies, makeup was simple. Very few people knew anything about it. It was made to hold against strong lights. Everyone used lipstick. The makeup was applied in the morning and powdered throughout the day. As a child, Diana Cary applied her own. Since both the makeup and the powder had a lead base, by the end of the day, Diana says, her face was two pounds heavier.

Ann Rutherford remembers makeup as a means by which they "tried to force future stars into molds. Everybody had their eyebrows plucked. One day, I ran away from the head of makeup, Jack Dawn. 'Don't you ever do that to me anymore,' I told him." Ann remembers a lovely young girl sitting in the makeup chair, getting ready for her first test: "Different casting directors came down and peered at her intently. After they'd replucked her eyebrows fifteen times, they plugged a cleft in her chin with some sort of material. Are you ready? Finally, someone with good sense looked at the test and decided she was more distinctive with that lovely dimple in her chin. The girl was Ava Gardner."

The use of makeup by all actors was taken for granted, even by the public. People (mostly blacks) asked Stymie why he let them put black grease on his face. That bothered Stymie. "You know they never did that," he told me once. "They never put black grease on my face."

Sybil Jason was with Warner Brothers doing a film with Humphrey Bogart when she first lost a tooth. They rushed her to a dentist "to put a falsie in." Mysteriously, a box of taffy appeared in front of her trailer. Someone saw Bogart put it there. Sybil doesn't know if he wanted to help her lose another tooth or if he was being kind, anonymously.

The absence of teeth caused particular anxiety for Diana Cary, coming as it did during a slump in her career. After Diana's father refused to renegotiate a contract on terms acceptable to the producer, two front teeth fell out at once. This happened in the 1920s, before the studios had acquired enough sophistication to have dentists waiting in the wings for instant repairs.

The "Our Gang" kids were supposed to be ordinary people. If one of the gang lost a tooth, it was accepted as normal. But Diana, as Baby Peggy, was a glamorous star. No one could imagine her without teeth.

As it happened, a producer chose this moment to interview her for a low-budget ("poverty row") picture. Diana's father told her, "Be pleasant, but don't smile."

The producer examined her and said he thought she'd do. "I can't pay her what she used to get, but I'll pay a hundred and fifty for the picture, ten days' work." Her father agreed and Diana was so pleased she had been accepted that she curtsied at the man and grinned.

"My God," he said, "what happened to her? What's that hole in her face?" Finally, they located a dentist who was able to fix her up with a plate, and she got the part. After that, she got a job in vaudeville and was on the road for four years and wore that plate till her own teeth came in, so it did yeoman service.

It was taken for granted that kids in pictures could do anything. Since risk to the protagonist was an integral element of audience appeal, acceptance of some hazard was normal.

A scene in a Baby Peggy film called for Diana to fall from the branch of a tree and land in the rear seat of a speeding convertible passing below. If she dropped too soon, the car would hit her. Diana was frightened, but said nothing lest her father disapprove. Another child actress who was supposed to fall with her screamed bloody murder and was fired. Diana thought her unprofessional.

Baby Peggy (Diana Cary) in one of her early films. Diana was a star at two. At five she felt that she was finished.

Baby Peggy as mascot of the 1924 Democratic convention. With her on the platform is the future President of the United States, Franklin Delano Roosevelt.

In Diana's day, children were the same as Brownie the dog, or any other actor. Diana's contracts said that if for illness or "any other reason" she was unable to perform, the contract could be canceled. Diana later understood that her father had been more terrified than she was, but for different reasons.

Movies popularized the phrase "The show must go on," but Hollywood did not invent it.

In vaudeville, Donald O'Connor didn't realize that some stunts he did were dangerous, even when his brother accidentally put a finger through Donald's ear. As he started to sing, Donald noticed "all this red stuff coming down" on his white suit and it scared him, so he cried. But his brothers got him off stage and put collodion on his ear to stop the bleeding. He went right back and finished the act. It didn't occur to any of them to stop the show.

Bronco busting, archery, knife throwing were among the feats Jane Withers tackled with her accustomed zest. She jumped off trains, drove cars. Once, she said, "Excuse me, gentlemen, are you aware that on page twenty-eight I am supposed to drive a car and almost hit this person?"

> They said, "You don't drive?" I said, "No, I am fourteen years old; of course I don't drive." They said, "Oh, my God, that shoots in two days." I said, "I told you four weeks ago I don't drive, so since you did nothing about it, I did. I have been going with my chauffeur and my bodyguard and they have been teaching me to drive."

I do not recall being placed in a really dangerous situation. Nor was I constrained from playing with neighborhood children. When a softball knocked the braces off my teeth, my parents had the damage fixed without suggesting that I not play ball. Other children weren't so lucky. Sybil Jason's contract had a long list of things she was not permitted to do, including swimming, climbing trees, and roller skating, because, says Sybil, "bruises would show up on my legs."

Stymie, too, told me he was kept on a tight leash. "I couldn't go

In this 1922 two-reel comedy, *Carmen, Jr.*, a takeoff on the opera, Baby Peggy, at three, played all four leading roles, two men, two women. Here, complete with cigarette, she was the villain.

in the street, play kick the can, or go under the house or nothing. I did it anyway. I got a whetz on my back for it, but I did it."

The work was hard; most of us thrived on it. Often, we rose before the sun was up, having learned our lines the night before, and arrived at the studio by 8 A.M.

If makeup was complicated and took longer than usual (blackened hair, slanted eyes, curls or wigs, etc.), we reported earlier. Location shooting invariably demanded an earlier start, so that every hour of sunlight could be captured.

If the distance to the location site defied commutation, the entire company was accommodated locally, most often in hotels. My favorite location was Malibu Lodge, on a lake in the Malibu Hills a short distance from the ocean. There, in our off hours, I fished, and the cook at the lodge served me my catch at dinner.

For me, Hollywood was not an industry. There was no relationship in my mind between the pictures I did and box office receipts, no equation of a film's success with personal achievement, wealth, or fame. I knew only that an especially good performance (free, letter-perfect, and without problems) brought approval from the people I most wanted to please.

Dean Stockwell had a sense of the larger view. When, at twelve, in 1948, he was filming *The Boy with Green Hair,* whose theme music, "Nature Boy," became his favorite song, Dean knew that it "had an important, universal, and politically loaded antiwar theme, and that the boy with the green hair was in reality a symbol that there shouldn't be any more war."

Though most of us were workaholics and the work was interesting and sought after, our time off was precious. Whenever he could, Jackie Cooper got on his horse in Palm Springs and hid out all day, convinced that if he returned, there would be a call that would take him back to town.

The professions that we hoped to enter as adults seldom bore resemblance to our lives as children. While most little girls fantasized that one day they might be movie stars, the top movie star of the decade longed to become a brain surgeon. But by the time she was eleven, she knew it wasn't going to happen. "I realized," she explained to me, "that no one would come to Shirley Temple for brain surgery. They would have to anesthetize the patient before the doctor showed up. Perhaps I could have been a pediatrician; that might have been a better idea."

6. Time to Study, Time to Play

Whenever any of the kid stars had a birthday party, Hymie Fink was there. Hymie Fink was Hollywood's most persistent and successful still photographer. His flashbulbs popped like Chinese firecrackers, his relentless lens was everywhere. Each month, *Modern Screen*, *Photoplay*, and other fan magazines of the era, so popular and so important to the industry on which they fed, were filled with Hymie's pictures.

Hymie Fink was not at my friend Butler's party. Butler wasn't under contract to a studio. His billing was inconspicuous at best, the roles he played were small. But his mother gave a birthday party for him and Mother took me, dressed in my patent-leather shoes and my sailor suit.

Butler and six other children—none of whom I knew—were on the lawn in front of their stucco bungalow as we drove up. His mother, a vast sea of guts contained in a flowered tent, swept toward our car, lifted me from the back seat of the convertible, and kissed me on the mouth. "Dickie Moore is here!" she cried to the one photographer present. He took a picture. "Well, now we're ready to start," Butler's mother said gaily.

"Is everybody here?" The photographer looked worried.

"Yes. What would you like the children to do first?"

"I want to open my presents," Butler whined.

"Where is Shirley Temple?" the photographer persisted. "My editor told me she was coming."

"Oh, Shirley couldn't come. She wanted to, but the studio couldn't shoot around her because they had a 'weather permitting' location call today. Mrs. Temple called me personally to say how disappointed Shirley is. But you have a nice group here, practically all the young elite. Let's start. Shall we pin the tail on the donkey?"

"Looks like you already have," mumbled the photographer.

Gifts were opened, the cake was cut. It had six candles. Butler told us he was seven. "Arithmetic is not his forte," his mother said, and winked.

"Isn't it a pity that poor Shirley couldn't come," Mother said, to no one in particular.

"Yes, a shame," another lady sympathized, "and such a big surprise."

I wasn't surprised. Shirley never went to parties as a child. Parties went to her. And Hymie Fink went with them.

One such gathering, when I was twelve, was a birthday party given by her studio while Shirley was shooting *The Blue Bird,* in which I had a tiny part. I worked less than a week in that film and shared the scene with forty other kids, Gene Reynolds among them. My career was languishing and I was acutely aware of being practically an "extra," so I hid from the camera at every opportunity.

The party was held in the Fox commissary, situated near the center of the studio, away from the main gate and the new administration building. On this day, the commissary was given over completely to the party. Scores of cars pulled through the front gate, parents flashing their studio-engraved invitations at the guards and steering their vehicles into the parking lot.

How far you drove your car into a movie studio was a matter

of considerable importance and something that was closely watched by those you worked with. At Fox, the main parking area was inside the front gate, tended by guards. To reach the studio, you had to pass through a second gate. If you could drive past the second guard right onto the movie lot, you knew your option was going to get picked up, or that they liked you at the studio.

The day of Shirley's party, all guests parked their cars in the main parking lot and were met by buses and driven to the commissary. There Shirley stood at the head of a long reception line, gravely shaking hands with all arrivals, telling each of us how glad she was we had come, and thanking us for the presents we had brought, which were passed along to join the growing mountain of unopened packages, most of which were later sent to an orphanage.

One boy, in an ill-fitting jacket, kept telling us that his mother had spent *fifteen dollars* for a makeup case for Shirley. Everyone ate cake, while the mothers tried to get Hymie Fink to take their children's pictures. There were many party favors, including a pen with a magnifying glass at one end and Shirley's name inscribed on it.

I fretted that my gift to Shirley—an embroidered handkerchief—was insufficient. You don't like to leave a birthday party with more stuff than you brought.

Shirley's parties usually featured creamed chicken and peas. "It was Mother's favorite," she explained at our interview. How did she feel about her birthdays? I inquired.

The parties were endless, because I would have three birthday parties every year. Fox would have one for a large number of people I didn't know, a lot of children I'd never seen in my life and never saw again. And I was hostess. It was kind of strange. I figured it was part of the job.

Fox would pay half the cost of the parties and my mother and father—or I—would pay the other half. Why I had to pay for the parties at all is a mystery, but that's how it went. And there'd be two hundred kids, maybe more. I thought those parties were a big bore.

Then there would be a party on the set, with the crew. That one I liked.

Finally, there'd be the one I liked best, which was the one at home.

Ironically, the guests did not enjoy the parties any more than Shirley did. Marcia Mae Jones summed up our reaction: "I felt very out of place."

Darryl Hickman recalled that when he worked with Shirley on *Young People*, on her birthday "some maharaja from India brought her a string of pearls." But the pearls were phony, Shirley told me, and so was the maharaja. Quickly discovered, he was just as quickly ejected from the studio.

"Fox gave marvelous favors at those parties," Shirley remembered. "One I'd love to have—and don't—was a clock in the shape of the world. It was a globe with stars and a beautiful dark-blue face with white numerals. But I don't have one. Two or three hundred other kids have them. Jane Withers will have one," she said cryptically, "but I don't know if she went to that party."

Jane wasn't at the party. "I was never invited to Shirley's parties," she said, emphatically setting the record straight. "And I always wanted to go so badly. I always invited her to mine. Of course, she never came. *Never!*"

Jane's birthday parties also were big events. Hymie Fink was always there. Gene Reynolds, who went to several of them, recalls that "there were more cameramen than kids." He hated the parties. Not because of Jane, who, like her mother, was an enthusiastic hostess, but because Gene was never comfortable at parties. "Everyone was posing. The whole business of publicity made the parties seem synthetic. If you have a party, it's just to be with people. But most of our parties were stunts to get pictures in the magazines, so where the hell was the fun in that?"

One of Jane's party invitations told the kids to "come as what you want to be when you grow up." Gene went as a convict, Marcia Mae Jones went as a nurse, and Freddie Bartholomew (the very personification of British elegance and refinement) went as a football player with a black eye. Marcia Mae recalls that she and Freddie "spent most of our time clinging to each other, we were both so frightened."

Cora Sue Collins enjoyed a Jane Withers birthday party with a

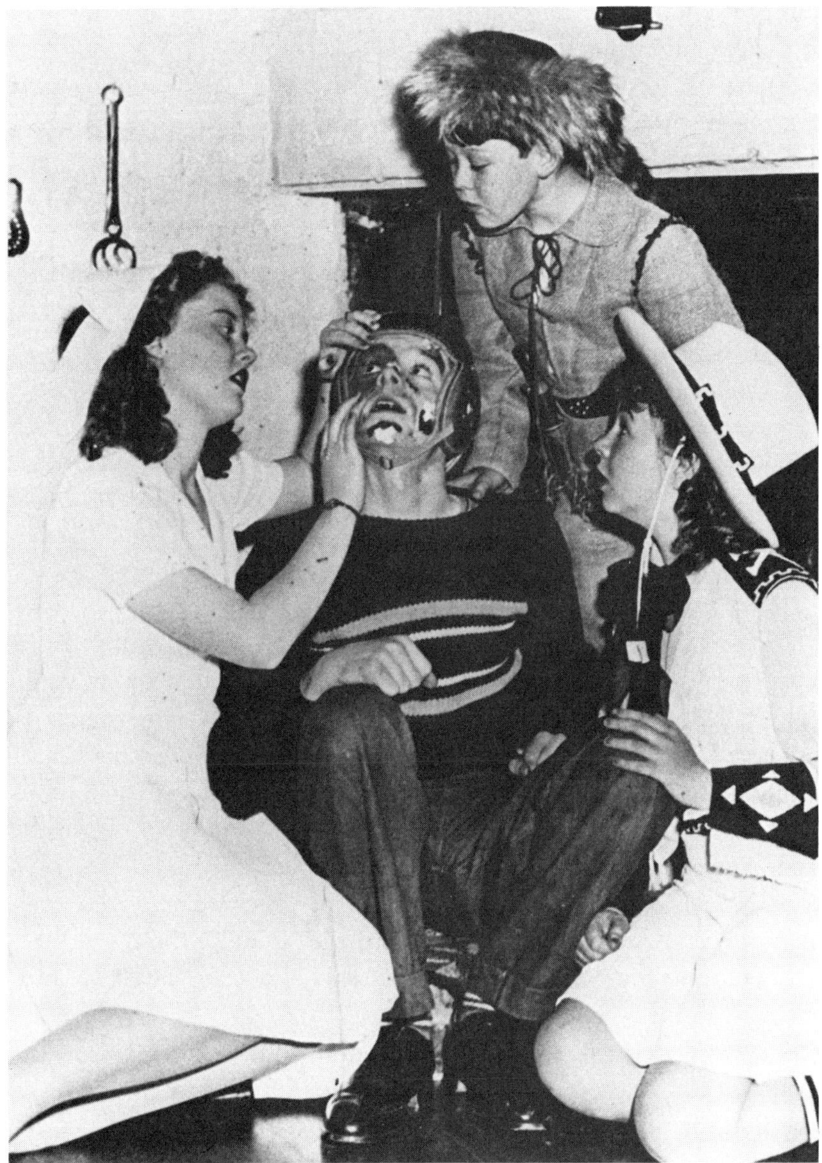

At one of Jane Withers's birthday parties guests were asked to come as what they wanted to be when they grew up. Marcia Mae Jones dressed as a nurse, Freddie Bartholomew as a football player, Bobs Watson was a backwoodsman, and Jane was a cowgirl.

circus theme, "but Jane was devastated because they wouldn't permit elephants inside the Beverly Hills Hotel."

Jane's fifteenth-birthday party, with a Western theme, caused Cora Sue discomfort. The scene: Jim Jeffrey's Barn in the San Fernando Valley near Hollywood. Many horses used in films were trained and boarded there, and the rustic Western buildings served occasionally as film locations.

Cora Sue developed early. By fifteen, she was a knockout, cleavage and all. At the barn dance, she wore a scoop-neck blouse:

> A photographer took me to a hay wagon and had me bend over—supposedly looking for a needle in a haystack. I was so foolish I went for it. When the picture came out in a magazine, after being airbrushed, Mother dutifully put it in my scrapbook. That's when I saw it. I thought I looked like Jane Russell. It gave me a terrible complex. So I burned all my scrapbooks and every still of myself I could get my hands on.

Many of the guests—including me—arrived at Jeffrey's Barn in chauffeur-driven hay wagons. Jane rode a horse. She wouldn't ride with any of us for fear of offending people on another wagon.

Leo Carillo, a popular adult actor who owned vast stretches of prime acreage, and who for years rode his magnificent palomino horse (with silver saddle) at the head of every Hollywood parade, rode with Jane. He stayed for the party.

Ranch hands were preparing the barbecue as we arrived. Gingham, denim, and cowboy boots were the order of the day. But I wore tennis shoes because Mother had said, "It seems a waste to buy cowboy boots just to wear at a party."

To my horror, the party got around to square dancing. "Swing your partner to the right!" the caller yelled into the microphone, as the fiddlers played. I went left.

During a break in the dancing, Sidney Miller took the microphone and introduced the guests: Judy Garland, Mickey Rooney, Darryl Hickman, Freddie Bartholomew, Jackie Cooper, Donald O'Connor, Gene Reynolds, Cora Sue Collins, Marcia Mae Jones,

Peggy Ryan, Edith Fellows, and members of the Watson clan, including Bobs and Delmar—these and many more.

Prizes were offered for the best costumes. Delmar Watson smiled as he recalled: "Sidney was on the podium and he kept trying to get people to come up to get a prize and nobody would go up. We were all bashful. He begged us: '*Anybody* come up—I'll give you a prize!' Finally, he ended up saying, '*I'll* take the prize.' "

Mickey Rooney played the drums and left. Donald O'Connor danced with Peggy Ryan. Bobs Watson (youngest of the guests) threw hay at cars as they went by. Edith Fellows and Bobby Jordan (a former "Dead End Kid") clung to each other, enraptured, paying no attention to the music. Suddenly, scores of balloons were released and Jane announced that attached to some of them were tags for door prizes. One balloon descended on Bobby and Edith. They won a baby goat. Edith's grandma let her keep it until it ate her flowers, then Joel McCrea, who owned a ranch, took it off her hands.

I worried that when Sidney called my name, he'd ask me to do something. Did he know I'd studied piano for seven horrible years? Would I be asked to play "The Swan"? "Oh, God," I thought. "Please, Sidney, *please* know how untalented I am; don't ask me to perform!" Recently, I talked to Sidney about my feelings on that day. My fears of being called on to entertain were understandable, he said. Sidney elaborated:

Dickie Moore was a cute, natural, sensitive child who responded to a director's direction. You were given lines to say within a given situation, like "Please, sir, can I have some more?" in *Oliver Twist.* You were always given material. Now you're invited to a party. "Dick, will you please get up and say something to the folks?" What can you say?

Everybody feels that way, but some work through it. I was always worried when I had to perform without Rooney or O'Connor, because we worked together so much. I did a Gulf radio show once with Jack Benny in his prime. He had the script in front of him and still he was shaking. Red Skelton used to throw up before he went on in his act.

Okay. I know that now. I didn't then. I just wondered what all the other kids were feeling—those who seemed so at ease and in control. Like Donald O'Connor.

"I'll tell you where my head was at the day of Jane's fifteenth-birthday party," Donald told me. He leaned back in his chair and stretched his legs.

I was making a lot of money for the studio, but I wasn't getting any. And I was working all hours. There were laws to protect minors at that time, but they didn't seem to apply to me. As long as I got my three hours of school, nobody cared how long I worked. Of course, they paid overtime, but I didn't get it because I was a contract player.

I had just written a note to my agent. I must have been too scared to mail it, because I found it the other day. I told him if I was going to work on Sunday, I wanted to be paid for it. And if I worked past eight o'clock, I'd want to be paid for that. They tried to finish all those pictures before I went into the service. We worked three pictures at one time: the one coming up, the one we were doing, and we dubbed the one we'd just finished. That's all we did: work. It's amazing we had as much fun as we did, grinding them out like that. That's what was on my mind.

At the party I felt out of it, never felt part of the group.

"I never went to any of those teenage parties." Jane Powell looked wistful. "I was never a part of the kids at all. I was never invited. I didn't even know they were going on."

I didn't know most of them were going on, either. Nor did Natalie Wood. "I didn't know one other child in films," she told me. "I never knew Margaret O'Brien until I was fifteen. My stand-in, Bonnie Brown, was the only one I knew. I remember one birthday when my mother hired a pony. That was the fanciest party I ever had when I was a kid. But it was *real.* It wasn't a Hollywood party. It was all arranged by my mother, and there were no photographers."

Tough luck for Hymie Fink. He fared better with Ann Rutherford: joyous, irrepressible Ann, who loved parties and whose favorites were progressive parties, which MGM helped her to arrange.

"And," Ann recalled delightedly, "the whole thing was free!" Guests would gather at her house and then everybody repaired to the Brown Derby (the chic restaurant of the day) for shrimp cocktail:

> This was great for the Brown Derby, because Hymie Fink went with us. He would take pictures of all the attractive young people sitting there eating shrimp cocktail. Then we would all get in the bus and be ferried to another restaurant, where we would have a salad. Then we would go to an Italian place downtown and have spaghetti, and wind up at the fun house on the Ocean Park pier, where we were all issued huge oversize pajamas and we would all ride the slides and the revolving barrels until three o'clock in the morning.
>
> One producer, Carey Wilson, who wrote and produced the "Andy Hardy" pictures, gave huge parties for the junior players at MGM simply because he wanted to refuel his memory of what young people said and did so he could write about them.
>
> Well, there was a boy I knew when I was about seventeen. He'd come over to my house and we'd neck a little, or he'd take me to a movie. Then I got so angry at him. Carey Wilson asked me at one of his parties, "Where's your date?"
>
> I said, "I didn't bring him because I don't like him anymore and I'm not ever going out with him again. He has a new car and all he does is pay attention to that dumb Model A. And it's a secondhand one, too."
>
> Well, he got a whole "Andy Hardy" picture out of that: Andy gets his first new car and pays no attention to Polly and Polly gets really ticked off at him.

A business purpose always lurked behind a studio-sponsored party. Sybil Jason was invited to a party to celebrate some woman's book of children's poems: "The author had dedicated her book to all the children of the world. We took publicity pictures. When we started to eat ice cream, someone said, 'Could you come over here and pose with So-and-so?' "

Jane Powell, then a teenager, spent New Year's Eve singing for Louis B. Mayer's party guests.

While Margaret O'Brien "never really got roped into the big birthday party thing," she went to many luncheons, "like the Home for the Aged, which was Mr. Mayer's sister's favorite charity. You'd have to give a speech and listen to all the other speeches. For a child, it was hard to sit there and be on display for several hours."

When Jackie Coogan had a party as a child, "they put up a circus tent over part of our golf course."

Jack's contemporary Diana Cary thought parties were a waste of time. They made her nervous because she could not relate to other children.

When I was in vaudeville, I had to go down to the theater lobbies before the morning matinees and sign balloons and hand out presents. Children swarmed around me, so I handled them the way you would handle a herd of buffalo. You tried to save the species, but from a distance because they were a threat. They would scream and yell obscenities and make all kinds of gestures, and follow us outside and try to tip the car over. So children in groups of more than ten were very threatening to me.

When I was five, the press association in New York City gave a birthday party for me in the banquet room of the Biltmore Hotel, with about five hundred people. It was an occasion for everyone to make a speech. One man spoke—he'd just written my definitive biography (I was five, remember)—and then Sol Lesser, my producer, got up and explained how he had discovered my dramatic talents. Then my father got up and said that my talent was really nothing at all, that I was just obedient and knew how to follow instructions.

Mrs. Coogan was there—Jackie couldn't come—and there was talk that Jackie and I were engaged to be married. Finally, they asked Mrs. Coogan to say something, and she got up and said, "Well, of course you all know me: I'm the goose that laid the golden egg." It stopped the whole party.

Edith Fellows had a party once. Since Edith had no friends her own age, her grandmother's cronies were the guests. Edith invited Cliff Edwards, a popular adult entertainer of the day, with whom she'd worked and whom she adored. By that time, Edith had a piano and Edwards brought with him a "nice, gangling, tall blond kid who played the piano." Skitch Henderson sat down and played. Then, said Edith:

> Cliff went over to my grandma. He said, "Where the hell are the children? Are they hiding?"
>
> Grandma said, "Who invited you?"
>
> "I did," I said. Then she said, "Well, it's none of his business."
>
> "It is my business," he said. "Why aren't there any children? What are these old farts doing here?"
>
> They left and my grandmother was furious.

There's more to life than work and parties, we kids found out early. There's also school. Child actors are required by law to attend school classes.

During the time I worked in "Our Gang" comedies with Stymie and Spanky, we attended school together at Hal Roach Studios. Even when the Gang wasn't filming, we arrived for school at 9 A.M. At noon, our parents came to take us home. There were Spanky, Stymie, and the other kids, and our teacher, Mrs. Carter, who drew clowns and wore a dark-blue dress with large white polka dots.

In our sparsely furnished classroom on the second floor of the long frame office building behind the facade of Hal Roach Studios, I glanced anxiously at the clock on the wall over Mrs. Carter's desk as noon approached. Sometimes Mother (or Dad if he was unemployed) arrived early and waited in the car.

Fidgeting in my seat by the window, I would see the Buick drive through the gate and park outside the building. Then—for the fourth or fifth time—I would raise my hand and ask permission to go to the bathroom.

"What on earth did you eat last night, Dickie?" Mrs. Carter asked one day. The other students smiled. I never did tell Mrs. Carter I needed help with the buttons on my pants.

My short pants were buttoned to my shirtwaist, and I could not reach the back buttons. Stymie, Spanky, and the other boys wore corduroys with belts and relieved themselves whenever necessary.

But each of my desperate, fruitless visits to the lavatory made me more uncomfortable, until the folks arrived to help.

That's all I remember of my two years in school at Hal Roach Studios.

After I left Roach, my parents considered putting me in a private school. Dad thought that the discipline of a military academy would cure me of wetting the bed. So we visited the Black Fox Military Academy nearby. We watched the boys salute and stand formation in their uniforms. They appeared to range in age from six to seventeen. A major from the real army led us around and we saw other boys climbing ropes in the gymnasium, swimming, shining up their brass. Later, we went to the major's office. Mother said, "We'll see," and Dad said, "Thanks, Chief. Mighty decent of you."

We also visited a private school for young professionals, which was oriented differently. Whereas Black Fox had trees, an athletic field, and barracks, this was a three-story colonial on a residential street in Hollywood. A Mrs. Grainley met us at the door. "Notice how centrally located we are," she began. "Four minutes from Paramount, seven minutes from RKO, eight minutes from Columbia, and just eighteen minutes from Warners, through the pass." Metro and 20th were farther out, but of course, "it's impossible to be right next to everything."

Mrs. Grainley steered us through the building. Dad peered into the bathrooms. "At least the toilets are clean," he muttered.

We saw a class in progress. Mrs. Grainley's narrative continued. "When one of the children is featured in a picture, we send his lessons to the teacher at the studio and work together in planning his curriculum. When our students are here, their agents or parents can reach us at any time. And of course, they can leave classes for interviews, and return to class when the interview is over." Mrs. Grainley hardly paused for breath. "A car owned by the school takes children to the studio in special emergencies. The scholastic average of our students is B-plus, and professional children blossom here, where our teachers understand their special gifts and talents."

"We'll see," said Mother.

Stymie and Spanky were still with "Our Gang" when this picture was taken. I had left to concentrate on feature films.

With studio teacher Mrs. West at Universal. Others in the class were not all in the same film. Mrs. West, one of our best-remembered teachers, would stop production if children were mistreated.

In the end, I went to Carthay Circle Grammar School. It was free. It was also the best choice, for while my academic standing was average at best, I got to ride my bike to school, play kickball, get into fights occasionally (if forced), make friends and enemies, and eventually become chief monitor of the Safety Committee, in which capacity I frequently arrested a boy named Clifton for urinating in the tunnel under Olympic Boulevard.

There followed John Burroughs Junior High School, where, because of work, I spent more time out than in, but where I fell in love with another student, Jane. Or was it Jean? Jane and Jean were twins, and to this day I'm not sure which one I loved. At John Burroughs, I learned to type.

Then came Fairfax High School. In and out, in and out. But I did appear in *Tom Sawyer,* the class play, become a sergeant in the ROTC, sharpen my chess game during chemistry class and flunk the course, along with French and algebra. I made them up in summer school.

Gene Reynolds envied my going to public high school. "I'd have taken a few lumps, but I would have had a more balanced experience," he reflected. "I would not have been isolated at an early age. There would have been coping and a few more successes with girls. As it was, I went all through Gaul with Julius Caesar and a teacher who didn't know Latin. So my whole high school was spent with one teacher when it should have been spent with thirty teachers."

Until the 1930s, there were no controls on the hours children could work. Baby Peggy emoted until she dropped. By the time I started school, work laws were tighter. If a child actor was too young for school, the presence of a licensed "welfare worker" was required. By law, from the time we started first grade until we turned eighteen, three hours of our workday—Monday through Friday—were devoted to study. We were always mindful that our schooling was infringing on production time. Production time cost *money.*

"I always felt guilty when the crew sat around waiting and I hadn't finished my three hours of schooling," Natalie Wood confided to me. "I always remember running to the set when I was called."

For Gloria Jean, "school was sitting down at a desk, picking up a pencil, and hearing someone say, 'We're ready for the next scene.' I never knew where I was."

Teachers also were under pressure, since they were being paid by the studios to enforce a law that cost the studios a fortune. And they did enforce the law. "If we started shooting at eight A.M. and hadn't finished our three hours' school by four, Mrs. Carter shut down the set," Spanky McFarland reminded me. "We could not be in front of the camera again for the rest of the day. It didn't matter whether we were on location, losing the sun, or what. We had to have three hours in school. It was the law."

Indeed it was the law, and it used to drive directors crazy. Kathleen Nolan told me it still does. Kathleen, former president of the Screen Actors Guild, joined her parents on the stage of a Mississippi River showboat soon after birth.

"There is always that constant pulling between director and teacher," according to Kathleen. "The director says, 'Can't you get 'em out here?' and the teacher says, 'They only have five minutes to go on their geography test,' and the director says, 'I don't give a fuck about their test—get 'em out here!' "

Not surprisingly, MGM filmed *Boys Town* during the summer, when school was out.

Each motion picture company had its own classroom, with blackboards and little desks fastened to the floor. Since each studio had at least one child actor in its stable, it employed a teacher full time. When many children were working, the resident teacher hired assistants temporarily, so that a teacher was always with us on the set.

"Free-lance" actors shuttled between regular school and the lot on which we happened to be working. Actors under contract went to their studio's school even when they weren't filming. This was fine, but if they dropped your option, you didn't have a school.

Peggy Ann Garner, after years in school at Fox, spent the twelfth grade at University High when the studio bought out her contract. "I just wanted to wear sloppy joe sweaters and skirts and be accepted,

Kathleen Nolan started acting early but got to Hollywood late. Her first big break was as Wendy in Mary Martin's *Peter Pan* on Broadway. Coming from St. Louis, Kathleen was disappointed when New York didn't turn out at the Greyhound bus station to meet her.

but I wasn't. I had been a straight-A student, doing concentrated work in French and Latin, and now I found myself sitting in each class for only forty minutes. I could just goof off," said Peggy Ann. "I wanted to belong to the Rally Committee, but the kids didn't like me. I was looked down on, totally. I did not want to be a spectacle. All I wanted to do was read my books and listen to my records."

Peggy's difficult experience was shared by Sybil Jason, who, when her studio dropped her, suddenly found herself in public school being kicked and pinched by other children, who refused to play with her.

Free-lance kids were considered oddities in public school, but we were seldom ostracized. When filming, we studied on the sound stage in little canvas dressing rooms. On days off, we went to the studio school until our jobs ended. There, one teacher nearly always taught all subjects to a class ranging from first to twelfth grades.

One who excelled in studies was Juanita Quigley, whose mother was a teacher. Juanita went to college and teaches now, as does her husband, near their home in Pennsylvania.

Those who did well in school "were the ones who got out of the business," Jane Powell believes. That's not entirely true. Natalie Wood, a straight-A student, continued on as an adult actress. Virtually the only one among us who excelled in math, she managed money well.

Most of us were unexceptional as students. School was an "infinitesimal experience for me," Roddy McDowall summed up.

Some child stars studied privately, including Temple, Coogan, Cooper, Bartholomew, and Jane Withers. But three hours of schooling were not enough for Jane. When she wasn't in a film, she demanded five hours, sometimes six, exhausting her teacher.

Cora Sue Collins, an exceptional student, looks back with pleasure on the personal and unusual interest L. B. Mayer took in her education when she was under contract:

> I remember he used to say to me, "You have such lovely hands," and I said, "Isn't it a shame that I'm going to ruin my fingernails." He asked

why and I said, "The teacher said I'll have to learn to type." Mr. Mayer asked me how that would hurt my hands and I told him, "It will blunt the ends of my fingers and it will ruin them."

So he assigned me a secretary and to this day I don't know how to type.

Mickey Rooney, who sometimes feels two ways at once about a subject, looked back upon his education: "The three hours of school on the set were a bit confusing until we got our heads screwed on correctly. Being an actor makes it tough to acquire an education, because you say to yourself, 'What the hell does it mean to me to know about the hypotenuse of a triangle?' It was very tough as a child to go from Ponce de León to playing a scene and out of the scene back to Ponce de León. And yet you found a great freedom in getting away from the educational conduit for a moment to return to what they call work, which wasn't work to me."

I let the subject drop.

Bonita Granville, Bunny to her friends, was one of those children who excelled scholastically. Her high school years were spent under contract to Warner Brothers, where, in 1936, she played my older sister in a picture called *My Bill.* Kay Francis was our mother. On the set of *My Bill,* Mother and Lois Horne, the head teacher at the studio, became friends.

Lois was strict but capable; since I wasn't under contract, though, the most she could do for me was to see that I brought in correct assignments from John Burroughs Junior High. But each day, Lois would focus Bonita's studies on a single subject, and she hired special teachers to instruct Bonita in foreign languages. When Bonita went downtown to take her annual tests at the Board of Education—as contract players had to do—she was graduated from high school at sixteen.

MGM's Little Red Schoolhouse was the most renowned of the Hollywood studio schools. Its distinguished graduates included Jane Powell, Judy Garland, Mickey Rooney, Elizabeth Taylor, Dean Stockwell, Margaret O'Brien, and many other stars and featured players.

MGM's Little Red Schoolhouse wasn't really red. Some of the students included Jane Powell *(left)*, Elizabeth Taylor *(center)*, and Darryl Hickman *(right center)*. Mrs. McDonald *(back row)* ran the show.

Miss McDonald was the principal. She also taught. "I think everybody was scared to death of her," Margaret O'Brien told me. "She was very strict and none of the children liked her and the studio didn't like her, either, because she obeyed the law and yanked us out of a scene when the time came, even if they only wanted to get that one last shot. I know Elizabeth was real glad when she got away from Miss McDonald."

High school graduation at the Little Red Schoolhouse was duly recorded for the movie magazines. Hymie Fink was there. So was Dean Stockwell, who shared his memories of that day with me:

> When we graduated from MGM, we had to do a magazine layout of a graduation party: Rusty Tamblyn, me, Claude Jarman, Jr., Elizabeth Taylor, and Jane Powell. They wanted a photo with all of us outside in the front of the schoolhouse. Elizabeth was so happy she threw her books in the air, and Miss McDonald came running out, screaming at the photographers, "Don't have her throw her books like that."
>
> Mary McDonald intimidated me. She didn't have the most beautiful visage in the world. She didn't teach me shit. But in retrospect, I love her because I feel she was intent upon educating us. In some way—a way she didn't realize consciously—she sensed that she was dealing with kids that were out of place in time and ties and culture. I tend to revere her.

Some teachers deserved to be revered. Lillian Bartley probably saved Edith Fellows's life.

Edith enjoyed public school, where she began. It was her first and only opportunity to be with other children. It didn't last. Sent to school with her hair in curlers—so that it would look perfect if an interview came up—Edith was forbidden by her grandma to play games. She might get bruises on her knees—not good for dancers. She was not to yell at recess—bad for her singing voice. Since she did not participate, the other children shut her out. Finally, the principal called her into his office, said she was disruptive, and asked her to leave school.

Grandma had no choice. The Hollywood Professional School

was—despite the cost—the only way to go. But soon there was no money for tuition. Don't worry, Edith could remain, the principal told grandma. Then Edith got her break. The film *She Married Her Boss,* with Claudette Colbert and Melvyn Douglas, won her a seven-year contract at Columbia. Grandma was sued for back tuition, but by then Edith had found Lillian Bartley, her teacher at the studio. They shared a tiny classroom. Edith was the only student. But she couldn't concentrate. There were problems at home. "What's wrong?" Lillian asked her. "Put your books away; let's talk." Here's what happened, as Edith told it to me:

From that point on, for five years, Lillian was not just my teacher. She was my psychiatrist, my friend, mother, sister—she was everything. She kept me from blowing to pieces. I didn't learn my three R's, but I survived. She knew that it was more important that I have someone to talk to than learn my lessons.

I never did catch up in school. First of all, when you're making a film, how can you study on the set? They're hammering. They're changing scenery. You're trying to remember the lines coming up for your next scene. How can you remember dates in history?

Lillian realized that the moment my grandmother suspected that we were close, she would move heaven and hell to get rid of her, because she wanted no one near me. No one. Lillian and I both understood this, and we discussed it and we kept our friendship hidden. Fortunately, Grandma did not go to school with me.

When it came time to graduate, I was still at Columbia. Lillian called Hollywood Professional School, where I'd gone for a while, and arranged for me to graduate with their class of 1940. So I was able to go to the prom. They even gave me a little speech to say.

But in order to graduate, I had to pass exams, and I knew *nothing!* Lillian took my tests for me. That's how I passed. That's Lillian's and my secret. Now it's your secret and everybody else's. But I know Lillian wouldn't mind my telling you. She's gone now.

7. Grownups Run the Show

During the filming of *Blonde Venus,* Marlene Dietrich gave me a bath. I shared the tub with a rubber duck, wore swimming trunks, and felt naked and uncomfortable—early sexual arousal, no doubt.

One would think that being given a bath by a beautiful woman would put you on intimate terms, but I had trouble calling adult stars by their first names, even when they asked me to.

In *Blonde Venus* I played Miss Dietrich's son. My function, as in most early films, was to serve as an emotional prop for the adults, in this case Miss Dietrich, Herbert Marshall, and a tall newcomer who smiled a lot (and who everybody said would be a major star), named Cary Grant.

I found Miss Dietrich warm and friendly. Our director, Josef von Sternberg, while not warm, was lively, pleasant, and obviously on close terms with Miss Dietrich. They yelled at one another constantly in German, but always ended up laughing and embracing.

With Marlene Dietrich in *Blonde Venus.*

Off the set of *Blonde Venus.*

Both owned Rolls-Royce convertibles, identical except that one was black and one was gray. I would sit behind the wheels and pretend to drive while the chauffeurs watched. Von Sternberg boasted to me that his car could beat Miss Dietrich's in a race. She said hers could beat his anytime.

Von Sternberg shot one scene 149 times. (I can still see the chalk mark on the slate.) He wasn't satisfied with the way the backlight came through a beaded curtain. In another scene, he wanted Miss Dietrich to throw her hat on the bed as she entered the room. She refused. A hat on a bed is bad luck, she said. A lively argument ensued. Much time was lost on these two scenes. Inevitably, the head of production at the studio, surrounded by his entourage, appeared on the set to see what the holdup was.

Mr. von Sternberg didn't take to crowds. He ordered them to leave. Visibly upset, the executive said that he could fire von Sternberg if he wanted, whereupon Miss Dietrich said, oh, could he now? Von Sternberg said, go ahead and fire him. With only half the picture in the can and the other half in his head, he didn't care. The visitor said he was the boss, and wouldn't leave.

Von Sternberg said, "Okay, boss, then stay; only no film will roll while you are here." If the boss liked to pay everybody just for sitting around doing nothing, that was up to him. Then von Sternberg sat in the chair with his name on it and had the lights turned off.

The executive was furious, but finally he left the set with his friends, who flanked him six abreast, and marched down the main street of the studio toward the front office. As he passed my dressing room bungalow, my Scottie, Rags, ran out and bit him.

Mother wondered why Rags had to pick the production chief out of a crowd of men, all of whom looked more or less alike. But Rags did. The man walked right into the front office and resigned.

Rags was often unpredictable like that, so we stopped taking him to the studio. Mother, being Irish, said he was temperamental because he was Scotch. Dad, being French, said that the Scotch were no worse than the Irish, and both of them were "too damned temperamental."

During the filming, Miss Dietrich gave me an enormous toy boat, over three feet long. It had a crank that went down through the cabin and wound up the engine. I took it home and put it in the bathtub. The engine couldn't function in such close quarters, but I was eager to float it. It looked beautiful, but it soon filled with water and sank. After Dad tried to repair the leak without success, we put the boat in drydock on a shelf in the garage.

All through the shooting, I was fascinated by a fifty-foot tape measure that hung in its leather case from the camera. It was used to measure the distance from the actors to the lens, so the focus would be accurate. Von Sternberg was amused by my interest in the tape. When the last scene ended, he yelled, "Print!" then unhooked the tape from the camera and presented it to me. It was a treasured possession, more desirable than any toy.

Among the greatest directors in the history of film was Ernst Lubitsch. He always had a twinkle in his eye, and wore old blue sweaters on the set, many sporting moth holes. I thought: "He's a very successful man. He's rich. He's a great director. He can afford the best. Why the moth holes in his sweaters?"

Lubitsch always was gracious, never raised his voice. On his set, there was a sense of zest and relaxation and, invariably, a piano. He relaxed by playing during setups for the next scene. Even as a child, I was aware that he was a highly accomplished musician. I asked him once, "How come you have time to play the piano?"

"Dickie," he replied, "Hollywood is a very funny place and we are in a very funny business. You never know. Someday I may have to make a living playing piano in a cabaret, so I always keep in practice."

He also told me, "When you become a director someday, remember, everybody loves Technicolor now." (The film we were doing was *Heaven Can Wait,* a Technicolor spectacle with Don Ameche, Gene Tierney, and an all-star cast.) "But be very careful what you shoot in color. Some movies, no matter what the fashion, should always be in black and white. Never shoot a serious drama or a mystery in Technicolor."

Three times I worked for director William Dieterle. In *The Story of Louis Pasteur,* I played the boy that Paul Muni—Pasteur—cured. When her husband worked, Mrs. Muni was always on the set.

Dieterle wore immaculate white gloves at all times. (Mother told me he had hemophilia, but no one confirmed it.) He was very German, screamed a lot, even at the Warner brothers, who did not come on his set. A large, exuberant man, he played all the parts for you and wanted you to imitate him.

When Muni finished a scene, he would glance quickly at his wife, who sat behind the camera, and she would nod or shake her head almost imperceptibly. Paul Muni would then tell the director whether or not he wanted to do the scene again. Dieterle never indicated how he felt about this. He gave no sign of noticing.

Some years later, I was in need of work. I was painfully aware that I was no longer getting many large roles. One day, they called me for an interview at Warner Brothers. There I saw Dieterle with Edward G. Robinson, who was to star in the film *Dispatch from Reuters.* Robinson, who knew I was being considered to play him as a child, clapped me warmly on the shoulder and smiled broadly, his eyes crinkling, and he said, "Oh, Dick, how wonderful to see you!" Robinson went on, "I understand there's a chance that we will be in the same picture, that you'll be playing me as a boy." I said, yes, I was there to see about it, and he said, with a sidelong glance at Dieterle, "I'm so very glad. That would be perfect. You know, you even look like me. You look more like me every day!"

I tested for the part with several other kids, Bobs Watson included, but there was no contest, really. Dieterle just went through the motions. It was clear that they had already chosen me. The test was awkward because all the other kids being considered were within sight and earshot, along with their parents.

Dieterle directed all the tests himself. (Often, that was not the case—an assistant would take over.) He gave me some business to perform and said, "Then smile."

I felt stiff, self-conscious. I was beginning to be aware of a feeling of great discomfort when I acted, especially if I had to smile.

Dieterle noticed, of course. "You're very stiff. You are not as relaxed as you used to be when you were younger."

I was sure I'd lost the part, but I got it. Forty-five years later, Bobs Watson told me he remembered what Dieterle said to me. It had embarrassed him.

Many who were kids in films, especially those who played in "Our Gang" comedies, remember Hal Roach well. I don't, even though I starred in his films for over a year. There was our meeting in his office with my mother, when we signed my contract. He smiled, but my only firm impression was that his office looked scruffy, like his studio. He also showed up at the Christmas party that he gave for the Gang, but we had no contact there, and little elsewhere.

With C. B. De Mille I had definite contact. I did *The Squaw Man* for him, much of it on location in Arizona. Mr. De Mille, wearing his puttees and carrying a riding crop, would walk across the desert, followed by his helpers, and sit unexpectedly without turning around, assuming that his canvas chair would be there. It always was.

We shot outdoors. I wore an Indian costume, complete with feathered headdress. My blond hair was long and blackened by mascara, which ran down my face as I sweated. The heat poured down on Castle Hot Springs, rolled like rain off the red tile roof of our hotel, and bounced off the parched adobe earth.

I was having trouble with a scene. Mr. De Mille was not pleased.

Many people stood around. Time was being lost. Finally, he called, "Print," then said to me so everyone could hear, "Young man, I didn't care for the way you did that last scene."

What was there to say? I didn't answer, so he said again, "I said, Young man, I didn't like the way you did that last scene."

Finally, I found my voice. "Who cares?" I said.

C.B. blinked, then raised his riding crop as if to strike. The teacher, Mrs. West, swooped down and whisked me back to the hotel. They had to shoot around me for the balance of the day.

Many years later, when I did the *Lux Radio Theatre,* Mr. De Mille greeted me warmly, but reminded me of "how rude you were to me."

De Mille was never known for his sense of humor, so it surprised me when Jackie Coogan told me a story that De Mille told on himself. It happened on another outdoor epic, with a cast of trillions, all milling about below a huge platform on which the camera was positioned. De Mille, from the platform, called out directions through his megaphone.

Somehow, he noticed in the throng one inattentive woman talking to the person next to her, so he called out, "Since the young lady has something to say that obviously is more important than what I'm saying, I would like her to come up here and say it through the speaker, so we all can hear."

At first she hesitated, but when De Mille insisted, she climbed the ladder and took the megaphone and told the crowd, "I just said, I wonder when the old bald-headed bastard is going to call lunch." De Mille called lunch at once.

Among all the women I worked with, Barbara Stanwyck was a favorite. Affectionate and demonstrative, she was easy to understand. She talked but didn't fuss. Her film that I appeared in was *So Big,* based on the Edna Ferber novel.

She was a direct and gracious woman, who seemed extremely interested in whatever interested me. She told me later how nervous she was on meeting Edna Ferber and how much she wanted Ferber's approval for the way she did the role; but Ferber never in any way acknowledged her performance.

After the filming of *So Big,* Miss Stanwyck wanted to give me an Irish terrier. I don't know if she preferred that breed or if she was influenced by Mother's pride in being Irish. Although I didn't have a dog at the time, I said, "No, thanks; it might fight with my cat."

Undaunted, she gave me a gold watch, a delicate rectangle on which is inscribed: "To Dickie, my favorite picture son, with love, Barbara Stanwyck Fay." (She was married at the time to Frank Fay.)

Mother seized the watch. "It isn't appropriate for a boy to wear," she said, but it looked fine on her. She wore it until age eighty-two, when we had to put her in a nursing home. I have it now.

On one of my rare forays onto the MGM lot, I played Joan Crawford's son in *The Bride Wore Red.* The picture was notable because the director was a woman, a virtually unheard of phenomenon in those times. Dorothy Arzner had come recently to Hollywood. She wore tailored suits, was a no-nonsense, rather masculine-looking woman (to me, at least), and was pleasant, businesslike, and patient.

The film was unusual, too, in that Joan Crawford and Franchot Tone, the co-stars, were negotiating a divorce. Their dialogue, when they were not before the camera, was sparse.

When we were both off camera, I liked to spend time with Franchot Tone in his dressing room. He taught me the rudiments of chess, but since I was more comfortable with checkers, we compromised by playing both—sort of.

On the set, Tone had one of the larger portable dressing rooms on wheels, which had just come into use. These replaced, for the stars at least, the folding canvas rooms that other members of the cast, myself included, still used. Tone and Crawford had adjoining dressing rooms. Hers was equipped with a telephone, his was not.

With my favorite movie mother, Barbara Stanwyck, in *So Big*.

Mr. Tone got many phone calls from women, all of which came in on Crawford's line. In the middle of one of our games, her maid would knock on the door and say, "Call for you, Mr. Tone, in Miss Crawford's dressing room." Tone would excuse himself and take the call, giving me needed time to study my next move. Miss Crawford never seemed to object to this frequent use of her telephone. Once I went with him to her dressing room. They nodded wordlessly, acknowledging each other. Then he took his call, hung up, and they nodded again. We returned to his room and finished our game.

One day, Miss Crawford and I were working alone in a scene when suddenly an electrician—a gaffer—fell from the catwalk above the set and landed not more than two feet from her. A light fell on top of him, also narrowly missing her. I was whisked away. Production, of course, was halted. The studio ambulance arrived and he was taken immediately to the studio hospital. Eventually, the scene resumed. I was impressed by Miss Crawford's concern for the man, for his family, for the medical attention he received. She wanted absolute assurances that he was cared for properly, that he remained on salary, and that his family was provided for. She would not resume shooting until those assurances were given, and she called the hospital each day for reports on his condition.

In my reflections on the men I worked with, the movie *Sergeant York* stands out. Strong, gentle men abounded, including Walter Brennan, Gary Cooper (I played his young brother), director Howard Hawks.

Hawks got precisely the results he wanted from me by making no demands. "Don't smile in this scene, Dick," he said to me early in the filming. "In fact, there's not one scene in this whole picture where you need to smile unless you feel you have to." Of course, I felt relaxed and free to smile throughout the film, and I was one of several people in the picture who either won or were nominated for an award.

Producer Jesse Lasky's younger son, Bill, was an assistant director on the picture. Bill was an expert falconer and herpetologist, and thanks to his influence, birds, reptiles, and other animals became an important focus of my life.

Cooper took pains to show me the proper use of a rifle. I was contemplating buying my first gun. "If Mr. Cooper says it's all right, then I suppose it is," Mother said.

Cooper thought it was not only all right, but a downright good idea. "Can't learn too young," he told Mother. I had visited the local sporting goods store and set my sights on a .22 caliber hammerless repeater. Before getting it, I asked Cooper's opinion. As we talked between scenes, he examined the contents of his wallet, carefully counting and recounting the twenty-eight dollar bills inside. Finally, he folded the wallet and returned it to his hip pocket. "If I were gettin' my first rifle"—he looked at me, his eyes bluer than Jane Powell's, if possible—"I'd get a Winchester 62-A pump. It's lightweight, easy to take apart, and the hammer is exposed so you always know when it's on safety. Costs less too," he drawled. That, of course, is what I bought, and I used the gun for twenty years.

Cooper also taught me how to throw a knife. "Good thing to know," he said.

Walter Brennan had come to Hollywood with Cooper—some said on horseback from Montana, where they were both cowboys. Brennan told me once, "As far as I'm concerned, I have the best deal in Hollywood. Coop"—everyone except me called Gary Cooper "Coop"; I called him Mr. Cooper—"is stopped on the streets wherever we go. People ask for his autograph. Dickie, don't ever be a big star. I work all the time. I make fifty thousand dollars a picture. And nobody recognizes me, because I always wear different makeup. I'm never pestered for my autograph when I go into a store, I can be completely free to do exactly what I want, and if a picture fails, I'm never blamed, because I'm not the star. Try to be the top featured player. You'll always work and you'll never be bothered."

Brennan, of course, later disregarded his own advice and went on to be the star of his own TV series, *The Real McCoys.*

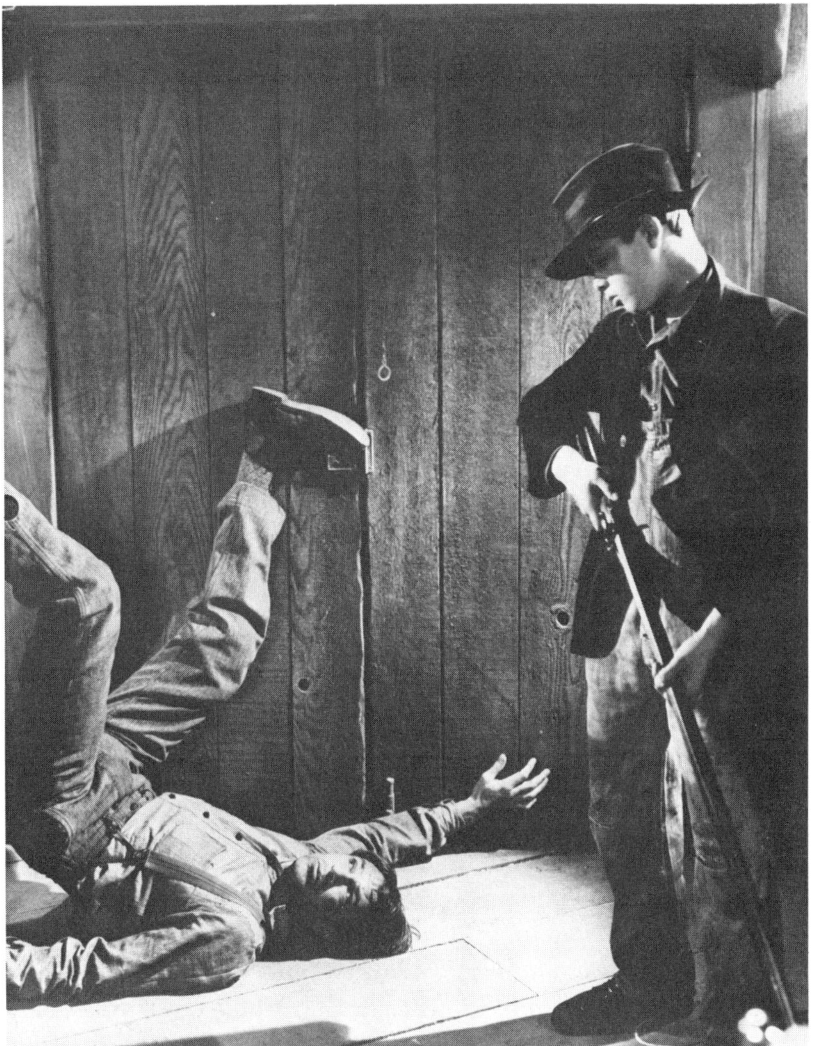

"Ma wants ya, Alvin," I said, fetching older brother Gary Cooper from the bar. Cooper fought and landed upside down when local toughs laughed at him. The picture: my favorite, *Sergeant York*.

Filming *The Arkansas Traveler* brought me into contact with two other entertaining men, humorist Bob Burns and Irvin S. Cobb, the famed journalist turned actor. In the film, Fay Bainter played my mother, endeavoring to run a rural newspaper against apparently insurmountable odds. Bob Burns was a hobo, a journeyman printer, the "Arkansas Traveler" who happened into town one day and stayed to help us out. Then the train whistle beckoned and the drama centered around whether he would stay on as our editor or succumb to the call of the rails.

I don't remember the outcome, but the picture was memorable because we were on location.

I loved locations. There seemed to be less pressure. The distractions of the outdoors reduced the feeling that you were the complete focus of attention when the cameras were turned on you.

Bob Burns brought along his famous bazooka, of course, and occasionally played it for us. Terrible sound, but fun. Bob had his own weekly radio show, and he had recently done a guest appearance on Al Jolson's show, which he told us about.

At the prebroadcast warm-up of the show, Jolson came on stage just before air time and told his audience, "This program, as you know, is sponsored by Lifebuoy soap. Lifebuoy is made for you people who stink."

Mother, who was with us on location, joined the hilarity, but was nevertheless shocked.

Mr. Burns and Cobb sat around the set discussing politics. They encouraged me to join in. I was an avid Roosevelt supporter. To me, our President was the ultimate authority figure, and I liked his voice on radio. Cobb sat calmly in his canvas chair, his cigar protruding from his mouth like an extension of his face. He was not high on Roosevelt, the New Deal, or anything FDR stood for. We argued endlessly.

Burns said one day that the Packard Motor Company had asked him to do a commercial extolling the virtues of its car and had offered him as payment their biggest, most expensive model. Bob told them, "Gentlemen, I'm a very modest man. I don't drive big cars. I wouldn't know what to do with such a fancy automobile. So just give me three little ones." They did.

Even allowing for Bob's bazooka and Cobb's politics, the most exciting thing that happened on that film involved Jean Parker, who played my older sister. Out of the blue, she invited me to go swimming with her in Lake Malibu one night. She was older than I, a nubile seventeen or so, and to my eyes, the most gorgeous vision imaginable.

She said, "Do you like to swim?" At that point, I didn't much, my sinuses and mastoids having chased me from the water.

I answered, "Well, I like to fish, but I don't swim too much."

"I'd love it if you'd go swimming with me some night. We could swim nude," she said.

The prospect of asking Mother to let me go swimming nude with Jean Parker in Lake Malibu one moonlit night was more than I could conjure. We never did go swimming, but I never forgot her invitation. She was one of the first stars of my erotic fantasies.

Of all the film people who acted with children, Wallace Beery, W. C. Fields, Errol Flynn, Spencer Tracy, Lionel Barrymore, and Bing Crosby (all men, you'll notice) are best remembered by them.

I worked with Fields once. Our few scenes together included Ben Turpin and Jack Oakie, and I spent most of my time looking down at them from a steam locomotive or shooting arrows into Turpin's rear. (The end of the film saw me running from an arrow —pulled along behind me on a wire—fired by him in retribution.)

Mrs. West, our welfare worker on the lot, was perhaps another reason I saw little of Mr. Fields when the cameras were not rolling. It was Mrs. West who had interceded with C. B. De Mille on my behalf. She and other teachers did not encourage their charges to associate with W. C. Fields, who unleashed a spate of merriment within the industry by spiking Baby LeRoy's bottle of milk with a couple of jiggers of gin. When the child was ushered before the camera, unable to walk, Fields, whose legendary abhorrence of children and animals had won him many friends, announced to the director, "See, I told you the kid was unreliable."

Mrs. West was not amused. She also was the teacher on a picture that Edith Fellows did with Fields, and she had occasion not to be amused then, either.

They were filming in the desert. As Edith walked down a path past Fields's tent, he called, "Hey, little girl, come in here." She obeyed and he told her, "You know, it's dangerous around here; there's lots of rattlesnakes." Edith said she knew; her teacher had told her to keep on the path. "Well, I have some medicine so that if you're bitten by a snake, it won't hurt you," Fields told her. He had a large dispenser, holding what Edith thought was water, and a bunch of Dixie cups, one of which he filled. He handed it to her. "You just drink this," Fields said.

Edith still remembers her reaction. "I took a sip and it burned my mouth. I threw the cup in the air and ran to the schoolhouse and told Mrs. West. She marched over to Mr. Fields's tent and chewed him out."

Whenever W. C. Fields's name came up, Jackie Coogan could be counted on as a witness for the defense. Coogan liked Fields:

> He liked me too, 'cause I used to play golf with him. I could beat his ass. Dad and I would go over to his house and he'd say, "Well, here comes Big Jack, my favorite person, and the little snot." And I'd say, "Still foolin' the people?" And he'd say, "Still foolin' 'em." And I'd say, "That swan's gonna get you," and he'd do a take, because there was one swan on the golf course that hated his guts. And all Fields had to protect himself was a five iron.
>
> When he'd forget and put down the club, that fucking bird would come out of the water and stalk him, and hit him on the legs. The bird would charge, while Fields in those English walking shorts, with legs like he was breaking them in for a hummingbird, would run around, calling it every name that you can imagine, until he could finally get his hands on the golf club. Then the bird knew it was time to head for the water.
>
> I used to enjoy just listening to him. I'd write down his words and try them on people. Oh, I heard the foulest things from that man.

He and my dad—two old vaudevillians—were inseparable. Mostly they would tell stories. And they'd sit and drink gin. Bill Fields could polish off a quart without batting an eye, and they'd talk and laugh. Fields laughed a lot, but mostly at his own stuff.

When Fields was making *The Old-Fashioned Way,* Paramount had three directors, and he told them, "This is shit you're getting. I want John L. Coogan to come here."

So Dad went over and Bill said, "I don't care what kind of a deal you make with them, but I want you to direct this movie. These cocksuckers don't know what I'm trying to do."

Dad said, "Bill, I want you to juggle. Just for forty feet of film. I want people to see you actually doing it."

So Bill did four or five of his old tricks that were absolutely stunning, stuff that other jugglers hadn't done before. That picture was a humdinger.

When Gloria Jean worked with W. C. Fields, he never ate. Between scenes, he disappeared behind a folding screen, where a waiter in a white coat served him drinks. The teacher (Mrs. West again) said to him, "One drink in front of Gloria and the whole set closes!"

"W. C. hated Mrs. West like poison." Gloria laughed, then continued:

Once I took a sandwich over to him. "Honey," he said, "that's very nice of you, but I don't eat," and he threw it into the bushes and went behind his screen for a visit with his waiter.

One day, just before a close-up, he took a little brown bottle out of his pocket. Mrs. West came storming out. "Caught you!" she said.

He said, "Relax, my dear, it's Listerine." It was!

They said he hated kids, but he invited me to his home and showed me his paintings and his poolroom. He taught me how to shoot pool.

Later, his grandchild, Ron Fields, came to my home when he was writing a book about W.C. and he said, "You know, I don't believe that he ever drank like people said he did." But I have to tell you, he did. We'd start out early and he'd be pretty sharp, but by two-thirty, W.C. was so drunk they'd have to close down.

Fields made Jane Withers happy when he chose her out of all the kids on the set to do a bit with him. At the time, Jane was about five and still doing extra work.

In one scene they played hopscotch, and Fields said, "Every time I start to jump, I want you to jump in front of me. I'm gonna try to get around you." So they tried it and it wasn't working.

Jane said, "Excuse me, sir, may I make a suggestion?"

Fields said, "What'd you have in mind?"

"Well, when I jump here, if you'll move here and then I jump here and you move there, it'll work."

"How old are you?" Fields asked.

"Five," Jane answered.

"Hmm," he said. They tried it and it worked. Later, Fields said, "Now, when I start to fumble at the door here, you come in with an ice cream cone and ask me—just ad-lib something."

"Anything?" Jane asked. "Well, you own this store, don't you?"

"Yes," Fields answered. "In the movie, I own this store."

Jane said, "Okay." So she ran in and said, "Can I have another ice cream cone?"

Fields replied, "Go 'way, little girl, you bother me." That line became a classic.

I never worked with Wallace Beery, for which, perhaps, I should be grateful. Jackie Cooper did "four long films" with Beery and ended up convinced that "they couldn't find eight guys to carry his casket."

"I don't know what his problems were," Jackie told me. "Working with him, I felt rejected. The crew used to say that he was jealous because I was stealing scenes, but as a kid I didn't want to believe that."

Margaret O'Brien maintains that she never had problems with any adults except Wallace Beery: "He didn't like children. He was a tyrant. They had to put a wooden box between us so he couldn't turn me away from the camera.

W. C. Fields and Gloria Jean liked each other. He taught her how to play pool.

Jackie Coogan, Wallace Beery and Jackie Cooper. Cooper "did four long films" with Beery. "I don't think they could find eight people to carry his casket," Cooper told me.

"And he stole my lunch," Margaret remembers. "We had just enough lunches for the cast and crew and he'd steal mine. But he had a marvelous way. He could look like he adored you."

To Jane Powell, Wallace Beery was a "very mean" man. "He used to steal the props off the set. Once he took a canoe that had 'Property of MGM' written on the bottom and he rented it back to the studio for retakes. He must have been sick. I wonder what ever happened to his daughters? I'm amazed he ever had a child. I'm amazed he ever had a wife."

Darryl Hickman found in Beery a kindred spirit. They both were loners. Darryl felt that neither of them fit into the Hollywood system. Apparently, Beery felt the kinship too, for he often asked Darryl's mother if he and Darryl could go out for lunch together. "In front of the camera, he was never generous or giving, and when we walked out of the MGM gate to go to a nearby restaurant, there would be a lot of kids waiting for autographs. They'd run up to him, and he would knock them aside. Yet," Darryl recalls, "he would sit in the restaurant and talk to me as an equal."

Jackie Coogan did only one picture with Beery. It was Beery's first, and Jack's dad directed it. Coogan agreed that Beery was difficult on the set. The reason, Jack believed, "is that Wally never knew what he was. He started out as a female impersonator, playing a Swedish maid. His brother, Noah Beery, was a pretty good actor and a gentleman with impeccable manners. You can see it in his son, Noah, Jr. He's as nice as Joel McCrea. But Wally had to go out and hustle."

Coy Watson and Wallace Beery were old friends. Coy worked as a propman on some of Beery's films. Beery had a three-carat diamond ring, which he would throw to Coy to hold for him during scenes. As Beery went up the ladder he became one of the highest-paid stars at MGM, getting $10,000 a week.

Bobs Watson, who appeared with Beery in *Wyoming*, remembers that during the first week or so of shooting, Beery was "very standoffish." After each scene, he walked away, ignoring Bobs and

Coy, never hinting that they'd known each other before. Bobs asked his dad, "Why did he act like that?"

My father would tell me, "He's got something on his mind." He'd always make excuses for Beery. The ice was broken one day when we were all sitting around running dialogue.

Beery was a terrible ad-libber. He would never give you the right cue. At one point, he stopped about three lines before my cue. He looked at me and said, gruffly, "Well, go on, kid. That's where you say your line." I said, "No, Mr. Beery, your line is . . ." and I went through his whole speech, adding, "And then I say . . ." and I repeated my line.

He looked up at the script girl and she put her hand over her mouth and nodded her head yes. And, by golly, everybody just started to roar. There was no way to pretend it didn't happen.

At first he was stunned. Then he began to laugh, and he reached out and pulled me over and put me on his lap. He said, "You see that old coot over there?" pointing to my dad. I said, "Yes." Beery said, "How long have we known each other, Coy?" My dad said, "Thirty years, Wally." After that, we were the best of friends.

"There were uglies and there were beauties. For me, Errol Flynn was the best," Dean Stockwell asserted. Dean thought of Flynn the way I thought of Gary Cooper. "He was the ultimate father figure for me."

I'm not saying I'd recommend him for the rest of society. It just so happened that at that time of my life—I was twelve or something—he was what he was: a truly profound, nonsuperficial sex symbol. He was *the* fucking male.

Okay, so I'm going to play this little Indian kid in Rudyard Kipling's tale of *Kim* and Errol Flynn is going to play the other guy. While they're building the sets, I come onto the sound stage with my mother and the studio teacher, the perfect Norman Rockwell portrait of middle America —sixty-three years old, sweet, giving, a long-suffering spinster with the rimless glasses and high lace collar. She was terrific with her rosy cheeks.

Didn't even have to blue her hair; she had her own natural white hair. She and my mother were flanking me.

Errol Flynn came up to me. Somebody said, "This is Dean Stockwell." Of course, he's bigger than me, and with this gleam in his eye, he looked down at me. He stuck out his hand and said, "Hi. Have you had your first fuck yet?"

There was a moment, it lasted an eternity, where both my mother and the teacher were going "Brrrr," like pigeons with a gnat up their ass, blushing and doing everything but bleeding on either side of me. Flynn is still staring at me, waiting for me to answer him, but I didn't know what the word meant. I'm just looking at this guy, thinking, I finally found a friend, a father.

Obviously, he knew I hadn't had my first fuck yet, or he figured that out right after he asked me. Still, he gave me one of the special lapel buttons he'd had made. It had beautiful hand-carved wings. In the center were three *F*'s, interlocked. It was "Flynn's Flying Fucker" club, and the part that went into your lapel was a huge erect cock and balls to hold it in. I had it hidden in my top drawer for four years. My mother finally found it. She didn't tell me until two years after she threw it out.

I had a hell of a good time shooting that picture.

Errol Flynn came onto the set one morning a little blurry-eyed, and told me about picking up a girl the night before, a waitress. He really liked waitresses and working girls—secretaries.

So he took this waitress to his place. Next morning, he said, "You know what she did? As I'm fucking her, she said, 'Oh, fuck me, Errol Flynn! Fuck me, Errol Flynn.' I mean, that really tells you where it's at. 'Fuck me, Errol Flynn.' Not 'Fuck me, Errol.' "

Flynn was a maniac practical joker. I had a horror looming up, one of those crying scenes—a real toughy—with Paul Lukas. He's a dying lama. The scene is a master shot inside a tent in India and I'm there with the lama and Flynn comes through the tent flaps and gives me food for the lama in a rice bowl, and I'm supposed to be—as the character Kim—on the job and I can't let the lama eat maggots. So I check the bowl. Flynn has a line and leaves. Then I have this big crying scene with the lama.

So we rehearse and do a take. I'm talking to the lama and in comes Flynn and hands me the bowl, piled high with fresh camel dung, still steaming. Now I'm supposed to look at it and say, "Is this okay for the

Jackie Coogan felt sorry for Wallace Beery. "He never knew who he was," Jack said, "because he started out doing female impersonations as a Swedish maid." Beery and Jackie's father were close friends.

Errol Flynn and Dean Stockwell in *Kim.* Flynn lost a $500 bet when he couldn't make Dean laugh by serving him a bowl of fresh camel dung in a serious scene.

lama to eat?" And he's supposed to say, "Yes, of course. I promise it's good."

I looked at the mess and said my line and he backed out. I played the rest of the scene and it cost Flynn five hundred dollars. He had bet everyone on the crew that he would break me up.

Stymie also liked Errol Flynn. After Roach let him go, Stymie was in *Captain Blood,* with Flynn and Olivia De Havilland. "It was a pirate picture, with big ships on the stage, with two-by-fours under them, and guys would sit on them to rock the boat." Stymie smiled. "Mr. Flynn took me hunting and fishing with him, and he introduced me to Howard Hill, the world-champion archer, who shot an apple off my head. Errol Flynn was a hell of a man. He helped me to get a lot of savvy."

Ann Rutherford was warned before going to work with Flynn to watch out and to wear her track shoes. "But," Ann reports, "there must have been something wrong with me, because I found him to be a perfect gentleman with a delicious sense of humor, very erudite and well-read, a joy.

"The only thing peculiar about him, he kept a monkey in his dressing room. He absolutely adored that monkey, which was a little gamy. But he was wonderful to work with."

Lionel Barrymore was, in Bonita Granville's words, "wonderfully interesting and kind," in spite of his crippling arthritis.

Bobs Watson, who played with Barrymore in *On Borrowed Time,* knew that "Barrymore was in a great deal of pain. He was on crutches, and his hands were all gnarled." Bobs "cried like a baby" the day the picture ended and he had to say goodbye to Barrymore.

"Barrymore gave back," Bobs said. "The one thing about him and all the people I worked with that I consider great—Rooney, Tracy, Edward G. Robinson, Loretta Young, Fonda—was their eye contact. As they looked at you, they became the characters they were portraying. This actor *was* my grandfather, that *was* Father Flanagan, that *was* Whitey. They literally became those characters in a very interesting way; they were performers at the controls, but they took on the personalities of the characters they were playing."

Margaret O'Brien remembers that Barrymore would tire at times because of his arthritis. "I'd run around the set and then sit and plunk on the piano. He finally had it taped so that it wouldn't make any sound. Then he felt guilty and he made beautiful rag dolls, which he'd present to me."

Cora Sue Collins played a little girl in *Smiling Through.* In one scene, all of the major characters, including Barrymore, appeared. "Nobody printed the first take in those days. They shot each scene at least ten times. So all of the very important stars in the film just walked through the first take, but Barrymore was letter-perfect; he was magnificent. But in every take *after* the first—I think they shot fifty-two—he transposed his lines or said them backward. Finally, they had to use the first take, in which he'd been perfect. Of course, he stole the scene."

When Spencer Tracy looked at you in a scene, you felt riveted. There was no place to hide. I did two films with Tracy: *Disorderly Conduct,* co-starring my friend Ralph Bellamy, and another with Loretta Young, in which I was a cripple and lived on the second floor. Tracy carried signs while walking on stilts and stopped to talk to me through the window. Tracy seemed warm yet distant.

Gene Reynolds, who did both *Boys Town* films, remembers Tracy as "very kind and encouraging, but you didn't have much conversation with him off camera."

Sidney Miller was proud and a bit awed to play with him:

> Spencer Tracy was the best listener in the world. When I did a scene in *Boys Town,* I swear those eyes bore into mine.

I also did a scene with him in *Men of Boys Town.* The cameraman said, "Spence, will you cheat your look to Sidney's right ear." He refused. He wouldn't look away from my eyes. If they wanted his full face, they were going to have to bring the camera around. A lot of stars wouldn't stay on the set when your close-up was being shot. But he would.

Bobs Watson found Tracy quiet but warm:

Often, after a scene, he'd reach over and hug me and take me on his lap. I felt like a little puppy. I would follow along and stand close, hoping he'd call me over, and often he would. He'd say, "How're you doing?" and put his arm around me.

Years later, after I'd joined the ministry, a member of my church who worked at Columbia came to me and said, "Hey, Spencer Tracy's making a film, *Guess Who's Coming to Dinner?,* with Katharine Hepburn. How would you like to come out and see him?"

I said, "Sure." So he took me in the back way to the set. Tracy was sitting by himself between takes. I walked over and said, "You may not remember me, but I have always called you Uncle Spence." He looked at me. "I'm Bobs Watson. I played Pee Wee in *Boys Town.*"

"Oh, my God!" Suddenly he was his old self again. "How are you, Bobbie? What have you been doing?" I said, "I'm a minister now. I should tell you that as I approached the ministry, I asked myself, who were the people that I should identify with? I thought back to all the people that I had known, and you influenced me most. Even though I knew you were acting, the way you played Father Flanagan always affected me deeply. Somewhere in my ministry, the way you treated boys has been incorporated."

I've heard that Tracy drank a lot, that he was a loner. I understand that he could be quite nasty, quite belligerent, but from my perspective, he was always a very kind man.

Jane Withers says she was so excited working with Spencer Tracy, she could hardly get her lines out.

In *Dante's Inferno,* I played a brat again. I had to throw a baseball and hit something to make the pig slide down the chute. And I'd say, "I wanna see the pig slide down the chute! I wanna see the pig slide down the chute!" Well, my aim was good, so every time I threw the ball, the trapdoor would open and the pig would come sliding down the chute, and I'd say, "Oh, I'm terribly sorry."

Spencer Tracy was hysterical. He said, "Your aim is too good, kid."

By all accounts, Bing Crosby was a complicated man. Some say he was distant and aloof, that his relationship with his four sons was less than perfect. I never met Crosby, but he left an indelible impression on Donald O'Connor, who appeared with him in *Sing You Sinners* and *Anything Goes:*

In *Anything Goes,* when I was an adult, Bing and I played buddies, chasing girls together, telling raunchy stories. It was very difficult for me to relate to him as a buddy, because I still had this feeling for him as a father figure.

Then a funny thing happened. You've heard that nobody could ever get close to Bing. You'd talk to him and then he'd leave. So, during this picture, I didn't want to bother him and I kept my distance. I knew he was busy. He had other things to do besides acting.

One day, a mutual friend said, "Donald, do you like Bing?" I said, "Of course. I love him. Why?" And he said, "Well, Bing doesn't think you like him. He feels he can't get to you." Bing laughed when I told him about it.

When Gloria Jean first met Bing, he walked over to her and said, "We're going to do a lot of singing together." The movie was *If I Had My Way.* Gloria describes their first recording session together:

We listened to the music. Bing was chewing gum. He chewed gum all the time. He took it out of his mouth and stuck it on the microphone and said, "I have a confession to make. I can't read music." And I said, "Well, you're looking at another one who can't read music."

What we'd do is this: They'd play the songs for us maybe two or three times and we'd learn them. Then we'd sing them together. Bing would say, "Birds never took lessons in singing, and they sing beautifully." He said,

"Just put feeling into a part or into a song." He taught me a lot of little singing tricks that I've always remembered, like throwing away some lines and not thinking about the music as much as about the feeling.

Edith Fellows associates Bing Crosby with laughter. "He was a great tease. You had to have a sense of humor with him around." When Bing made *Pennies from Heaven* in 1936, his last boy, the fourth, had been born. Bing had wanted a daughter.

Soon after they started the film, he said to Edith, " 'Fluffy'—he nicknamed me Fluffy—'would you mind, since we're going to be on this film for two or three months, if we pretend that you're my daughter and I'm your papa?' " Edith didn't mind.

I said, "Oh, I'd love that." I hadn't seen my father very much throughout my life. "But do you want me to call you Daddy?" He said, "No, just call me Bing." I said, "Okay, you still call me Fluffy, but we'll know, won't we?" He said, "Yes, we'll know."

Bing knew that I couldn't swim, though I wasn't afraid of the water. We were on location when he said, "Oh, look at that beautiful lake, Fluffy. Too bad you don't know how to swim."

At lunchtime they put up this huge table for the cast and crew, outdoors, near the lake. I was in my dress for the next shot after lunch, and during dessert I noticed everybody moving away from me. Usually they hung around, smoked a cigarette, or had an extra cup of coffee. But they were backing away and disappearing to the point where it was eerie.

Of course, Bing had it all set up. So, sure enough, he picked me up and plopped me in the lake right at the edge, where nothing could happen to me. The whole crew laughed, but the water felt good because it was so hot.

Bing said, "Would you like to swim around the lake?" "You know I can't swim," I said. He said, "Put your arms around my neck and I'll swim around the lake with you hanging on." Which he did, with all his clothes on. It took almost an hour to dry our clothes, a whole hour lost in the shooting.

Some years later, I did a Broadway play, *Marinka.* During a Saturday matinee, I was singing my first song, when I looked out and there in an aisle seat in the second row was Bing. No notice, nothing. I remember

With Spencer Tracy in *A Man's Castle.* When you played a scene with Tracy, his eyes consumed you. He never looked away.

Edith Fellows with Bing Crosby and Donald Meek in *Pennies from Heaven.* Crosby substituted for the father Edith didn't know; they both pretended she was his daughter.

thinking: "You are a professional. You do not play to him. You do not know he's there." And I never once looked at him after that.

He came backstage after the show and he said, "Well, I didn't know my little girl could sing like that. Why didn't you tell me?"

I said, "Well, you were so busy throwing me in the lake, you didn't have time to hear me sing."

He said, "I was so proud of you today. There was my little girl all grown up. I've never been prouder."

He had his toupee off and he was practically unrecognizable. Bing stayed very much in the background. It wasn't his style to come backstage, but that day he did.

8. Standouts and Bugbears

Whether through repeated and intimate contact (as with Jackie Coogan and Charles Chaplin) or brief encounters (such as Cora Sue Collins with Greta Garbo), our personal encounters with legends of their time left us with indelible impressions. Casual incidents told volumes, and affirmed or contradicted what the world believed about its heroes.

As youngsters, we had a vantage point that frequently was better than that of adults. We saw, from time to time, unsuspected cruelty, kindness, stubbornness, humor, and fear. And we witnessed eccentricity that was notable even by the bizarre standards of Hollywood.

Most movie people, including Jackie Coogan, will tell you that Groucho Marx was mean. But not Gloria Jean. Most think of Henry Fonda and Clark Gable as self-assured and confident. Not Jane Withers or Darryl Hickman. Most think that Joan Crawford was born tough. Coogan knew better.

Most think that Humphrey Bogart lived his life and played his

Kay Francis played a mother of four in *My Bill.* I was Bill, and twelve, when we did the low-budget Warner Brothers film, which won unexpected critical acclaim. Kay Francis was pleasant but she worried that her role was not sufficiently important.

roles his way. He did. When Sybil Jason was seven, Bogart played her father:

They were preparing to shoot a scene with Bogart alone. I was off to the side. There was a big to-do between William Dieterle, the director, and Bogart. He wanted to do it one way, Dieterle insisted he do it another way. Finally, Bogart said, "Okay, let's shoot this thing and get it over with." Dieterle, of course, thought that Bogart had conceded.

The bell rang, the dialogue began, and then suddenly there was silence. Someone called, "Cut." Bogart had unzipped, exposed and relieved himself on camera. He told Dieterle he'd keep on doing that until he could do the scene his way. He did it his way.

I got an education as a child.

Jane Withers was in Henry Fonda's first movie, *The Farmer Takes a Wife.* Fonda was terrified. Jane felt sorry for him. She said, "You're awfully nervous."

"Well, sure I am. I've only done stage work. This is a whole new world for me."

Jane said, "Okay, now you've just got to get over being scared. That's a pretty normal reaction. I get scared too, but then I say my little prayer and God always helps me and I don't get scared anymore." She took Fonda's hand in hers and she said, "God, he really needs help. He's new in this industry, but I think he's going to be awful good. And *he* does too. So he just needs to have a little more confidence." Jane has what she considers "the most wonderful" autographed picture of Henry Fonda. On it he wrote: "To Jane, who helped me to break into this racket. With confidence and love."

Darryl Hickman played Clark Gable's son in *Any Number Can Play.* Gable's hands would sweat badly before a take. He would have his wardrobe man, Brownie, hold his jacket while he put it on. Then his makeup man would bring a mirror and comb and Gable would comb his hair. A propman would bring a towel and Gable would wipe his hands.

Darryl was a fresh fifteen or so, and one day he said:

"Why are you wiping your hands with a towel?"

Gable put his big paw into mine and said, "Feel that." It was sopping wet. "It's either that or it drips," he said. A propman would hold a towel for him before a take, especially before a close-up.

He was The King in those days, and he played the part well. It's all such bullshit. But he was a gentleman. He was there at nine o'clock. He knew his lines. He went home at five o'clock. He couldn't have been nicer to me. He called me Junior. Those were the days before he had a son, and he wanted a son badly. He used to spar with me and cuff me around and we'd play with each other in the most wonderful father-and-son way.

Jackie Coogan and his father gave Joan Crawford her first job in pictures. Jackie found her "wonderful," even though she was in trouble all the time.

She was a very loose-living girl and she was banging everybody in town, and she was a hell of a dancer.

We had to get this one big crying scene from her, so Dad, who was producing the picture, had a couple of detectives tail her for two weeks and learn everything about her.

The scene called for her to enter alone and come down the stairs and start to cry. Well, in a silent picture the director could talk to the actors. So Dad brought her in and ordered everybody off the set. (I stayed on the catwalk.) Then Dad started in on her and while the film rolled he told her everything she'd done, skipping nothing. He tore her right in half and she cried as though her heart would break.

Gloria Jean remembers Groucho Marx as a very quiet man. "People thought he was a cutup, joking all the time. He wasn't at all."

I was in my teens when I made *Copacabana* with Groucho. Steve Cochran was one of the stars. Steve was a tyrant with women. Groucho was like a father to me.

Every day we'd all have lunch, and Steve Cochran would have one of the Copa girls. Later, he would tell people which one he was going to have tomorrow. Naturally, I listened. Groucho didn't like it. He said, "Close your ears. You don't need this yet." And he'd take me away for a walk. He was one of the best people I've ever known.

Jackie Coogan saw Groucho differently:

He was the worst horse's ass in the world. Nothing ever came out of Groucho's mouth except puns and putdowns. He had a great delivery, great stage presence. But take a look at some of the old TV shows of his, and you can see how his hatred of everybody, even the contestants, comes through. And poor George Fenneman, the announcer. Groucho's not ribbing, he's on the level when he says, "There'll be a new boy around here."

Directors were, in many cases, teachers, father figures, ultimate authorities. We had more daily contact with them than we had with our own parents. It was the director who gave us our marching orders and whose approval we—and our parents—wanted most. No wonder they frequently made lasting impacts on our lives.

Frank Capra was the best, Delmar Watson says. Several Watsons worked with Capra in *Mr. Smith Goes to Washington.* Capra started as a film cutter, so when he became a director, he shot with an eye to how he would cut. If an actor blew a line, Capra, rather than redo the entire scene, would pick up a speech or two before the flub, and cut to cover the mistake.

Clarence Brown gave Gene Reynolds a sense of worth and freedom, and wanted to adopt him until he learned Gene had a father.

John Ford, whose reputation as a tyrant was deserved, stopped shooting on *The Grapes of Wrath* every afternoon at four, while the company had tea and cake.

"Do you trust your Uncle Mike?" Michael Curtiz asked Sybil Jason just before a scene in which she was called upon to scream, but couldn't. Sybil said she did. "Then trust me—you will scream." As the cameras rolled, he poked her in the fanny with a hatpin. She screamed, and loved him for it.

In their dealings with children, directors erred most when they tried to make us cry. If we were lucky, tears would flow on cue to start with. But scenes were shot many times. Then the cameras moved in for medium shots, then close-ups. We were dry by lunchtime.

It's true that the director pretended to have Jackie Cooper's dog shot to get him to cry.

In any case, we judged directors largely by how they handled us in crying scenes.

Elia Kazan was tops. He arrived in Hollywood when most of us were adolescents. Peggy Ann Garner gave him credit for the special Academy Award she won for *A Tree Grows in Brooklyn:*

A Tree Grows in Brooklyn was the first picture Gadge Kazan ever did. I was supposed to cry in one scene, and after lunch Kazan said, "Do you have a dog, a cat?" I said no, and he said, "Gee, if you did, what if something happened to your pet?" He talked some more about it, and soon I was ready to cry hard, so he said, "I think we better go inside." Then we shot the scene.

Kazan had a marvelous quality. In *Tree,* he even knew how to handle Dorothy McGuire, and there was a certain way you had to handle that lady. Then there was sweet, warm, buxom Joan Blondell. And Jimmie Dunn, with his hands shaking until someone said, "Knock off the booze, or else." Kazan was like a kid with a new toy, doing this film.

Two weeks into shooting, Darryl Zanuck came on the set. He seldom did that. Gadge often printed two takes, something Zanuck didn't like. Gadge said, "If I'm going to do this picture, I'm going to do it my way."

Another day, Mr. Zanuck came on the set and said, "The picture is so great we're going to scrap it and start over in color." Kazan hit the ceiling. At that time, the only type of color used was Betty Grable–Technicolor, and this picture was very low-key—Brooklyn tenements and all. Anyway, Gadge won.

Natalie Wood was also grateful to Kazan, and to Nicholas Ray as well. "They changed the course of my professional life. Nick introduced me to a new way of working, doing improvisations. It opened the door to a whole new world; it was just glorious. Here were things that I had never dreamt of—improvising, motion memory, sense memory, attending classes, going to the Actors Studio in New York, perhaps even doing theater. All this was just incredible to me." Natalie warmed to the subject:

I had an opportunity to do *Rebel Without a Cause* with Nick if I agreed to sign a seven-year contract. Well, I would have signed almost anything to play that part, so I signed. Then I was stuck under contract and I did some films I wasn't happy with—cranked-out pictures, really. I was forever going on strike, and they put me on suspension.

Then somehow it got straightened out; I guess because Kazan decided that he wanted me. Jack Warner finally agreed I could do *Splendor in the Grass.*

Working on that with Kazan was like being reintroduced to that golden world that Nick Ray had given me a glimpse of. There was nobody an actress could want to work with more than Kazan in the 1950s and '60s. He was God. Nick was sort of his disciple. So here I was with Kazan, the real number one director.

Working with Kazan was different than I'd expected. I thought he would teach me everything. I expected him to teach me how to cry. Instead, I got a different kind of lesson. He tried to demonstrate to me that crying on cue wasn't so all-fired important. Here's how he did it: There were two actresses in the film who played smaller parts, and there was a scene in which crying was not called for. He said, "Come here and watch this." Then he said to the girls, "Now, next time you do that scene, cry for me, okay?" And they said, "Oh, okay," and they did it, just like that!

He tried to impress on me how unimportant the ability was, that it didn't fit, that just crying itself was not the ultimate goal. But I was so neurotic I took it as a further example of my failure as an actress. Here were these girls who could cry when it wasn't necessary, and I had to sit in a corner and think of horrible things and get myself all worked up to do it.

Kazan taught me other things that were very important—about being bold, not being afraid. I was very inhibited, actually. I found it very hard to utilize rehearsal. Normally, I didn't like to rehearse. I would always hold back because I felt I only had one or two takes in me, especially if the scene was emotional.

Kazan showed me different ways to play a scene. He said, "Try things, risk it, don't worry about making a fool of yourself; be bold; be brave; don't be afraid; don't play it safe. What's the worst that can happen?" he said. "Suppose you make a complete fool of yourself; we'll do the scene again." He was trying to get me to be free. To loosen up. His teaching was a wonderful gift.

Greta Garbo wanted to be alone. Marjorie Main saw ghosts. These eccentricities Hollywood could tolerate, if not relate to. What it couldn't understand, and didn't like, were eccentricities—contrived or real—that blew the budget. Despite the mythical public perception of nonconformity, most Hollywood stars conformed in everything that really mattered to the studios. Orson Welles, probably the first certifiable genius to invade the town in some time, refused to conform. Natalie Wood played his daughter in Natalie's first big picture after she went to Hollywood.

Orson Welles had a fight once with Irving Pichel, the director of *Tomorrow Is Forever.* It had something to do with moving his chair. He had to sit in an armchair and I had to sit in his lap. As he sat down, he shifted his chair off its mark and the cameraman said, "Mr. Welles, would you mind shifting your chair back so you will be in the light?"

He said, "This is the way I'm going to sit," and they got into this incredible beef and Welles made them change the lighting rather than move his chair.

He was always doing magic tricks. He had a valet who was a midget. We became great pals, Shorty and I.

Claudette Colbert played my mother in that film. She was always dieting. My mother used to be amazed that "Miss Colbert doesn't seem to eat any food, she just drinks fruit juice and vegetable juice." She was thin as a reed. She had a little atomizer and she sprayed it into her eyes. I think it was just air. She wanted them to sparkle.

Cora Sue Collins recalls that Greta Garbo would invite her to her dressing room for tea. "I was very impressed by her soft, gentle manner. I never saw her with other people around, because I would be left at the door and then picked up afterward."

Cora Sue continued: "One time, Miss Garbo came on the set to watch me work and they surrounded her with black screens. Whenever she worked, the entire area would be screened off so that only the people who had to be within her line of vision would be able to see her."

Margaret O'Brien learned that Marjorie Main was funny, really nice, but that she was afraid of germs. "While we were on location for *Wyoming,* we'd go into town and play the slot machines. Then at night Marjorie would come in with toilet paper wrapped around her arms to keep germs away. And she had a place set at the table in the log cabin for her dead husband and she'd talk to him during dinner."

Often the encouragement that adult stars gave us affected our careers directly. During a period of cutbacks, when Jack Warner was laying off a clutch of contract players, Sybil Jason waited for the ax to fall. "I hadn't been assigned to a film for three months, and that wasn't a good sign. Kay Francis helped me. She said she wouldn't do *Comet Over Broadway* unless I played her daughter. She was kind. But she never could pronounce her *r*'s. Kay 'Fwancis,' she said."

Irving Berlin was particularly helpful to Donald O'Connor and Sidney Miller. Donald told me the story:

> Sidney Miller plays piano in five flats, on the black keys. He can't play any other way—like Irving Berlin.
>
> When I was making *There's No Business Like Show Business,* I told Irving about it. Irving had five unusual pianos. When he pressed the middle pedal, a lever underneath would shift the piano to another key. He still played on the black keys, but he could go up half a tone, a full tone, or whatever he wanted. Out of kindness, he gave one of the pianos to Sidney and me, so we could do the same. With Mr. Berlin's piano, we were able to extend our repertoire.

Charlie Chaplin taught Jackie Coogan "the moves"—how to protect himself. Preventive scene-stealing is what Jackie called it. "It was pretty elemental and worked better in silent movies, when they shot full-length figures.

"Chaplin would make a move to upstage me," Jackie explained, "and I'd have to counter with my elbows, or by putting my foot behind his heel. This fooling around with Chaplin proved very helpful when I worked with Lon Chaney, who played Fagin in my *Oliver Twist.* Chaney was an irascible man. He'd had such a miserable life. All of a sudden he was a big star and meant to remain one."

When Jack met Chaney before they started shooting *Oliver,* the first thing Chaney said to him was, "Come well armed." Jack asked his father what Chaney meant by that, and his dad explained that Jackie had to thwart Chaney when he tried to upstage him.

"Chaney did great things with those mythical hands of his and wove his little spells," Jack said, admiringly. "He was beautiful, a top-notch actor. It was lucky that Chaplin had shown me how to hold my own."

Many of Hollywood's big stars were not so much actors as personalities. In movies, they played themselves. Gene Autry, for instance. Gene didn't impart any tricks of the trade or lasting inspiration to any of us, but Edith Fellows and Jane Withers remember him fondly for his sense of fun and his personal appeal. Interesting that young girls should find this dogged straight shooter so likable —and so funny. Jane says that Autry was a dreadful actor, but she loved him anyway:

When I was twelve, I wanted to do a picture with Gene Autry, so I went to Mr. Wertzel, my producer at Fox, and asked him. He said, "No way they're going to let him come over here. We wouldn't let you go to Republic."

I said, "But if he could come to Fox, could we do a picture together?"

"I'd leap at the opportunity," he said.

I called Republic Pictures and asked who was the head of it, and the lady said, "Herbert Yates."

So I called Mr. Yates and we made an appointment to meet.

Mr. Yates thought that a movie starring Gene Autry and Jane Withers was a fantastic idea. He said, "But what are we going to do about this thing? They won't let you come here."

Cora Sue Collins is crowned in her first film, *Queen Christina,* in which she played Greta Garbo as a baby. Later, Cora Sue burned her photographs and scrapbooks.

The publicity caption on this behind-the-scenes photo, taken during filming of *The Holy Terror,* claimed that "because of the power of Jane Withers's larynx and lungs, the microphone had to be placed at an unusual distance."

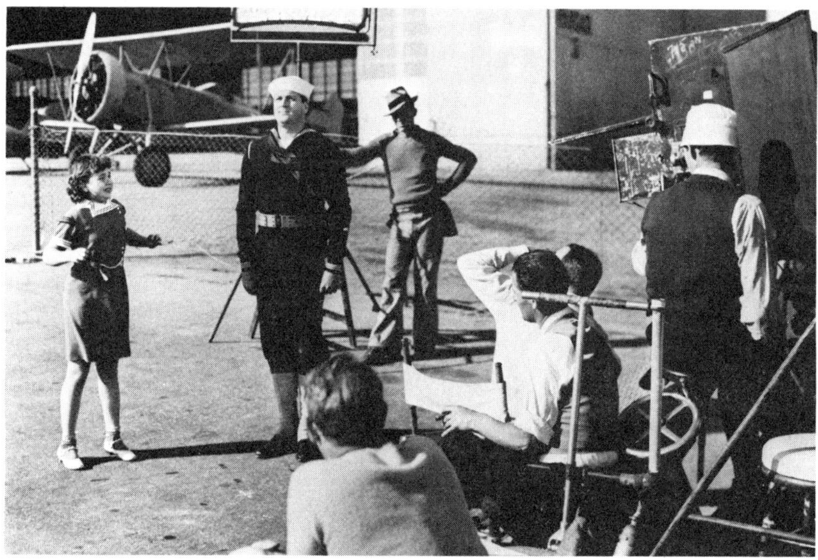

"No, sir," I said. "You're the only one that can make it happen. Maybe there are stars at 20th Century–Fox you'd like. I read in the papers that you swap folks around."

So Gene Autry came to Fox and we did a movie together. It was one of the biggest-grossing pictures of 1939.

I never did find out what stars went to Republic in exchange for Gene, but that's the only picture of all the pictures he's ever made that he doesn't own. He bought all of his other films.

To Edith Fellows, Gene Autry was a nut, a funnyman, a delightful practical joker. "Gene's idea of fun was to pour horse shit down my cowboy boots," Edith reminisced. She retaliated by doctoring his makeup with the same ingredient. Obviously, he soon discovered this and knew who did it, but he never mentioned it to Edith. Then one day:

> There was a scene where a horse bucks me off. So they had to have a close-up of me landing in the dirt on my fanny. They had a two-step for me to jump from so I would roll into the dirt. I was just getting ready to shoot when the cameraman—now this was all set up, of course—said, "Oh, her nose is shiny. Makeup!" And they twisted me around and started powdering, and while my back was turned, Gene was throwing horse shit all over where I was supposed to land. "Okay, roll 'em! Action!" I turned around and leaped. Too late, I saw where I was headed.

For most of my career I was a free-lance actor, but children of some prominence usually were under contract to a single studio and had personal encounters with Louis B. Mayer, Darryl Zanuck, Harry Cohn, and the like.

Since agents handled negotiations for me and I seldom visited the front office, I didn't have strong feelings about the moguls of the industry. But other child stars did.

Jackie Coogan felt that "of all the movie moguls, Cohn was the filthiest. At his funeral, somebody asked Red Skelton, 'How come so many people are here?'

" 'Give the people what they want, they'll all show up,' Red said."

Edith Fellows recalls that Harry Cohn had a speaker into all sound stages and could also listen in to check on whether people were working. If he thought they were goofing off, his voice would boom over the speaker:

The first time I heard Harry Cohn's voice was on *She Married Her Boss*. I was twelve. Gregory La Cava, the director, also wrote the screenplay. He wrote the scenes the night before we shot them. We'd sit around and talk about the scenes. In retrospect, I realize we were improvising, but at that time we didn't know what improvising was.

When Harry Cohn tuned in on the set, he heard nothing happening, just Claudette Colbert, Melvyn Douglas, and me sitting around discussing the scene, while La Cava gave us an idea of the feeling he wanted.

All of a sudden this booming voice: "What the hell are you doing down there?" I thought: "It's God speaking." It scared me to death. Grown men looked ready to cry, it was that frightening.

The first time I saw Cohn close up was when he commanded me and my grandmother to go to his office. It was a long walk to his huge desk. He invited us to sit down. I sat behind and to the side of my grandmother.

Without preamble, he lit into her. She has to stop putting this cheap crap on my back. It reflects on the studio as well as on me and she has got to dress me better, and those are his words and that's the law.

Meanwhile, I'm sitting there smiling because I'd no idea that my boss was my friend. I almost started falling in love with Harry Cohn. He used a few colorful words that I didn't know then.

Grandma said, "Well, Shirley Temple's mother gets a salary for taking care of Shirley, so I certainly think I deserve a salary for taking care of Edith." She was ready to fight.

He screamed at her, "You'll get nothing, and good day!"

I think that shook her up, and I just loved it.

Darryl Hickman's mother named him after Darryl Zanuck, the boss of 20th Century-Fox. Young Darryl thought it was a "sissy name." Zanuck would grin when they passed each other. Young Darryl doesn't think he ever got a part because they shared the name.

Jane Withers, who, more than any of us, loves all God's creatures, makes an exception of Darryl Zanuck:

> Darryl Zanuck was the only man I've ever met in my entire life that I didn't like. I didn't respect him, his attitude, or the way he treated people. I felt strange around him, like I wanted to go take a bath. Luckily, I didn't usually have to worry about him, because I was in "B" pictures.
>
> I had to go to conventions for exhibitors because they demanded to see me. It would make Zanuck so mad, and it used to tickle me to death. Those guys would say to me, "Hey, kid, we can always count on your movies to save us from those tacky things that he puts out."
>
> When they introduced Shirley Temple, of course, she'd get thunderous applause. But when they mentioned my name, those exhibitors would get up and scream. And Zanuck would be furious. He would get red in the face, he'd be so angry. Instead of being thrilled and proud that mine was another film from his studio, it just killed him when they carried on so.

Hal Roach spawned more kids' careers than any other man. Scores of us touched base at Roach at one time or another. Spanky (George) McFarland and Stymie were most identified with the Gang. As a baby, Spanky, born in Dallas, modeled clothes. An aunt sent Hal Roach a photo, then Spanky and his parents drove to Hollywood, where Spanky had a screen test. Roach signed him to a four-year contract on November 4, 1931. Spanky was still three. He stayed at Roach longer than any other child—eleven years—and appeared in ninety-five "Our Gang" comedies.

While Spanky remembers little of his early years in films, he remembers what his mother told him about his former boss: "Roach was not really interested in the kids. He was a businessman, not the fatherly type who had our welfare at heart, like everybody thought. He was cold as a fish. Only when there was a camera around or somebody was asking him about the comedies did he ever display

An early picture of Spanky McFarland.

any warmth or feeling toward the kids, and then it was contrived."

MGM was the top of the heap and Louis B. Mayer was the top of MGM. Or so it seemed. Vastly different perceptions of L. B. Mayer are held by those who worked for him. Elizabeth Taylor has described him as "a monster." The first time Jane Powell was ushered into Mayer's office, it seemed immense to her. With each succeeding visit it got smaller.

Jane recalls L. B. once waiting for a "message from Garcia in New York." She wondered who Garcia was. Jane felt close to L. B. Mayer:

> He was like my father. I was still with the studio when they kicked him out and brought Dore Schary in. He couldn't understand it. I think it killed him, and from then on, the studio went right down the tubes. I went to see him on his last day and he was in tears. They made him out to be such an ogre, and he wasn't that way at all, at least not to me. I loved the man. I think what they did to him was a shame.
>
> It's true that I told him I wanted to play more adult roles, and he'd pat me on the top of the head. "You will, you will." But I understood his reluctance. When you've got a good thing and people are still buying it, you don't want to change. It was a business, and I was an employee, and I was getting a very good salary—five thousand dollars a week—to do what I did. I didn't have to do it if I wasn't happy.

Jackie Cooper recalls that after *The Champ,* when he was around ten, he was put on suspension for six months—no salary, and he couldn't work anyplace else. Finally, an intermediary got Jackie's mother and L. B. Mayer together:

> Mayer insisted that I go to his office for the burying of the hatchet. I remember being kind of bored and sitting there watching him behind his huge desk in his white-on-white shirt, practically crying and telling my mother how I'm family and she's family and these things should never happen again, and life's going to be wonderful.
>
> As we were leaving, he opened the door and my mother said, "Say goodbye to Mr. Mayer." And he grabbed me. I had a little coat on with

an open-collared shirt, and he grabbed one lapel and shook a finger in my face and said, "It's a goddamn good thing you came back to work today, young man." I started to cry and he yelled, "Get him out of here! Get him out of here!"

When Cora Sue Collins was about four, she was under contract to MGM. One day, Cora Sue and her mother were in Mr. Mayer's outer office with Ida Koverman, Mr. Mayer's secretary. Suddenly, the door to Mr. Mayer's private office opened and a very beautiful star—perhaps the studio's most illustrious and ladylike actress of the day—opened the door, and with her back to the waiting room, said to Mr. Mayer, "Don't give me that crap. I've fucked every producer on my way up and I don't have to take that!," slammed the door, and walked out.

Cora Sue turned to her mother and said, "What does 'fuck' mean?"

My mother, a proper Southern lady, turned nine shades of red and said, "I don't know." So I asked Miss Koverman and she was just as nonplussed. I said, "When I go in to see Mr. Mayer, I'll ask him. He must know what it means."

She said, "Please don't discuss it!" so I never did ask Mr. Mayer.

Virtually equal in status and power to the Zanucks, Mayers, and Cohns were Louella O. Parsons and Hedda Hopper, whose syndicated Hollywood columns could (and did) make or break pictures and careers. They were widely feared and their loathing for each other was honed to a fine edge. But both were cordial to me whenever we met and generous whenever they wrote about me.

Parsons, who imbibed, had the air of a plump and addled old-maid aunt. Her access to the front office of any studio was unquestioned. Often, she sat in on crucial meetings. At one such, in the office of Louis B. Mayer, Miss Parsons excused herself and made her way through an outer office to the rest room. Her task accomplished, she wandered back across the hall and into L. B.'s office, trailing behind her an unfurling roll of toilet tissue, the end of which was snugly tucked underneath her girdle. Lolly Parsons never noticed.

Hedda Hopper was sharper than a serpent's tooth and just as lethal. An attractive actress, fifth wife of matinee idol De Wolf Hopper, she retained her acting credentials and was set to play Jane Powell's mother until her unfavorable review of an MGM film caused her temporary banishment from the lot. Jane, who got on well with Hedda, dropped by to visit her at home.

As Jane was leaving, Hedda said, "Come upstairs. I want to show you something." Jane followed. Hedda opened a door to reveal a room crammed full with packages and boxes. "Jane," said Hedda Hopper, "these are gifts of fear."

9. Our Pay and What Happened to It

"Dickie Moore pulls down more money than all the other 'Our Gang' kiddies together, for he is a drawing card in features and head gangster, too," read the photo caption in the movie magazine. The picture showed me dressed as Santa Claus, presenting Mother with a dress. The caption continued: "Dickie's dad was a bank teller before Dickie got in the big money. So the fact that Dickie is making more than most bank presidents even aspire to must give dad a rather comfortable feeling. . . . Dickie can and does bring home the right sort of things when Christmas rolls around. A nice convertible coupe for dad. A beautiful evening gown for mom. And a dozen smaller but also wonderful things. And it doesn't impoverish Dickie to do it. There is plenty left to satisfy his own wants."

The year was 1933, when, as Stymie recalled, you "could take a dollar bill and get you three pork steaks, a half a dozen eggs, a loaf of bread, a quart of milk, and get eight cents in change."

The Great Depression gripped the land. I could buy a Baby Ruth candy bar—many times its present size—for a nickel. A stamped postcard cost a penny, a newspaper two cents; ninety-nine cents bought a four-course dinner in a restaurant that had tablecloths. Dad almost died when he wrote a check for $1,200 for the new Buick, a convertible sedan with leather seats. A three-bedroom bungalow in Hollywood could be yours for $3,000, and when cost overruns on our Fifth Street house brought the final tab to $6,600, Dad exploded: "That damn Ray Fargo has no business building houses! He just pissed our money down the drain, or stole it!"

I don't know how much I earned. Money and work were not consciously connected. I remember only brief episodes associated with money, an out-of-sequence montage in my mind.

At six, I was called downtown to see a judge, who asked me if I was happy with my contract with Warner Brothers studios. I told him, "Sure."

Dad complained about the rising income tax, which took nearly a dime from every dollar of my salary. What's an income tax? I asked him. His answer didn't make sense to me.

I left my baby teeth under my pillow, hoping that the Tooth Fairy would leave a quarter. She always left a dime.

Our Boy Scout troop met every Friday night. We paid ten cents weekly dues. When a movie part came along, I missed ten weeks of meetings. On returning, I handed in my dime. "You owe a dollar more in back dues," the leader told me. I asked Mother for the money. "You shouldn't have to pay for meetings that you missed," she said. "That isn't very nice." I quit the Boy Scouts.

One day in junior high school, the teacher called me out of class. Mother paced the hall, in tears. Her appearance frightened me. "Dickie, I must talk to you," she sobbed. "My mother died—your grandma in Toronto. Your father won't give me money to go to her funeral. Dickie, dear, what can I do?" I hugged her, awkwardly. We decided to send flowers.

Dinner at Sammy's Steak House, with my sister, four: Mother

read aloud selections from the menu. Pat announced, "It's Sammy's Steak House. I'll have steak!"

Mother was furious. "Don't you realize that steak is the most expensive thing on the menu? Just who do you think you are, ordering steak?" Pat cried. (To this day, she anxiously consults the right side of the menu and never orders steak.)

Our friend Alfred Fay, an insurance agent, told Dad about a new invention, a fishing reel which, in return for a modest investment, would yield substantial wealth. Dad got his checkbook. "I need an extra thousand too, to tide me over, Jack," said Mr. Fay. Dad, unsmiling, wrote a check.

A drawing of me sitting in a director's chair, holding a shiny new dime, appeared in magazines. The caption said: "Whenever Dickie Moore finishes a picture, he gets a shiny new dime." It was true.

Most kids find ways to supplement their allowances. I sold Kool-Aid off the curb, two cents a cup.

At eleven, I had a magazine route. Dad, then working, was worried that I didn't "know the value of a dollar." He hit on the idea of my selling magazines door to door. A man from Macfadden Publications visited the house with forms for me to fill out weekly, a canvas shoulder bag to hold magazines, and a supply of *Liberty* (five cents) and *True Story* (twenty-five cents). I worked on commission.

I hated ringing doorbells, certain that no one would buy my magazines. Each week, I returned most of them unsold. One day, a man invited me inside and closed the door. He bought every magazine, then unfastened my pants. "Let's see what you have," he said gently. Something was wrong. He took my penis in his hand and said, "That's cute." Quickly I retreated to the door and ran outside.

Two days later, I told Mother what had happened. She and Dad whispered urgently when he got home from his "hard day at the bank." Next day, the man from Macfadden settled our accounts and took back the canvas bag.

In my early teens, one summer when I was unemployed, Mother spoke to our neighbor Mr. Rossi, the buyer for the May Company. Could he find me a job? He did, not in the downtown store, but in the new emporium on Wilshire Boulevard. "It's a marvelous opportunity," Mother said, pleased, "and right in the neighborhood. You'll be meeting the public and you can walk to work."

I sold sporting goods. People bought volley balls and other equipment for me to autograph. When they asked what I was doing there, I answered awkwardly, "Getting experience." My salary was $28 a week, which I kept. When school began, I quit.

Every Tuesday, Mother picked me up at school and drove me to the Department of Employment, where I signed for unemployment compensation: $18.50 a week. I was the only one my age in line. "What are *you* doing here?" adults would say, and stare at me.

"Tell them it's your money and you earned it," Mother encouraged me. "After all, Adolphe Menjou collects, and he's the best-dressed man in Hollywood. He even has his chauffeur wait outside while he signs for his check."

Bobs Watson didn't like going to the unemployment office any more than I did. When he filled out the form, he figured it was just another autograph and wrote, "Yours truly, Bobs Watson."

After school one day, Mother, in the kitchen, was preparing dinner for some guests. "Dickie." She wiped her hands on her apron. "I have to talk to you." Her voice was high and tight. "Your father feels that you should be paying room and board. We've discussed it and we think fifty dollars a month is appropriate. You don't have to start till the first of the month."

My stomach sank. The room became a roller-coaster poised for the big descent. I leaned against the sink, then found my voice. "No. I won't pay it. I can't." The first time I ever said "I won't."

"Things cost more these days, and your father doesn't earn that much. You haven't worked in three months, and you're getting unemployment compensation. You don't need all that money."

"I'm saving up to buy a wire recorder. I need it for my work."

"But you're not working. Anyway, that's just a toy. Now the

subject is closed. If you won't contribute, you'll have to move until you do. Your father insists. He made me talk to you."

"This is my house," I murmured. "I paid for it; I won't pay rent to live here. What happened to all the money I made?"

"You never earned more than six hundred dollars a week. You never got what you deserved. There is nothing to discuss."

That night at dinner, Edie Lake, Aunty Ruth, Aunty Jo, and her new friend, George Germain, were at the table. Pat was visiting a friend.

"Why are you so quiet, Dickie?" Aunty Jo teased. "Cat got your tongue?"

"I don't feel like talking," I replied.

Dad filled the gap with how Roosevelt was driving prices up. "My life insurance premium cost four hundred dollars. I don't know what the hell I need insurance for, but I've kept it up for Dickie's sake, so he'll have something if I die."

"Thanks," I said, "a lot."

From where Dad sat I felt the anger roll like silent waves across the table. Edie Lake said nothing; Aunty Jo, Aunty Ruth said nothing. Mother offered more baked beans and all accepted. Instantly, a scene flashed through my mind, from *Oliver Twist,* one of my early triumphs: me standing with an empty porridge bowl, looking up at a stern-faced man, imploring, "Please, sir, can I have some more?"

I left the table and went to my room.

"Hi, big shot," Dad greeted me one Saturday when I joined him in the garage. He had finished tying several stacks of newspapers into neat bundles and had placed them next to three cardboard cartons of discarded clothing which he had collected and folded with great care. Alongside, on the garage floor, stood some coils of copper wire and balls of tinfoil, peeled from candy wrappers and packs of cigarettes.

It was the day the junkman drove his horse-drawn cart past our house, ringing his bell and calling, "Junk! I buy old clothes, old papers, junk!" Hearing his approach, Dad hurried to the sidewalk to hail the junkman, then led him up the driveway to the garage and exhibited the products of his labor. The junkman examined the boxes. Dad, serious, waited for his verdict. "Well, how much?" Dad asked.

The junkman paused, then said, "Two dollars for the lot."

Dad went gray. Finally, he said, "Hell, I'd rather give it away."

Involuntarily I smiled, a secret smile of pleasure at Dad's powerless frustration, a guilty smile I tried to hide, even from myself.

Money was the only reason that Lillian and Dorothy Gish—two of the most celebrated actresses ever to appear in theater and films—began acting as children.

Tiny, delicate, astonishingly beautiful at eighty-eight, Lillian Gish poured tea for me in her New York apartment as she reminisced about her life when Theodore Roosevelt was President.

To support the girls, their mother, who had never worked, got a job in a department store. "She gave Papa the money to pay the man when he came for the furniture we were buying on the installment plan. But he didn't pay it, so she said, 'Well, look, I can support three people, but I can't support four. You go out and get a job, and when you can support us, you come back.' " Miss Gish spoke precisely.

To supplement her earnings, her mother rented out the girls' bedroom to two actresses, who encouraged her to try the stage. The Proctor's Stock Company hired her as leading ingenue. An actress with a company that needed a four-year-old girl took Lillian with her on the road. Another actress took Dorothy. Each girl earned ten dollars a week; their mother, fifteen dollars. They saved enough to get them through the summer, when theaters closed; air conditioning hadn't been invented. Came summer, Lillian, Dorothy, and their mother visited Aunt Emily in Ohio:

In Ohio, hotels had signs saying: "No actors or dogs allowed." We asked Mother why. We thought actors were such nice people. Mother said

When father wouldn't support the family, the Gish sisters, Lillian *(left)* and Dorothy, and their mother, were forced to earn a living. The girls became actresses at ages three and four.

it was because actors often got stranded and had no money to pay their hotel bills, so they slid down the water pipe at night and left without paying their bills.

After I went into the movies, Grif [D. W. Griffith, in whose films the Gish girls starred] ran out of money while we were filming *Birth of a Nation.* He had only fifty thousand dollars and the picture cost sixty-one thousand. We all worked without salary because we knew he was honest, and we wanted to help. Mother had saved three hundred, which was a fortune for us, and she went to Mr. Griffith and offered to put it into the picture. But he said, "No, I won't take it. You might lose it all."

I earned a thousand a week in the movies. Mother said, "You think you're getting a thousand a week? You're getting fifty dollars, five percent. See that you live on that." Mother put the rest away for us.

By the time Jackie Coogan came along, the Gish sisters had grown into popular adult stars of the fledgling motion picture industry, first headquartered in New York.

Vaudeville was still big business then, Jackie recalled, and when W. C. Fields played a town, he'd open a bank account, usually for $5,000. Many old-time vaudevillians did that. But Fields opened his accounts under different names and he kept no written records. Instead, he kept track of his deposits through association, and he memorized a code: "Let me see, what town did I play? Ashtabula. Ashtabula . . . I got a dose of clap in Ashtabula. Clap . . . *C* . . . Citizens Bank. Yeah, I put some money there!"

The trouble with this system was that in his last days Fields was so far gone that he didn't remember where his money was, or what name it was under. To this day, nobody knows.

Jackie Coogan laughed delightedly when he repeated this anecdote. It was one of the few stories about losing money that amused him. He remembered with less relish how his fortune vanished.

"Did you feel used?" I asked him.

Jack fell silent, then: "Not until much later, when I was twenty-one, after my dad died. That's when I knew I'd been had."

By the time Jackie was ten, pencil boxes, lunch pails, chewing gum bore his name and picture. He received $50,000 yearly for the use of his photograph on an Erector set. For a weekly royalty of

$2,000, his name went on the label of a line of boys' clothes. More than 200,000 Jackie Coogan dolls were sold, paying Jackie a royalty of fifty cents apiece. Jackie Coogan chocolate (in the shape of Jackie's head) paid him half a cent on each nickel item sold. The Coogans set up a finance company that earned interest on short-term loans by factoring department stores. Arrangements were made with a large Chevrolet dealership to finance all the cars it sold on time. World heavyweight champion Jess Willard opened the first supermarket on Vine Street in Hollywood by borrowing $30,000 from the Coogans, pledging his 28-carat diamond ring as security. When Jackie signed his Metro contract, the studio gave him a bonus of $500,000 to keep him from signing with Goldwyn.

All this, in addition to the revenues from Jackie's pictures, was funneled through Jackie Coogan Productions, Inc., the company founded by the Coogans, which employed five secretaries and paid Jackie $20,000 a week, his father $5,000, and his mother $1,000. The door of Coogan Productions was open to anybody with a good idea.

Still, Jack said, his dad was "not a businessman, he was an opportunist." So, as the business grew, Jack Coogan, Sr., who produced all of Jackie's pictures and directed many of them, was persuaded that he should get somebody else to handle business details. Friends introduced him to Arthur L. Bernstein, who became the Coogans' business manager.

Bernstein was, in Jackie's view, an "angle man," who "got us in trouble with the government on income tax, so we had to get the highest-priced woman attorney in the world, who had a pipeline into Washington. We paid off," Jack told me.

By the time Jackie reached his teens, his career had waned and his dad could not find work as a director. Deeply hurt, Jack Coogan, Sr., retired to the Coogans' ranch in Mexico. "Half of Hollywood owed him money," Jack remembered bitterly. "He was owed over half a million dollars just in tens and twenties."

Still, Jackie was happy sharing his adolescence with his dad. There was still plenty of money. Best of all, there was the ranch, where Jackie and his father hunted. It became their haven.

One day, returning to Hollywood from the ranch after a dove-hunting trip, Jackie, his dad, the ranch foreman, and two friends rounded a turn in the highway fifty miles from San Diego. In the middle of the road, moving at high speed in the opposite direction, another car appeared. Jackie, in the rumble seat, reacted quickly as they swerved to avoid a collision:

We hung up on the edge of a riverbed, then we went over, and I dove for the floor of the rumble seat. We had eight shotguns in the rumble seat with us and about 350 doves in bags. The doves were like feather pillows. That's what saved me. The car went seven times end over end into a dry riverbed, bouncing off boulders as big as houses. I was the only one who stayed in the car; everybody else was thrown out. I guess one of the rocks or a gun hit my back and hurt a vertebra, but I didn't know it until later.

When we stopped, I got out of the rumble seat, or rather, I fell out. I found my dad and carried him up to the side of the road. Then I carried my friend, Junior Durkin, up. People were stopping by then. One of them was a nurse and she gave my dad, who was still alive, a drink of brandy. Everybody else was already dead. Junior Durkin was unrecognizable, Bob Horner was caved in, the foreman, who was riding with me in the rumble seat, had his head taken off.

Somebody took me to the general store in Pine Valley, about eight miles from the accident, to the nearest phone. I called my mother. I didn't know what else to do. When I came out of the phone booth, I fell through a display case. That's when I knew I had hurt my back. After about three hours, the ambulance came and took me back to San Diego.

Then my doctor flew down with my mother and Bernstein in a chartered plane. They moved me up to Physicians and Surgeons Hospital in Glendale.

Jack walked out of the hospital three days later—against his doctor's wishes—to attend his father's funeral. A year later, Lillian Coogan married Arthur Bernstein. Jack went to the wedding and accepted Bernstein into the family. "I had no reason to dislike him then," Jack remembered. "Actually, I didn't pay much attention to him. Oh, I'd get mad at him. He said something to me once down at the ranch and I knocked him on his ass."

There were jokes about Jackie's money by some who knew the family. One such friend, songwriter Sully Violinski, had a habit of pinching people when he saw them and telling ladies they were cute. One day on Madison Avenue in New York, Sully pinched Jackie's mother. She hit him with her purse and knocked him down. Lying on the sidewalk, looking at the people gathered around, he said, "No wonder—it had all of Jackie's money in it!"

Jackie's mother gambled. So did Arthur Bernstein. "Bernstein lost the ranch one night playing chemin de fer. We had paid $380,000 for it. To this day, I never found out exactly what they lost between them. The nearest I can figure was that they lost about two million after my father died," Jackie calculated.

On his twenty-first birthday, Jackie got a gift of a checking account with $1,000 in it. He asked his mother, "What am I supposed to do now? Do you want me to go to the office?"

"What for?" she asked.

"Well, how am I going to earn my salary?"

"What salary? There is no salary."

More time elapsed. Jackie married actress Betty Grable. Forced to live mainly off her earnings, Jackie decided to hire a lawyer:

> I went to a law firm and told them that I had nothing coming from any of the money that I'd earned, and I recounted the estimates of what I had made, ten million. I showed them a photo of the five-hundred-thousand-dollar check that Metro gave me just for signing the contract with them.
>
> They were aghast. They said they'd handle it, and they told me to keep quiet. I was to maintain the normal relationships while the suit was being prepared, because we were a big business.
>
> Before the suit was filed, I went to Charlie Chaplin. Usually I visited him to pass the time of day. This time I said, "I'm broke. I need ten thousand."
>
> He said, "What's the matter with Moody?" He still called my mother Moody, like I did. So I told him. He sent for Arch Shreves, his business manager, and whispered something to him. About fifteen minutes later, Arch came back with an envelope containing $10,000 in cash. Chaplin was a real friend, the only person I could count on.

The suit broke. So did the publicity. *Newsweek,* in its April 25, 1938, edition, led off with this: "Ten years ago Walter Winchell reported in his gossip column that, when Jackie Coogan's mother turned away a caller with the excuse that her son was 'with his private tutor,' the caller snapped: 'Don't ever teach him arithmetic, because some day he's going to wonder where all of his money has gone to.' "

The *Newsweek* article continued: "April 11, Coogan sued his mother and Arthur L. Bernstein, his stepfather, in Superior Court, Los Angeles. According to the 23-year-old plaintiff's arithmetic, they had withheld from him $4 million of his money. . . ."

The May 2, 1938, issue of *Time* magazine reported that "out of the liveliest family shindig Hollywood has staged . . . had come two amazing bits of news. The first was that out of his vast earnings Jackie Coogan had got virtually nothing. The other was that if his billowy, multi-chinned mother and his slick, slanty-eyed, beaky stepfather and former adviser, Arthur L. Bernstein, had anything to say about it, he never would."

Time expanded on the subject: "A fortnight before, Jackie, at 23, a slight, blotchy-faced young man with a thinning patch of muddy blonde hair where once grew the Kid's famous Dutch-boy bob, had sued for an accounting of the great fortune he was sure he had amassed. From the San Fernando Valley mansion that Jackie's talents paid for, came the hurt and indignant cry of an outraged mother, the shrewd two-cents' worth of a story-book stepfather.

" 'Jackie has had all he is entitled to and more,' shrilled Lillian Coogan Bernstein. 'He isn't entitled to that money. It belongs to us.' Added stepfather Bernstein: 'The law is on our side. Lawyers tell his mother and me that every dollar a kid earns before he is twenty-one belongs to his parents. . . .' "

Time also reported that when Jackie had wanted to marry Betty Grable, his mother telephoned Betty's mother and told her, "If Betty thinks she's marrying a rich boy, she is mistaken. He hasn't a cent. He's a pauper." Betty married Jackie anyway.

Continued *Time:* "Confronted in . . . court last week with all this niggardly evidence, the Bernsteins put on a great show. Weeping wetly, Jackie's mother squalled: 'I love my boy. . . . I've always tried to do the best I knew how for him. . . .' At week's end, with Mrs. Bernstein heartily protesting 'I'd go through fire and water for that boy,' old friends and thousands of admirers were rallying to Jackie's cause."

Indeed they were. But many important people in Hollywood worried that the furor would give movies a bad name.

Jackie wasn't answering the phone. His wife, Betty, was. "It's somebody that says he's Louis B. Mayer," she said, covering the receiver.

"Does it sound like him?" Jack asked.

"Yes," Betty replied.

Jack picked up the phone.

So Mayer starts off with the old bullshit. "Oh, Jackie, boy," he said, "I read about this terrible thing. Why aren't you working?"

I said, "I don't know. I'm still around. Maybe I'm too old for kid parts and not old enough to play juveniles. I don't know."

Mayer said, "Well, come out here and we'll sit down and we'll tide you over. We'll give you a two-year contract for fifty-two weeks a year, twenty-five hundred a week the first year and three thousand the second. Is that all right?"

I said, "That's wonderful. That's the answer to 'most everything."

Then Mayer said, "Just one little thing. Call off that silly suit."

I said, "I can't. It's a contingency suit. I didn't have the money to pay a lawyer, so I had to give it to them on contingency."

Mayer said, "You can't cancel it?" We argued back and forth, and then he said, "You dirty little bastard!"

The next day, my agent, Arthur Landau, called me. "Do you know you've been blackballed? I can't talk about it. But you're dead. There isn't anything I can do."

The lawsuit went on, then all of a sudden my lawyers suggested we come up with a settlement. I later wondered if there was hanky-panky between my lawyers and Bernstein's and my mother's. I got about eighty thousand net out of the whole friggin' mess.

If I hadn't been so much in love with Betty, I wouldn't have settled, because I had a real hate in my heart for Bernstein; and my mother was a giddy woman who never grew away from vaudeville.

But I fumbled it. If I'd said to the lawyer who came out at eleven o'clock at night to get me to sign this agreement, "Tell 'em to go fuck themselves," they couldn't have made a settlement without my signature.

Jack later attended Bernstein's funeral, holding up his mother while "she did the widow bit." And, he marveled, "I noticed in the casket Bernstein was wearing my pants."

On June 20, 1939, the governor of California signed what is universally known as the "Coogan Law," which added sections 36.1 and 36.2 to the state Civil Code. No one consulted Jackie. "Out of shame, they never came near me when they wrote the Coogan Law."

Technically, the law relates "to the compensation and net earnings of minors for services rendered pursuant to contracts approved by a court."

But "contracts approved by a court" were long-term contracts to a studio. If a youngster worked free-lance—most did, including me—the law did not apply.

The provisions of the law that matter most, and protect working children least, state that: "The court shall have power . . . to require the setting aside and preservation for the benefit of the minor . . . such portion of the [minor's] net earnings . . . not exceeding one-half . . . as the court may deem just and proper. . . . Net earnings . . . [are] the total sum received for the [minor's] services pursuant to such contract, less . . . taxes and . . . reasonable sums expended for the support, care, maintenance, education and training of the minor; expenses paid [for] maintaining employment of the minor; and fees or attorneys for services rendered in connection with the . . . business of the minor. . . ."

Most of us earned the major portion of our salaries before the Coogan Law was passed. But even when the law applied, its language invited more violation than compliance.

Peggy Ann Garner's mother found the Coogan Law no challenge. For a time during World War II, salaries were frozen, but the studios got around that by giving their contract stars a bonus at the conclusion of a picture. Peggy Ann did three important pictures in one year: *A Tree Grows in Brooklyn*, *Nob Hill*, and *Junior Miss*. Since Peggy was under long-term contract to Fox after 1939, she thought the Coogan Law protected her. She was mistaken:

During the war years, my mother was very big with the army, navy, and marines. I never knew which branch she was going to bring home. If there were ten men at a table, my mother would pick up the check. She spent all my money. Here's how she got around the Coogan Law.

The only way you could get a child's money released under the law was to petition for it, and the expense had to be in the interest of the child, to buy a house or whatever. By now, I was so cut up—there was a guardian of the person, which was my mother; guardian of the trust, which I believe was a bank; guardian of the estate, guardian of whatever. My mother was obviously guardian of the person, and she decided she wanted to buy a house. So everybody had a powwow in court. The lawyers came from 20th Century–Fox, the lawyers came from the bank; my daddy was in absentia, fighting a war.

My mother petitioned to get the money, whatever was in trust, to buy the house, and the judge asked the studio lawyers, "Is there any reason in the future why the studio would drop this child?" and they said, "No," so the money was released to my mother and she bought the house. Two months later, Fox dropped me.

So she mortgaged the house a couple of times to raise cash. That's what happened to my trust fund. Until I went into the play *Bus Stop*, some twenty years later, I was still paying off debts.

Like Peggy Ann, Sybil Jason was under long-term contract, first to Warners, then to Fox. By the time the Coogan Law was passed,

Sybil's uncle was ensconced in Hollywood. He had come from England to be with Sybil and her older sister.

While Sybil's uncle didn't handle Sybil's negotiations with the studio (her agent, William Morris, did), he took a lively interest in Sybil's career. Sybil remembers how her uncle "almost wiped the slate clean financially" and got around the Coogan Law:

> What he did was to keep going back to court, always claiming he needed money to maintain my career, to keep up my image. He said he had to give parties, which he did. He gave fantastic parties and Christmas presents. He never bought his clothes off the rack. He had everything custom made for himself, with monograms. Meanwhile, he was shipping a lot of money over to England.

Sybil's uncle tried to interfere in her career and Jack Warner barred him from the lot. So he returned to England, to rejoin most of Sybil's money.

In addition to the obvious loopholes in the Coogan Law, there was another obstacle—you had to sue your parents to be protected by it. No one I know did that. We wanted to be loved.

In fact, the ex–child stars I talked to didn't know the Coogan Law's provisions, even as adults. I didn't know them until I wrote this book.

Arthur Bernstein wanted to manage Baby Peggy's fortune, but Diana Cary's father would not relinquish control. Instead, he founded the Baby Peggy Corporation, modeled after Jackie Coogan Productions, Inc. Her contracts guaranteed that Diana would get half of all the profits from her films. In fact, she got less because the studio would "block book" unprofitable films along with hers and charge their expenses against her films' receipts. Despite this common practice, the family prospered. Diana, like Jackie, got royalties from merchandising. There were Baby Peggy dresses, purses, dolls, prunes, even spinach. Companies paid to use her name, and

Diana appeared in the promotions. But when Baby Peggy Spinach, for example, was due to pay its royalty, the company disappeared. Her father, unsophisticated in business, couldn't cope. The Baby Peggy Corporation was dissolved.

Diana in the 1920s made $2 million before she turned six, with practically no income tax. When her film career declined, she toured in vaudeville for three more years, earning more than $2,000 a week. Then her father bought a ranch in Wyoming, where Diana spent the three happiest years of her life. Diana's dad was happy too. He'd always wanted a ranch. Eventually, he lost that, and, Diana told me, her parents blamed each other for bursting the balloon:

They fought all their lives over me and my money. They spent a tremendous amount on houses and cars, Duesenbergs and Packards. My father was crazy over cars. My mother had fur coats and servants. They spent a lot on entertaining. They were young. Mother was twenty-three, a small-town girl from Lancaster, Wisconsin. My father ran away from home at thirteen and became a cowboy. They spent it all, and because they never apologized for spending it, I grew up trying to apologize for them.

In 1936, I was rediscovered by a *New York Times* reporter, who asked me what happened to my fortune. My folks were sitting there and I heard myself say, "Well, you know, we had a lot of money from my career, but then the crash came in 1929 and wiped us out. We even lost our ranch."

Actually, Father never invested anything in the stock market. He used to say, "I wouldn't put a dime in it." But I wanted to protect him, so I made the story up, and they were off the hook. From then on, that became the story: We had a lot of investments, but lost them in the crash.

My father gave up the beginnings of what might have been his own career to concentrate on me. They didn't intend that mine was going to be a long career. It was supposed to last five days, but like slipping on a banana peel at the top of the stairs, it kept going and they couldn't stop; they couldn't leave Hollywood and all that money.

My father wanted to be something himself, other than Mr. Baby Peggy, but my success turned the family relationship upside down. It put great stress on his ego, on his relationship with my mother, my sister's relationship with me.

Baby Peggy, Jackie Coogan, and the Gish sisters were pre-Depression stars. We who came later were products of the squalid days that gripped the land after 1929.

Our parents, reading of our popularity and "wealth" while we were growing up, succumbed to the illusion that our careers would last forever, even while professing to the contrary. In Diana's words, "Nobody had gone broke yet, so there were no dead bones around to show what had overcome the others."

Marcia Mae Jones's parents were typical—more typical, perhaps, than some because Marcia Mae was not a star but a talented child actress who worked constantly and whose many films became the key to her family's survival in the 1930s and '40s.

Marcia's parents always worried about money, and Marcia felt it was her responsibility "to get the part, to get the money. My father didn't make much. I had this fear that we weren't going to eat or pay the rent if I didn't get the part, and if I didn't get it, I felt it was my fault."

Money problems seldom surfaced until we reached our teens or early twenties, after our incomes had dwindled, when we needed money for ourselves. If it wasn't there, feelings of anger and confusion stirred. Witness Marcia Mae:

> I was resentful that my money had been spent. One time, my father lost a great deal of it gambling, but I don't know how much. Maybe I enlarged on how much they spent, maybe I thought it was much more than it actually was; I really don't know. I know that my mother bought me clothes that were more expensive than they should have been. I said, "We shouldn't spend this," and she said, "Oh, don't worry." And I like clothes.
>
> The first time I bought a car, it was with my brother, because that was the only way he could get one. Yet every time I wanted to use it, they told me I was a spoiled brat.

Gloria Jean never thought of money, although today, she says, "I think of money all the time because I have to." Gloria's parents "weren't sophisticated," so they engaged an attorney recommended by people at the studio, who, to put it kindly, "made mistakes." When the government seized almost all of Gloria's money for back taxes, it almost killed her father, who had scrimped to see that Gloria would "not be wanting in her older age." Her attorney, who also managed the affairs of several other stars, then left for Europe.

Gloria succumbed to bad advice from her agent as well. "He talked us into leaving the studio to go on personal appearance tours. What I didn't realize was that the agent was making lots of money from my being on tour—much more than the normal ten percent."

Edith Fellows's earnings caused dissension in a family she never knew she had until her mother rang the doorbell after Edith was successful. Edith hadn't seen her mother since age two. The upshot of the reunion was that Edith's mother sued Edith's grandmother for kidnapping. When the trial began, Edith was working on *Pennies from Heaven* with Bing Crosby. The shooting schedule was adjusted so Edith could work and study in the mornings and testify in court in the afternoons. Edith testified for Grandma, and as the trial warmed up (Grandma had put a detective on Edith's mother's trail), Bing Crosby offered to testify as a character witness for Grandma if the need arose. It didn't. The judge barred unsavory evidence and designated the Bank of America as Edith's legal guardian. Before the trial, Edith's earnings had bought outright an eight-room house ($17,000) and a car, and had paid the bills for Edith, her grandmother, Edith's uncle (Grandma's older son) and his family. When the bank took over, Grandma was put on an allowance. The Bank of America, of course, received a fee for being Edith's guardian. In addition, Edith paid her own attorneys to watch the bank.

"I really wasn't that aware of money. I knew what I could do, and I knew that being under contract meant security. I knew that I had started at $150 a week, and I knew I was making $850, which was pretty good in the 1930s. But all the money meant to me was that I could do nice things for Grandma," Edith told me.

Columbia dropped Edith in 1940, Grandma died in 1941, Edith sold the house for $22,000, sent the money to the bank, traveled on the nightclub circuit, and sent everything she didn't need to live on to the bank. Turning twenty-one, she "zipped back to Hollywood to get my savings. The Bank of America handed me a check for $900.60 and hundreds of papers which I didn't understand."

Jane Powell became a star with her first film and earned $5,000 weekly, forty weeks a year, plus extra money for personal appearances during the customary twelve-week studio "hiatus." Jane didn't have a manager, but "everything was fine. My gosh, from Portland to five thousand a week! We hadn't made that much in one year."

Although Jane was one of MGM's top stars, the Burces lived modestly. Mama made Jane's clothes and gave her an allowance of $10 a week, out of which Jane bought lunch and gasoline. The family lived in a little house in the valley, and Daddy had a couple of donut shops, where Jane helped out on Saturday nights.

When, at twenty-one, Jane married Geary Steffen, Sonja Henie's ice-skating partner, she left all her money with her mother:

> I didn't take anything but my clothes. I left the house, even my bed, everything. I felt that that was the least I could do. I thought it would take care of my parents for the rest of their lives, which wasn't true. Within six months of my marriage to Geary, my mother and father divorced; Daddy never got any of the money.
>
> So when I got married to Geary I really started all over again. That was the year I needed to pay $25,000 in back taxes—thanks to our accountant—and I had no money left.
>
> Then when I divorced Geary we split everything I had made since our marriage down the center. I paid him alimony. So I spent my whole life trying to catch up.

Part of the money problem was that our parents wanted nothing to change. Going to college, for example, would be expensive, and worse still, we would learn to question things, a sure sign of growing up. I got to college after World War II because it cost nothing. The G.I. Bill paid for it.

Roddy McDowall didn't go to college because he didn't have the

G.I. Bill. He seemed surprised when I asked. "How could I go to college? There wasn't enough money. Who was going to do the work? The problem was very painfully explained to me. 'Of course, dear, you can do anything you want, *but* . . . ' " So Roddy didn't go to college.

But he did leave home. As a young adult, Roddy went to New York to learn to act and live an independent life. Jane Powell, his close friend, urged him to go, still convinced that if he hadn't, he would eventually have had a breakdown.

Like Jane, Roddy left everything with his parents, who, after his departure, rattled around in the big house in Cheviot Hills, ignoring the unused swimming pool:

> When I moved to New York, I gave my parents everything. Mother sat for years playing canasta. Eventually, I told them they had to sell the house. I could no longer make a living in New York and support the system in Los Angeles.
>
> After I left home, I never really had much money until I did the movie *Cleopatra,* and by that time I had a lawyer in New York to take over the parental role of managing my finances. I had given him power of attorney, which he held for ten years. But still I had no money, although I'd made over a hundred thousand a year.
>
> Eventually, I decided that I needed to learn about dealing with money. I knew nothing, partly because my mother never wanted me to know. My father knew, but he couldn't get at the money. If he hadn't been so mesmerized by my mother, if they'd done what *he* wanted, I would have had every dime I ever made. My father was scrupulously honest. And he was not a gambler. But she had such control over him that he was powerless.

Jane Withers's parents were happy exceptions to the general rule. They taught Jane bookkeeping at age seven. Mr. Withers, an executive with Goodrich, could not match Jane's earnings, but his salary paid the family's everyday expenses. When she was still a child, Jane's father told her, "Even though you have a job and I have a job, your money is not being used for the groceries. That's my responsibility as a parent, and I want you to know that."

Merchandising of Jane Withers's name on paper dolls, books, dresses, hair bows, shoes, gloves, and socks provided more income than her acting, and, Jane says, "Whenever this 'new money' came to me, we would have a family discussion about how to use it." That's what built Jane's home, Withering Heights, where she still lives. Jane says she has always "tithed at least ten percent" of her income to help others. Today, she has no money worries. "There were seven different funds set up for me," she told me proudly. "I understand now how unique that is. I didn't know it then."

Like Jane's dad, Juanita Quigley's father was successful in his own right. He owned five grocery stores in Culver City. "Money was put aside for me," Juanita told me.

Margaret O'Brien believes that MGM "would have had me working for a hundred and fifty a week" if her mother hadn't yanked her out of *Meet Me in St. Louis.* "The studio was frantic," Margaret said softly. "Mother walked into Mr. Mayer's office and said, 'We'll come back when you pay Margaret seven thousand a week.' " Stuck with an unfinished picture, Mayer capitulated. Margaret's mother put the money into bonds. "But she also liked to spend, and so did I, so there was a lot we didn't save. Still, there was a good sum set aside, so I didn't have to work when I grew up. Also, my mother got a salary from the studio. She spent all of hers."

When Jackie Cooper returned from World War II, he came home to the "better part of half a million dollars." But, Jackie says, "I never made the kind of money that Coogan or Temple made. I started at Metro at eleven hundred a week in 1930 and I left making twenty-two hundred and fifty six years later."

Jackie's mother saved his money for him. During the annual hiatus—that twelve-week period when studios didn't pay their contract players—Jackie worked in vaudeville, his mother's training ground.

I earned more in ten weeks of vaudeville than in forty weeks at MGM. The studio wanted to send me out at my regular salary, but my mother said, "No, we can get seventy-five hundred a week. His pay here is only twelve hundred." My mother withstood a lot of gunfire. She had no business acumen, just a sense of what was fair. She invested my money—much too conservatively. She bought things like thirty-nine-year endowments instead of putting it into AT&T.

Hal Roach once told Mother that he felt guilty about having made so much money off of me, and he suggested that she invest ten thousand in a new venture that would reap big profits. She refused because it was too risky. It turned out to be Santa Anita Racetrack.

Natalie Wood decided, as a young adult, to educate herself financially. At eight, Natalie earned $1,000 a week from Fox, but she had "no conception about money whatsoever. I just knew that whenever I got a part I would get a present." Once she wanted a typewriter, so that was her reward:

Otherwise I never worried my head about money at all. After I grew up, it was something that I realized I had better think about, because I had worked all my life and I was totally broke. I confronted my business manager when I was twenty-three, and I said, "I don't understand this. How can I make these rather large sums of money and not have any? At this rate, no matter how long I work and how much I make, I'll never have any money."

By that time there was a very large tax and you ended up with very little unless business managers were clever enough to put you into investments or tax shelters—a world that I was totally unaware of. Somebody else had always handled things, my father or R.J. or the business manager.

I never felt my parents did anything wrong. They put aside more than was required by law. They never took anything from me. I realized, too, that the business manager wasn't necessarily doing anything wrong; he was just not being very creative or very helpful. He was only doing simple things that any accountant could do.

As I began to think about it, I became more responsible for myself. I knew at some point that I would have children and I would be responsible for them also. So I started rearranging the way my business affairs were being dealt with. I found a very good lawyer, a very good business manager, and began to think about things like investments, and the fact that sometimes financial security goes hand in hand with emotional security.

Ann Rutherford took charge of her affairs as a teenager. She rode the bus to MGM while she saved to buy a house. Ann saw others under contract earn good money and spend it all. "Then, when option time came, either they wouldn't get their options picked up or they had to stay on at the same price." Ann was determined not to share this fate.

I'd seen too many girls in tears in the dressing room say, "Oh, I have to stay on without getting a raise." So I put all my money in the bank. The first time the studio pulled this tactic on me, I got a phone call—they didn't even call your agent; they were very devious about it. "Please come to Mr. Mayer's office." I had been warned, so I was well prepared when Mr. Mayer gave me the same routine I had heard the other girls describe: "We like you a lot. We have big plans for you. But the studio hasn't been doing too well. We want to exercise your option for the next year, but keep it at the same salary."

I reached into my purse and pulled out my little bankbook and coughed delicately into it and said, "Well, I don't know about you, Mr. Mayer, but I've saved my money. So if you can't give me a raise, I'll just have to go someplace where I can get one, because I'm buying a house."

It always worked and I always got my raise. But I did not buy a house until I could pay for the whole house in cash.

When young Bonita Granville married multimillionaire entrepreneur Jack Wrather, he was, Bonita says, "absolutely floored that I'd worked all those years and had all my money in cash in the bank." Bonita's mother, though thrifty, was "not smart about money."

Wrather steered Bonita into oil stocks and other investments, which, she told me, "have been absolutely fabulous." After nearly forty years of marriage, Bunny still has a lot of stock she bought when she and Jack were married.

Donald O'Connor's mother could handle money when she got it, if she didn't lose it gambling. "She knew nothing about business," Donald reminded me, since she'd run away from home at twelve, joined the circus, met Donald's dad at thirteen, and borne her first child at fourteen. Until Donald was seventeen, he filched money out of his mother's purse. Then he found a way to get hold of his own earnings.

I ran over and got my checks before Mother got them. Don't misunderstand, I was never denied anything. I had my tailor-made suits, patent-leather shoes, my spats. But I didn't take hold of my money until I was seventeen, and I got heavily into business in my late twenties.

The only time I ever got any real money out of the studio was when they sent me to South Africa at twenty-one to cement relationships between the Schlesinger chain of theaters and Universal. Schlesinger's thought they might leave Universal and go with J. Arthur Rank. I was the goodwill ambassador; Schlesinger stayed with Universal.

When I got there, a guy from the studio said, "We have some frozen funds here if you want to call upon them."

I said, "How much do you have?"

He said, "At the moment, we have about forty-five thousand pounds."

I said, "Well, that's wonderful. We'll start with that." So we started with that and we had a ball. The pound was worth a lot in South Africa at that time. I even brought elephant tusks back. If I could have got a live elephant on the plane, I would have brought that too.

When I left Universal after something like fifteen years, after I had made hundreds of millions of dollars for the studio, they had a nice little party for me in the commissary. And they gave me a nice little Minox camera with fourteen rolls of film. That was my going-away present.

What else can I tell you about those people?

10. Sex Can Wait?

When I kissed Shirley Temple in *Miss Annie Rooney*, I was sixteen and I hoped the world didn't know my secret: I had never kissed a girl before. Under any circumstances. And here I was getting paid to kiss Shirley Temple! The director encouraged abandon, urging me, in effect, to renounce the patterns of a lifetime. It was weird. Should I want to kiss her, paid or not? Kissing was something I just *knew* I shouldn't do at all, with any girl, let alone the Princess of the World. What if I got an erection while Hymie Fink and a wall of other cameramen recorded my first sin?

Of course, no one had told me in so many words not to kiss a girl. There was never admonition. Rather, I had absorbed an atmosphere. Continence was in the air I breathed.

Adding to my consternation, Shirley's breasts pressed hard against the party dress, her dimpled face was a map of mischief; her legs, firm and round, covered in this scene but well remembered from the days preceding, were suggestively outlined beneath the skirts she wore. America's Sweetheart was no longer a baby. She was sexy and seductive.

For the first time, I was seized by a paralysis of fear. For the first time, I could not conceal the twitching of my facial muscles when the script called for me to smile.

Edwin Marin, the director, called me over. He wore a tight little suit and a tight little collar, with a tight little knot in a tight little tie. "You seem very self-conscious, Dickie. Have you any inhibitions about kissing Shirley?"

Oh, no, I said, neglecting to admit I didn't know what inhibitions were.

After the torment I'd been through, it was strange to read Hollywood columnist Erskine Johnson's calm, unemotional description of the scene: "They're driving to a party when Dickie has to suddenly stop his car. He throws his arms around Shirley to stop her from going through the windshield. And then it happens. He pecks her on the cheek. 'Gosh,' he says, 'I'm just a cad. I won't blame you for being insulted. Now you won't even go to the party with me.' 'Well,' Shirley wells, 'I'm not *that* insulted.' "

Perhaps, if Joan Hamman had cooperated three years earlier, I might have found myself better equipped to handle romantic scenes.

My folks and I vacationed in Balboa for three weeks every summer when I wasn't working, and age thirteen was not a banner period for my career. But it was a splendid time for *me,* because I liked to fish, and it was a splendid time because of Joan.

We rented the top floor of her family duplex at the beach. Too large for the house, the mounted thirteen-foot, five-inch, six-hundred-and-ninety-two-pound marlin, the world's record at that time, caught by Joan's father, Alphonse Hamman, in one hour and fifty-two minutes, was kept in the garage. I looked in on it daily. Mr. Hamman was the local postmaster, Mrs. Hamman was a pleasant lady, and Joan and her older sister went to church on Sunday with their parents.

It was instant love. Tan, with hair bleached by the sun, her wide-set eyes huge sapphires, she lived in bathing suits, wore them more remarkably than any twelve-year-old in history, seldom bothered with shoes, was not afraid to unhook a captured fish, and was a dolphin in the water. Joan didn't say a lot. She didn't have to. We were together constantly, except for church. I hated Sunday mornings.

That she was Catholic worried Mother.

Physical intimacies included touching fingertips, wiping sand off backs, seemingly accidental brushings of one leg against another as we lay outstretched on the warm sand.

Summer ended, but we bridged the sixty miles between Balboa and L.A. with almost daily letters, mine virtually illegible, hers in a straightforward, clean, feminine script.

Through months of planning there emerged a rendezvous, catalyzed by Aunty Jo. Arrangements were made to visit the San Diego Zoo the next time school was out, and to spend the night in a hotel, with Aunty Jo as chaperone. We would pick up Joan en route. Anticipation grew, a field of butterflies; I thought of nothing else. Our letters grew obsessive in their heat.

At Balboa, Mrs. Hamman emerged from the house, down the short ribbon of concrete that crossed the sandy yard to the curb. Joan couldn't come, she said. Joan wanted to, she had tried, but the thought of leaving home, of staying over even for a night, had frightened her. She'd dressed and then undressed a dozen times this morning, but much as she wanted to, she simply couldn't come.

I imagined Joan undressing as Mrs. Hamman talked. Immersed in disappointment, I didn't really hear all she said.

The remainder of the trip did not exist. Aunty Jo and I went on to San Diego and saw the animals, but I don't remember it. On returning home, I cleaned my room for five straight days, emerging for necessities and meals. You wouldn't believe the stuff I threw away. "Cheer up," Dad said one night at dinner. "There's plenty of other fish in the sea."

Next day, a letter came from Joan, loving, contrite, and—in retrospect—courageous, telling me her fears at the prospect of a journey, since she'd never been away from home. She hoped I'd understand. I read the letter eighty times, but never answered it.

A bit later, I played Gloria Jean's brother in her first picture, *The Under-Pup.* I had pimples, and I knew my part was small and that she was the star. But I just wanted to go off with her someplace where pimples and billing didn't matter. Gloria, sweet and soft and smiling all the time. I liked her legs and hair and arms and gentleness and her buckteeth. Nothing came of that passion, either.

When I was seventeen, I had a crush on Katherine, an actress in the radio series I produced. She was seventeen also, and tall, with brown hair, hazel eyes, slight overbite—a smash. My first car, a used 1939 Ford, was a one-seat coupe, a model selected to discourage others in the cast from asking for a ride.

One night after the show and a drive-in hamburger, I took Katherine home. She couldn't ask me in, her mother was ill, but maybe we could sit in the car and talk. So we did, for hours: I, wise and rational, filling every lull with my worldly philosophy. Finally, I kissed Katherine, if you can call it that.

She put her arms around me, pressed her face hard against mine, and kissed me again, mouth open. Was there trouble with her teeth?

"I want you," Katherine said, and I said, "Well, I'm here."

Our show went off the air soon after. I drove by to see her once. She was sitting in the living room with an older man, twenty-two at least. She introduced me awkwardly, walked me back outside, and said goodbye.

So much of life is wasted.

I was much more successful with the ladies when I was six, as attested to by an article in *Silver Screen* magazine, November 1932: "There's a deep blush of shame on the Dietrich cheeks these days and a sad, so sad expression in her large blue-gray eyes. And the Bankhead sighs and sighs and looks reproachfully at a mundane world from under long, heavy lashes. And the Stanwyck tears her handkerchief nervously and listens and listens for the telephone to ring . . . and it never does. Now who's the Cause of It All? Who is Hollywood's Great Lover?"

It was me, of course. The article was headlined: "Dickie Moore's Women," and it was one of several like it that dominated movie

As a child, Marcia Mae Jones, pictured here in 1939, went to work with scarlet fever so shooting time would not be lost.

One magazine described Tallulah Bankhead as "Dickie's latest conquest." She gave me an electric train but our house was too small to lay the tracks.

magazines that year. The headline on another story was: "Dietrich's New Romance Has Hollywood Agog."

"The New Don Juan," all about a "heartbreaker who has the ladies in a dither," featured photos not only with Miss Dietrich, Miss Bankhead, and Miss Stanwyck, but also with Iris Hendron, the girl next door, age five.

There were other articles, but the story was the same: This six-year-old kid with those huge brown eyes is Hollywood's new great lover. A writer named Patricia Keats reported that the "Mystery of this Great Lover is his Great Unconcern. With his adorable puckering lips and his big beautiful eyes he looks like a soft, clinging baby of a fellow—but he isn't. He's all male and as undemonstrative and unspoiled as they are made. . . ."

Not bad for six. If only I could have bottled that fatal attraction and stored it up for later.

"If Dickie can have the Hollywood ladies languishing at the age of six, just imagine what will happen when he's 26," the article in *Silver Screen* concluded. "Pity the next generation."

The next generation, as subsequent events proved, had nothing to worry about.

The one thing I was sure of as I grew up was that my peers were wallowing in sex beyond my wildest fantasies. There was a joke I'd heard that went like this: Question: What's the definition of a Hollywood virgin? Answer: A three-year-old girl who can outrun her four-year-old brother.

I knew that *literally* that wasn't accurate, but I figured it wasn't too far off. Everybody knew much more about sex than I did, I was sure. Especially kids in pictures. And they were *doing* it. Of all the people in the *Motion Picture Academy Players Directory,* I thought I was the only one who knew nothing about dealing with the opposite sex.

I was wrong. Edith Fellows remembers her first kiss.

Grandma had told me never to let a man kiss me on the mouth or I would become pregnant. I did two pictures with Leo Carillo when I was thirteen or fourteen. One was *Little Miss Roughneck* and the other was *City Streets.* Leo Carillo kissed me on the mouth one day and I watched my stomach for weeks and I swear to God it blew up.

Leo was wonderful until he kissed me. Then he went right down the tubes for me. When I got my period, and knew that I was safe, I had the courage to speak to my teacher, Lillian. I said, "It's not true, is it? You don't get pregnant if a man kisses you on the mouth?" And she said, "Where in the world did you ever hear that? Don't tell me! Let me guess!"

Gloria Jean feels that she grew up very late, that the things she should have done at eighteen, she did at twenty-three. "As for anything romantic, we children had the *feelings* when we were young, but we never did anything about them."

Diana Cary, analytical as always, has thought considerably about our seeming retardation. "The problem," Diana feels, "especially for those of us who were in our early teens, was that our parents would tell us nothing about sex. Nobody mentioned it and yet it was all around us. At the time we were being told nothing, Clark Gable and Jean Harlow were doing something suggestive on the screen at our neighborhood theater. Most of us could probably guess what it was, but we really didn't know. We were very dumb, and I, for one, was not a confidante of other children my own age, so I didn't ask."

Donald O'Connor had to kiss Marilyn Monroe just before he launched into one of his acrobatic dance numbers—and he was nervous: "My lips were shaking all over and I couldn't find Marilyn's lips and she couldn't find mine, and I had to turn my back to the camera so the audience couldn't see these four lips trying to find each other."

Dean Stockwell was seven when he first became aware of sexual feelings. The experience made a deep and lasting impression on him. It was during Dean's first movie, *Anchors Aweigh,* in which he played Kathryn Grayson's nephew. Dean remembers vividly:

Kathryn Grayson was gorgeous and sang like a lark. I remember her long black curls and the song she sang with an accent, "Pennsylvania Polka."

She had the most beautiful, fine, filamenty blond hairs on her bosom. These tiny hairs would catch the light bouncing off the makeup on her skin. Then, just before they called, "Roll 'em!" I would lay my pancake-laden face on her bosom. It was unreal because the hairs were so fine and so downy and yet the skin was covered with the fucking body makeup; and the secret beneath the bodice was super naked then to me.

When Peggy Ann Garner was making *Junior Miss,* she "discovered something." She was terrified and feared telling her mother.

By the time I got home, I was so uptight I said, "I've got to talk to you." And I told her what had happened and she said, "Oh, well, that happens once a month." And with that, she threw me a box of Kotex and said, "This is what you do." Period. That was it. That was the explanation of what was happening to me.

God knows how many times I was accused of being pregnant. I don't know how that could have happened, unless somebody phoned it in. She always put the fear of God in me, about anything and everything. I didn't even know how you got pregnant, but she'd have me convinced that I was. And this fear, I'm sure, followed me when I grew to be an adult and when I got married.

This profound ignorance about sex was echoed repeatedly in my conversations with former child stars.

Diana Cary: "Everybody thought we were swinging and wild, sexing it up at ten years of age. But nobody ever told me anything about sex, menstrual periods, anything, ever."

Cora Sue Collins: "We were the squarest group of kids in the world. I was terrified of sex. So were all my girlfriends."

When I asked Darryl Hickman about this, he was ready, as usual, with a thoughtful response: "I think one of the reasons is that we didn't have the normal social or classmate situation. We were isolated in the studios, working, separated from our peers. The isolated life of a child actor contributed strongly to our sexual inexperience. We were also so involved in the work ethic and so imbued with responsibility that we tended to work all the time. We didn't have the normal opportunities to be with other kids and form relationships.

"And we lived in a world of fantasy, so the romance in our lives tended to be at the MGM commissary rather than at a prom or beach party," Darryl concluded.

Need I add that our parents and our studios found it in their interest to keep us pure, unspoiled, and single?

Mickey Rooney, the most visible, envied, and uninhibited member of the group, seemed to have had no trouble with girls, or with growing up. Ann Rutherford made many "Andy Hardy" pictures with him and witnessed his exploits firsthand:

> Everybody thinks we were such swingers. Oh, no! Except for Mickey Rooney. He was a swinger. I remember when Mickey was about thirteen, we were in the MGM commissary and a beautiful brunette came in and we said, "Hi," and she walked on. And Mickey said, "*Who* was *that?*" And he came out with a wolf whistle. I said, "That's Leah Ray." He said, "Well, get me an introduction to her." I said, "Mickey, for Pete's sake, you're only thirteen. She's nineteen." He said, "What the hell. I like 'em older than I—then the law's on my side."

Gene Reynolds confirms that Mickey was very successful with women when he was very young. Gene feels that Mickey had a great advantage: "He had humor, and humor is a great seducer. I think he would just laugh them into bed, and he had this incredible energy and gift for comedy."

Gene recalled a time in Omaha, when they were filming *Boys Town.* "Mickey said to me, 'You gettin' laid?' I was a wide-eyed fifteen-year-old kid, and I said, 'No,' like a little kid that had never seen a circus. And Mickey kind of smiled and said, 'Well, everybody else is.' I thought he was really the big time." Gene shook his head, remembering.

Despite our sexual immaturity, or possibly because of it, crushes were rampant. Most of us weren't capable of handling the tensions we felt, but our passions were normal, often painful.

Jane Withers had a mad crush on Peter Lawford. So did Peggy Ann Garner:

In *Leave Her to Heaven,* a jealous Gene Tierney *(left)* let Darryl Hickman, Cornel Wilde's crippled brother, drown. The picture was "the most traumatic experience" of Darryl's film career. The water was so cold his double wouldn't work, so Darryl spent three weeks immersed while the scene was shot and caught pneumonia.

Ann Rutherford and Mickey Rooney in one of their many "Andy Hardy" films. Ann, like most of us, was amazed by Mickey's boldness with women.

Didn't everybody? In fact, Barbara Whiting—my God, what she did! We were doing a little project in school on the 20th Century–Fox lot; we were etching initials in glasses for our mothers. Well, Barbara took the tube of etching stuff home and wrote on her bedroom windows, "I love Peter." "Peter Lawford." "Peter." And her mother had to have every window in that bedroom replaced.

Usually, Peggy Ann reserved her crushes for adults. So did Shirley Temple and Bonita Granville. Among Bonita's unrequited loves were Joel McCrea and Ronald Reagan. Bonita was impressed with the firm stand Reagan took with the "Dead End Kids," who, through their lack of familiarity with professional conduct plus an unending quest for fun, had terrorized the *Angels with Dirty Faces* cast and crew by throwing firecrackers under people's chairs and putting mice in women's dressing rooms.

Sybil Jason, too, remembers Ronald Reagan: "He got kicked off the location set of a picture I did with Jane Wyman because the director thought he was taking up too much of her time. That was in 1936, before they were married, and he was kind of courting her."

Sybil fell in love with Dick Powell when she worked with him on *Broadway Gondolier.*

When I was taken off that picture to star in *Little Big Shot,* I started knitting him a scarf. I'd learned to knit in London when I was four. The scarf was red, white, and blue, and by the time *Little Big Shot* ended, it was long enough to go around the necks of three men and still have some left over. I packaged it up in a real neat box with a ribbon on it.

About a year later, I was rushed to the hospital for an operation—tonsillitis or something—and when I got home there were two packages from Dick Powell, for *me.* One was a beautiful little evening purse with my initials in gold, and in the other package were a dozen handkerchiefs with my name on them.

Soon afterward, I went back to South Africa and I took them with me. While there, I heard that Dick had been ill, but I didn't know how ill. I wrote him a little letter and I enclosed one of those handkerchiefs and said, "Dick, when you're a little better, I will come and call for this again in person."

About two weeks later, a letter came. Enclosed was my handkerchief. "I'm afraid Mr. Powell has passed away. He's gone." I still have that purse and those handkerchiefs.

Gloria Jean and Donald O'Connor went to school together at Universal. They worked together too. Donald never knew how much Gloria loved him as an adolescent. Here is Gloria's unabashed account:

Donald would walk into the schoolhouse—the little canvas schoolhouse on the set—wearing his teenage sweaters and I couldn't concentrate on my schoolwork, I was so crazy about him.

I often thought: "One day, I'm going to kiss Donald, and I wonder how that'll feel."

Then one day on the set—it was kind of dark—Donald grabbed me and hugged me, really hugged me, and something snapped. It was my rib. Donald was thin, but strong. The doctor taped me up and I worked through the rest of the movie. I never told Donald. So to this day he doesn't know he broke my rib.

Edith Fellows got a crush on Bobby Jordan the moment she saw him in *Dead End.* And then, to her great joy, there he was at her sixteenth-birthday party.

Everybody lined up to give me my Sweet Sixteen kiss, and I see Bobby getting closer, and then suddenly he's back at the end of the line. Finally, he was the last one and he gave me a quick peck on the cheek. That night I held the cheek in my hand and fell asleep.

I'd see him here and there and he'd look at me like *yuch!* A year later, we met at a benefit. The studio had dyed my hair blond—they wanted to start changing my image—and Bobby came over and sat beside me and he took my hand and I'm thinking: "I don't believe this. Maybe blondes do have more fun." Of course, Grandma was there, so he had to watch it.

Darryl Hickman's first date was Elizabeth Taylor, but his "first crush in the world" was Peggy Ann Garner. Darryl was "nuts about Peggy Ann Garner." When he was fifteen, they had a date, but

Gloria Jean was in love with Donald O'Connor when both were at Universal. Donald never knew it, but he hugged her once and broke her rib.

Peggy called to cancel and gave Darryl an excuse. A friend of Darryl's saw Peggy with another boy on Hollywood Boulevard that night. Darryl was devastated. "I got the impression that her mother felt the fellow was somebody she should go out with. But I never asked Peggy out again, I was so hurt."

When Jackie Cooper was sixteen, girls his own age didn't appeal to him. Yet older girls usually made him feel too young, so for a while he went back to girls his own age. Jackie says he was "constantly falling in love and wanting to stay in love with that person forever. I think it was because I always wanted a family, because I was born into a small, highly emotional, poverty-stricken family that tried to be very close but could not get along. They just tore each other up."

Judy Garland and Jackie went steady at age thirteen, and he and Bonita Granville were a steady item from the ages of sixteen to nineteen.

Diana Cary fantasized very early that she and Jackie Coogan would marry one day. "Baby Peggy marries Jackie Coogan." Like the prince and the princess. After all, that's what Diana had seen in magazines since she was old enough to read.

When Diana was ten, she and Jackie met again. Diana and her parents were staying at the College Inn in Chicago, and Jackie (then about fifteen) and his father came over to their table in the restaurant.

> Jackie was very handsome and my little heart went pitter-pat and I thought: "Wow!" Jackie asked me if I would care to dance. I nearly swooned and I said, "Yes!" Then someone found out who we were and turned a spotlight on us and everybody else on the dance floor just melted away. We were talking and all of a sudden we realized this white spot was on us and we froze. We danced until the music finally stopped and everybody in the restaurant applauded. I was just scarlet; so was he. We sat down and very soon Jackie and his father left.
>
> The next time I saw Jackie, I was about eighteen and we were both fetched up for one of those awful, dreary parties at some godforsaken

studio. It was Jackie's birthday and they brought a big birthday cake and there were newsreel cameramen. It was one of those "And here we caught them making a movie on the same lot" things. We'd both been conned into coming, with the hope that we would be seen and maybe both of us might have our careers reactivated. I took the bus there and Jack drove me home. By that time, he was married to Betty Grable and I was in love with somebody else. It was just one more dreadful afternoon for me, and I guess for him too.

Jackie Coogan never did marry Baby Peggy and carry her off on his white horse to his palace. Still, romantic dreams persisted in our gradually maturing hearts. Purity and virtue also abounded. Witness Jane Powell: "I was a virgin when I got married the first time, and it bothers me. Maybe I was the second time too. No, I'm kidding —I had two children."

If it bothers Jane, at least she's in good company. Peggy Ann Garner, Margaret O'Brien, Sybil Jason, Jane Withers, Cora Sue Collins, Edith Fellows are among others who were virgins when they married.

I was married at twenty-three. My wife, Pat, was twenty. World War II had been my first excuse for leaving home. Marriage was my second.

The scene was journalism school at Los Angeles City College, where I was going on the G.I. Bill. Pat was president of Gamma Delta Upsilon, the honorary journalism society; editor of the women's page of our weekly college paper; active in student government and political affairs. Liberal, articulate, she knew more answers than I had questions for. We shared classes, talked politics, necked in the car.

Our mothers didn't socialize, though our fathers did play nine-hole pitch and putt, and Pat and I played with them.

On her agenda was a winter trip to Europe, financed by Aunt Kitty, her family's frequent backer and leader of the New York branch. Pat planned to stop off in New York, her point of embarkation, while I remained in California. An offer came to do a play—

not Broadway, but a second-string road show rehearsing in Chicago. Our letters settled it; we'd marry in the East and tour together. Pat never went to Europe.

Pat handled all the wedding arrangements. She knew whom to contact, where to take the vows and spend a honeymoon, how to make it *happen.* And there was her Aunt Kitty: doubtful though cooperative, always helpful when the chips were down. She had a house in Mount Pocono, Pennsylvania; the wedding would be there. A friend of Kitty's, Monsignor Something, would find time to marry us. I wasn't Catholic, but that could be worked out, so long as I'd been baptized and agreed to take instruction.

Did I have questions? the monsignor asked as our private meeting ended. I wondered about birth control; what did we do, exactly? The words arranged themselves with difficulty. Misunderstanding was afoot: I was seeking medical advice; the monsignor, an icicle frozen in his chair, told me, "You do nothing." Pat, on hearing my report, was reassuring: Naturally, he'd had to say that, but these were modern times.

I called the folks. "I don't think we have a baptism certificate, dear," Mother said. "I haven't seen one lately." But I was baptized, wasn't I? "Not that I know of," Mother said, but she *had* found the perfect ring for Pat. A friend had gotten it wholesale.

An emergency called the monsignor away prior to our wedding. Nor could we be married in the church. An understudy, a priest so young his acne hadn't cleared up, performed the hasty ceremony in the dining room of the rectory, a residue of breakfast on the table. Staunchly, Kitty stood by.

Seven years together saw passion choked by fear. Pat made guilty by prevented pregnancy; I fearful of unwanted parenthood: the sum, an inability to bind our feelings for each other with that magic mortar, lust. Two fumbling children, feeling, far below the surface, that the part of life that matters is always just around the corner.

I was unable to reveal that I felt deficient somehow, that I didn't know what was expected, how maleness is defined or, for that matter, femininity. When you can finally say, "I'm ignorant, but curious and eager, and I trust you, so let's learn together what it means to be a mate," you no longer have to say it. Children can't say that.

My son Kevin was born while I was unemployed. You can't be parent to a child when you are a child yourself. A just-closed prestigious Broadway play was going on the road. It offered work, an opportunity to be on stage with Fredric March in a play by Lillian Hellman and—although I didn't know it then—a third chance to leave home. Six months on the road, unpacking with my baggage every week the feeling that I was a father without ever having been a man. A bright, assertive ingenue my age soon filled the time off stage.

Pat found work when I returned: a needed contribution to our family and to her creativity. I could not feed my son or change a diaper.

We separated, reconciled, separated, tried again, and failed. If there was an answer for us, Pat said, it lay in psychotherapy. She found a place for me to stay, the apartment of a male acquaintance in Greenwich Village, with whom I shared the rent.

As before, the decisive action fell to her: She got a divorce, with my agreement, asking just enough to help me keep my pride in future dealings with my son. She quickly remarried. I began my first encounter with psychotherapy and for the next few years spent my nights in the arms of every lady in New York who wanted company.

Marcia Mae Jones, too, got married the first time to get away from home, but it was some time before she actually left:

> That was a very bad marriage. It was during the war and he was in the merchant marine. After he got out, he didn't want to assume any responsibilities for me or the kids. I got a divorce to force him into getting us a home, but it never happened.

So I waited eight years after my divorce before I remarried; and that's when I finally left home.

Cora Sue Collins married a man much older than herself. The marriage, she feels, was a terrible mistake. "I was so independent I wasn't capable of being a good wife."

Even Shirley Temple's first, storybook marriage ended in divorce. Shirley had no knowledge that her husband wanted to be an actor. "He wasn't an actor when I married him. He was a phys ed instructor in the Army Air Force, as it was called then. I didn't find out about the acting until later."

Diana Cary also first married a man whose eyes were on a movie career, and she has a theory to explain how this situation affected such relationships.

The first marriages of young women like me and Shirley Temple were usually to men who were trying to break into pictures. We were finished with acting. We no longer found it interesting. But our husbands were trying to make it, and they were using us, or we *felt* they were using us. After the ceremony, you discover that he didn't marry *you,* he married Baby Peggy, or Shirley Temple, or Deanna Durbin.

Poor Judy Garland used to say, "They're all in the Judy Garland business"—and they *were.* I didn't go through that many marriages, thank God, but one failure was enough. It's one of the most dreadful things you can experience.

I know that feeling, that sense of devastation: You're the only person left on earth when atomic war is done. How many times have you been with someone just to fill up time when, instead, you should have asked yourself, "Would I be better off alone?" But then you think—at least I did—"I'm a man and that's a woman; if I'd rather be alone, there must be something wrong with me." So you welcome the company of strangers to convince yourself you're not deficient.

The sound of silence can be either foe or friend. It starts out as an enemy. If it becomes a friend, you've grown up; for silence says you are alone, and must fill that time and space with some awareness that you're happy with yourself.

The catalyst for Natalie Wood's going into analysis was that her marriage broke up. She had gone from living at home with her parents to being married to Robert Wagner. Natalie made *Splendor in the Grass* in 1961. During filming, she became romantically involved with co-star Warren Beatty, and ended her four-year marriage. Natalie attributed the affair and the breakup of her marriage to a combination of things.

Before *Splendor,* I had gone from one movie to another without a day off in between, and *Splendor* had been a very emotional experience, a very demanding part. I always had a bit of inner resistance to doing that part, because I felt that in order to play some of those scenes I would have to open doors and relive a lot of feelings that I had put the lid on. I had a hunch that it wasn't going to be good for me to do that part in terms of my emotional life; and I was right. It did open up a lot of wounds and led to the marriage breaking up. Then I knew I had to get to a doctor.

My parents wanted me to go back to them, but I felt strongly that I didn't need my parents. I needed to get, in today's words, my "head together."

I knew I needed psychiatry. And I knew I needed to be independent; I went to stay with friends. I was still terrified of being alone, because I had always been dependent, first on my parents, then on R.J. This feeling that it was somehow dangerous to be alone was deeply instilled, maybe in part from having welfare workers always hovering, and directors to tell me what to do. It was as though there was some great danger in being independent.

Nearly all of us, it seems, shared Natalie's early fear of independence, and of loneliness; often we saw marriage as an excuse for leaving home. We needed an excuse and we needed, too, a safety net. We didn't see the people we were marrying, evaluate their qualities or ours, or our chances of growing together in a way that offered promise of a happy life.

Also, marriage was a way for us to prove that we had grown up. Children don't get married, right?

Wrong! But we didn't know it then. Not surprisingly, nearly all of us entered into at least one marriage that failed: Jane Powell, Donald O'Connor, Freddie Bartholomew, Deanna Durbin, Shirley Temple, Jane Withers, Gene Reynolds, Peggy Ann Garner, Bobs and Delmar Watson, Cora Sue Collins, Gloria Jean, Sidney Miller, Mickey Rooney, Elizabeth Taylor, Stymie, Jackie Cooper, Jackie Coogan, Judy Garland, Margaret O'Brien, Kathleen Nolan, Ann Rutherford, Darryl Hickman, Marcia Mae Jones, Edith Fellows, Dean Stockwell, Spanky McFarland, Diana Cary, me.

Mickey Rooney was married the first time when he was twenty-one, to Ava Gardner. "I needed to be married like you need to paint Shea Stadium at midnight," Mickey told me. "But I'm happy I did it, because it was part of growing up."

Lillian Gish is among a handful of former child stars who were never divorced. Miss Gish believes that "an actress shouldn't ruin a good man's life by marrying him," so she never married anybody.

11. After Stardom, What?

What do you do when you are eleven years old and your peak earning years are behind you? You hit the road. So I tackled vaudeville.

Vaudeville was tailor-made for those who sang, danced, or did comedy routines. I could not fill that bill, so a special thirteen-minute act was written for me by our friend Arthur (Dagwood Bumstead) Lake. The skit required two characters, a painted canvas drop, a fishnet, a table, and three chairs. The plot: I lived happily with Gramps, an aging fisherman; but unbeknown to me, my parents wanted me back. Gramps knew I would be better off with them, but he knew, too, that given a choice, I would stay with him. So he pretended that he wanted me to leave. After twelve and a half minutes of pleading and crying, I reluctantly returned to my parents, leaving Gramps alone, bereft but knowing that he had done his duty.

Usually, we did four shows a day. I was the headliner on each bill, so my skit was next to closing. We toured the East in the summer of 1936—no school.

For most child actors, these "personal appearance tours" marked our first forays into the world outside Hollywood.

Reading the marquees on the theaters, I saw: "Dickie Moore in Person," the title of the current movie, and sometimes another name below that, Mitzi Green or Larry Adler or Baby Rose Marie. Often, another sign advertised that the theater was "Cool Inside."

When I wasn't on stage I played in my dressing room, watched the other acts, or sneaked out front to see the movie. I particularly enjoyed Larry Adler's act. When our week in Detroit ended, he gave me one of his harmonicas.

Mother's parents lived in Toronto, a city on our schedule. One day, Mother told me I was going to meet my grandpa and grandma. Our driver pulled up to a spare frame building in a seedy section of town. Mother studied the names posted inside the front door, then bade me follow her up the narrow wooden stairs. The car waited at the curb.

Mother was strangely silent as we climbed to the third floor. She knocked and the door opened at once. Mother's daddy, Grandpa Orr, looked like Mark Twain. His mustache was yellowed from tobacco. Despite the summer heat, he wore a jacket, buttoned. Grandma hovered behind him, a plump St. Patrick's Day parade, gray hair tied in a knot behind her head, loose-fitting flowered dress. Awkwardly, I kissed them both. Mother hugged them and we stepped inside. Grandpa closed the door.

Straight lace curtains over big windows, a square room, bare wooden floors, bleached from years of scrubbing; a sofa, two wooden chairs, a pea-green painted table set with doilies, cookies, four jelly glasses, a pitcher of lemonade. Another room adjoining: a quilt, clean faded sheets on a lumpy double bed; on the wall, a photograph of me. Beyond the entrance, to the left, a tiny kitchen with an icebox, a cupboard, and a stove.

"Sit down, Nora," Grandpa said. "Dickie, sit you down."

I don't recall the conversation, so palpable was tension in the room. I ate a cookie, drank some lemonade, Mother rose, we left. Were they coming to the theater? If possible, they hoped to see me there.

That night in our hotel—I shared the room with Mother—I lay in my twin bed while Mother, with her back to me, sat at the little desk, writing Dad a letter. I cried, hoping to get her attention. I cried harder, as if playing a scene, determined to be noticed. Finally, she turned to me. "What's the matter, Dickie? Why are you crying?"

"It's Grandma and Grandpa." I stared at the ceiling.

"What about them?"

"They're so poor," I cried.

Mother bit her lip, picked up the pen again. "Not really, dear. They'll be all right. Anyway, I'm going to send them money."

"Send them a lot," I urged.

"I will," she said. "Now go to sleep."

Next morning, a friend of Mother's from the past picked us up in her chauffeur-driven convertible. The lady owned a champagne business and we were taken on a tour of her winery. I smelled a cork, took my first sip of champagne, and a few minutes later threw up all over the back seat of the lady's fancy car.

I never saw my grandparents again.

Our next stop was Chicago, where I acquired a new white linen suit for our summer tour. Short pants. At Mother's insistence, I wore it when we left Chicago on our way to Washington. Cinders from the belching locomotive poured through the open windows of the train. When we got to Washington, my beautiful white suit was gray. Photographers took pictures of Mother and me smiling at a man who greeted us. Two well-dressed men stood quietly nearby, then ushered us into a waiting car and drove us to the Willard Hotel, downtown. The two men were in the lobby when we came down for dinner. They were there next morning when we came down for breakfast.

A lady from a newspaper joined Mother and me in the dining room. "Are you enjoying Washington?" the lady from the newspaper inquired. I said I thought so, but I hadn't seen it yet. The lady whispered to Mother: "You know, when Shirley Temple was in town, our paper got a letter from a person who threatened to spirit her away. Some people are so strange." Mother, glancing quickly at me, said, yes, she'd heard about it.

My interview completed, Mother and I joined the two men in the lobby. "Dickie, is there anything special you would like to do today?" the tall one asked. The White House and the FBI were high on my list, I told him. He spent a few minutes on the phone, then both men walked us to their car.

Sitting in Franklin D. Roosevelt's chair in the Oval Office, I wondered how the President signed papers with all those knick-knacks on his desk. And who dusted all that stuff? "President Roosevelt is in Philadelphia today, Dickie," a man apologized. "He said to tell you he's sorry that he couldn't visit with you." "That's okay," I said.

Better luck at the FBI, where a chunky, smiling man walked around his desk to greet us, hand outstretched. One of our escorts said, "Mr. Hoover, this is Mrs. Moore and Dickie. Dickie tells us that he wants to be a G-man."

"Well, let's get you started, then." J. Edgar Hoover smiled at me and Mother. "Let's get you fingerprinted and show you the shooting gallery. Is that all right, Mrs. Moore?"

Not long before, John Dillinger had been shot dead by agents of the FBI in front of a Chicago movie theater. While in Chicago, I had scrutinized the sidewalk where he fell, for signs of blood. During the course of our tour, I had also visited the governor of New Jersey and, after much cajoling, sat in the electric chair in which Bruno Richard Hauptmann, kidnapper of Charles A. Lindbergh's infant son, was fried three months earlier. For me, such things held a fascination far transcending anything Hollywood offered. This was really *living!*

I briefed J. Edgar Hoover on my adventures in New Jersey and Chicago, whereupon he took us to the basement, picked up a tommy gun, and punched a life-size paper target full of holes. Mr. Hoover offered the gun for my inspection. "It has a kick, and the barrel keeps moving up. You have to hold it down. Try it." My marksmanship was not as good as his, but had my target been a real man, he would have died. Mr. Hoover urged me to shoot a pistol at other targets, which he autographed for me, then he said goodbye and left us with his assistants. "You're in good hands." He winked at Mother. "Call me if there's anything you need."

Later, as Mother, our two new friends, and I were leaving, we found ourselves in the same elevator with Mr. Hoover and a colleague. On seeing Mother, they removed their hats. Mr. Hoover said he hoped we had enjoyed our visit and that he would stay in touch.

"How do you get to be a G-man?" I asked J. Edgar Hoover.

"Study accounting or the law, Dickie," Mr. Hoover answered. "Don't worry; I think we can get you in when the time comes."

On parting, I inquired, "Mr. Hoover, do you carry a gun?"

"No, Dickie. The rats don't come out in the daytime."

A week after our tour ended, I received a letter from J. Edgar Hoover, telling me how happy he was that I had visited the FBI. He sent a photo of himself, on which he wrote: "To Dickie, my future G-Man, J. Edgar Hoover."

After the demise of vaudeville, actors continued to make personal appearances. Those who made them were by no means on their last legs. Often, during the twelve-week hiatus, studios sent their stars to perform or take a bow at theaters in major cities. It was good promotion for their pictures, good publicity for studios and stars alike. Each tour left most of us with at least one vivid impression.

In her teens, Jane Powell played eight shows a day at the Capitol theater in New York, but all she saw of the city was her dressing room and the Edison Hotel. Years later, Jane sang at the White House for President Eisenhower, who told her that he had just had "a hard day on the Hill." Later that night, Eisenhower had his heart attack.

Natalie Wood hit the road at eight to publicize *Miracle on 34th Street.* Her mother was pregnant with Lana, "so my father went with me," Natalie remembered. "People pulled on my pigtails and my father didn't know how to braid my hair."

Marcia Mae Jones went to San Francisco to promote a picture with Bill Robinson. "We stayed in the best hotel, but they told Bill Robinson, the star, that because he was black he had to use the servants' elevator."

MGM always assigned an attractive young man from its publicity department to escort Ann Rutherford when she visited New York. "He would leave his poor wife sitting home in Brooklyn and show up at the Hampshire House with a limousine and corsage and take me to a premiere, and smile broadly while I was being photographed. I wondered how his wife explained that to people."

One of the most widely touted tours in history was the trip Jackie Coogan made in 1924 to raise food for Greek relief. Among the heads of state who greeted him was President Calvin Coolidge, described by Jack as "the dullest asshole I ever met." Jackie also met Benito Mussolini and, on the same day, Pope Pius XI. Proudly, Jackie showed me the autographed photo given to him by the Pope. It hung over his bed.

Margaret O'Brien and Gloria Jean are among those who met President and Mrs. Roosevelt while touring. Gloria remembers that the First Lady "took me by the hand and led me through the White House and showed me her favorite shoes. I sat on President Roosevelt's lap and he sang to me." The President told Gloria, "I play your records over and over, but Eleanor gets tired and says, 'Will you turn that off?' "

Not all of Gloria's travels are so happily remembered. After she left Universal, Gloria toured extensively, accompanied by her mother. Her father and two sisters stayed at home. They were an extremely close-knit family, and all suffered from the prolonged separations. For Gloria, personal appearance tours were "the unhappiest times of my life because I was never home for Christmas." Finally, after touring England, Gloria eagerly returned to Holly-

Karo syrup advertised its offer of a free Karo Cap for "every boy and girl who gives a can of syrup" to Jackie Coogan's 1924 food relief program to help orphans of the Near East.

A crowd greeting Jackie Coogan during his food relief tour. Jackie and his father *(wearing derby)* are in the back seat.

wood to rejoin her family and to resume her film career. But in her absence, times had changed and so had Gloria.

I had the clothes ripped off my back and had to run out of offices—terrible things from very famous people.

The producer who discovered me, Joe Pasternak, had left Universal for MGM, and many people suggested I go to Joe. A dose of reality: The man who discovered me said, "I have no place for you here. I have enough singers."

I had to turn quickly to other things. I worked as a dental assistant for a week, but I was lousy and the doctor threw me out. I did everything I could to pick up the pieces of my life.

When I was completely alone, someone happened to take a picture of me working as a restaurant hostess. Jerry Lewis saw my picture in the paper and called me to the studio. He said, "I felt sorry when I saw that you were a hostess. How would you like to be in my picture?" "Well," I said, "it's like asking how I'd like to breathe. I'd love to." So he said, "Okay. You're going to be in my picture. You're going to sing songs. I'll make a star of you again. You'll make a comeback and be bigger than ever."

Can you imagine how I felt? But I worked for a couple of months on the picture and I not only didn't sing, I didn't even utter a word. I was one of a bunch of girls, and if you saw the movie you wouldn't even know that I was in it.

But Sammy Davis, Jr., also learned that I was working in a restaurant. He was doing the Dick Powell show on TV. Sammy said, "How would you like to do a show with us?" "I'd love to," I said. It was a very good show and I had scenes with Dick Powell and Sammy Davis. And the first day I walked into my dressing room, it was filled with roses and there was a card that said, "What a pleasure to work with you. Sammy Davis, Jr." What a marvelous gesture after I'd been cast aside like an old shoe!

Sometimes we went on tour during the "Awkward Age," a phrase used to explain why we lost the appeal we'd had as children. Usually, the Awkward Age began when we got pimples, or when we entered that coltish phase—not quite child, not quite adult—that comes with puberty; when new awareness of our sexuality, combined with inhibitions, caused self-consciousness.

The Awkward Age announced to the world that child stars were no longer children. Nervous time for parents who had become dependent on the earnings of their kids.

For most of us, the Awkward Age was frightening. For Dean Stockwell, it was Nirvana.

> When the Awkward Age arrived, I would no longer be a child star, right? So I would get the fuck out of it! I couldn't wait to get pimples. I couldn't wait to get awkward. I ruined my posture. I did everything, just to get out of it.

During the filming of *National Velvet,* in which she played Elizabeth Taylor's older sister, Juanita Quigley realized that MGM, where she and Elizabeth were then both under contract, "didn't need two people who had similar hair and coloring, and Elizabeth had more talent, more beauty, so the handwriting was on the wall." Juanita quit, saying to herself, "When I get over this awkward teenage thing, I will come back." She never did.

> I began to really enjoy my anonymity. I enjoyed being liked for who I was, not what I did. I remember leaving MGM with Elizabeth by the side gate one day. People crowded around the car asking for her autograph and my autograph and somehow I wanted to be on the outside of the car, not on the inside. I just wanted to be me.

Natalie Wood and Elizabeth Taylor seemed to skip the Awkward Age completely, though both felt it internally.

Shirley Temple "never went through that phase of 'Who am I, where am I going, why am I here?' because I was always doing something. If you're busy," Shirley speculated, "you don't have time to sit around and wonder who you are." When Shirley's film career slowed down, she starred in a live television series, *Shirley Temple's Storybook.* The limitation she was most aware of then (and since) was an inability to scream.

Nor did Mickey Rooney seem to question himself. Outwardly self-assured from childhood through adolescence, Mickey was the epitome of macho confidence. But when Mickey was sixteen, Andy Hardy in full flower, number one at the box office, Ann Rutherford saw another side of him:

> One day the director said, "Mickey, I think I'll be through with you by eleven o'clock. You can go to the football game."
>
> But an actor had to be replaced and it wrecked the schedule. The director had to say, "Sorry, Mickey, you have to work this afternoon."
>
> Mickey wept. I can see him now, tears running down his cheeks, this young man who was bowling the girls over and copping a little feel whenever he could. Suddenly there was returned to us a small boy who was bitterly disappointed because he was missing a football game.

Most of us who hoped to continue our careers had to change our image. No longer could we get by with childish charm. Our smiles and pouts could no longer be trusted to captivate the hearts of audiences and movie makers alike.

Changing our image meant getting out from under wraps, learning how to do through craft what we had done intuitively as children; it meant changing other people's conceptions of us—conceptions that had been cultivated at great expense, over many years.

At best, that isn't easy. It's tougher still when growth and change are actively discouraged by parents and by employers, who bind the wraps still tighter.

Being under wraps takes many forms besides the literal binding of young breasts with gauze to hide the evidence of approaching womanhood.

Donald O'Connor was not allowed to cross a street until he turned thirteen. His sister's death beneath the wheels of a car had traumatized Donald's mother. Once he forgot and walked Judy Garland back to his theater in San Francisco to meet his mother, who "slapped me across the face in front of Judy because I had crossed the street. It was completely emasculating."

Judy, too, had image problems as a child. "You know what

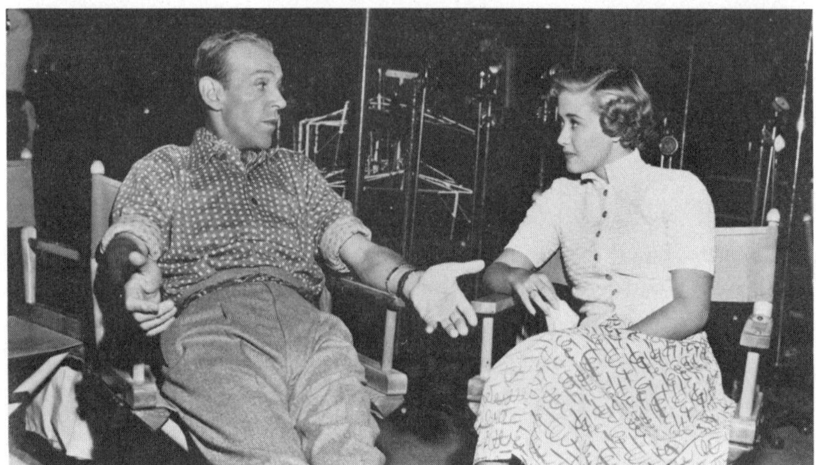

Young Jane Powell was awed at meeting Fred Astaire in *Royal Wedding*. To break the ice, she asked, "Tell me, Mr. Astaire, when did you stop dancing with your sister?" He told her 1929. "That's the year I was born," said Jane. They didn't talk much after that.

Natalie Wood and James Dean in *Rebel Without a Cause*. Dean, said Natalie, was fascinated by fame but at the same time didn't want it.

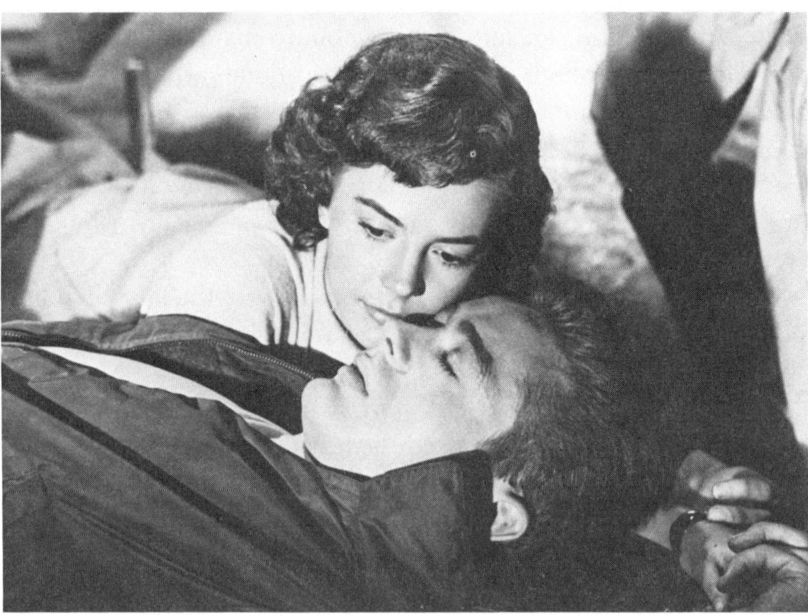

Judy's biggest disappointment was?" Sidney Miller asked. "In the MGM commissary, they named various dishes after stars, like the Joan Crawford Casserole. Judy's biggest pain was that on the menu she was just a sandwich; and out at the Universal commissary, Deanna Durbin was a salad."

As a young adult, Donald O'Connor went through an image problem during filming of the "Francis" pictures. "I was twenty-five and I told the studio I wasn't growing, that I wanted to become a man on screen instead of playing all those silly parts. Finally, I refused to make another 'Francis' picture unless they released me from my contract. I don't know where I got the guts to do it, but they said, 'Okay.' "

At nineteen, Jane Powell got ulcers. At twenty-five, she left MGM because, "being a mother of two children, I felt I just had to grow up." Earlier, while she and her first husband were being divorced, Jane and dancer Gene Nelson made *Two Sailors and a Girl*. "We became enamored of each other, but the fans and the studio were shocked. MGM wouldn't allow Gene to put his foot on the lot. The magazines wouldn't touch us, and they were terribly important at the time."

While Gene and I were going together, I got an award from *Photoplay*. The awards already had been announced or I would not have gotten it. At the ceremony, nobody had anything to do with us. The "Girl Next Door" shouldn't be involved with a man while she's still legally married to someone else. It almost killed my career and almost killed his. Here I was, the "Girl Next Door," with the wedding and the diapers and the babies and the dogs, the picket fence, the cookies, and everything, and all of a sudden, it's shot to hell.

In my teens I tried to grow through writing, producing radio, taking acting lessons. With Mother, I went to private acting coaches, asking each if they thought I ought to continue as an actor, hoping they'd say no. But all agreed that "it would be a shame" to waste my talent, and so I studied acting when I wasn't working or in school.

Whenever I got a role, I asked Mother and my agent to arrange for the studio to bill me as Dick Moore. The name Dickie was, in my view, childish. Reports came back: No one will hire Dick Moore because they don't know who Dick Moore is.

At seventeen, Roddy McDowall was loaned by Fox to MGM, where Lillian Burns, the studio drama coach, told him: "Until you're twenty-seven, nothing is going to happen to you again." It didn't make sense to Roddy that he was through professionally. "I talked to people about it. But Wynn Rocamora, my agent at the time, told me I would never work again, because I'd grown up."

To compound his difficulties, Roddy's mother "was dumb enough to believe Joe Pasternak, who told her, 'If you can get him out of Fox, we'll take him at Metro.' So she got me out of 20th, but there was no bridge to Culver City. She was left holding the bag." Roddy did a vaudeville tour. Pasternak was not Roddy's mother's only blind spot.

Once, Mother was desperately afraid that I was in love with Kim Stanley. I had done a television show with Kim in New York and I adored her. While I was in New York, I had written home every day, about everything, including Kim.

When I was back in Los Angeles, Kim was testing for *The Goddess.* Mother would say, "Now, that girl you did that show with, Kim Hunter . . ." I'd say, "No, Mother, Kim *Stanley.*"

"Oh, yes, Kim Stanley. She's old, isn't she?" And she never could remember her name, but she said, "Do bring her to dinner."

I brought Kim home and Mother didn't even wait for us to get into the house, but took one look at Kim and, with great expansiveness, said, "But you *are* pretty!"

That was for openers. She didn't leave a stone unturned in her advice and her caring. She took Kim into the back room and wept over Kim's talent and told her how the studio was killing her with terrible lighting. She did every rotten thing she could think of, poured out with her treacle.

Edith Fellows got out from under wraps when Grandma died. Grandma's funeral, says Edith, was one of the best performances she ever gave.

When I found her dead one morning, it was a terrible shock, but it didn't last too long.

At the service, I kept my head down because I couldn't cry. I knew I was supposed to cry. I kept saying to my teacher, "Lillian, I can't cry." And Lillian whispered, "Don't worry about it."

After the church service, Lillian and Bobby Jordan and I rode together to the cemetery. I knew there'd be photographers and lots of people there, but I could not cry. I felt a great relief. I was almost laughing all the way to the cemetery, where we had to trudge up the hillside, and I said, "Lillian, I can't do it, I'm going to get the giggles."

Sure enough, there were photographers. Can you just see it in the papers, that I laughed at Grandma's funeral? I said, "Lillian, I'm gonna laugh, what shall I do?"

She said, "You start to faint and Bobby will hold you by one arm and I'll hold the other and we'll take you to the car and go."

So I pretended to fall forward, and down the hill we went and zipped off in the limo, and I laughed all the way home.

Ed Sullivan, the noted columnist and television host, and his family came to Peggy Ann Garner's rescue when she needed a helping hand. Peggy and the Sullivans' daughter, Betty, were friends. When Peggy was sixteen, they invited her to live with them in New York. They knew the score at home. Peggy spent her happiest years with Ed Sullivan and his wife and daughter. At last she had a family, emotional support, and the courage to confront her mother for the first time, and to tell her father "all the things that had been going on for years."

Mrs. Garner and her flamboyance with a checkbook remained a subject of concern. She followed Peggy to New York, but the stay was brief. "To this day, I'm the only person who can see through her," Peggy says. Mama headed west again, Peggy stayed in New York.

Teenagers Margaret O'Brien, kept under wraps by her mother, and Natalie Wood, who enjoyed a much freer social life, became friends. They had not met as children. Most of the boys Margaret dated were Natalie's castoffs. When Natalie was tired of them, she'd tell them to call Margaret. Still, Margaret didn't go out much, Natalie recalled.

> Margaret called and invited me to spend the night. I drove over. I was much more independent than Margaret, though I was a couple of years younger. I was fifteen, but I had an illegal driving license that said I was sixteen. I was in a very rebellious phase, feeling that my parents were too strict. And then I saw Margaret's home life and I was absolutely astonished. When we went to the movies, both her aunt and her mother took us. We were not allowed to wait outside. We had to wait for them inside the lobby. Margaret had this extreme overprotection, which I had been rebelling against for a couple of years. She seemed to accept it, but I was absolutely horrified by the way her diet was watched. She had dolls around. I couldn't wait to get home and tell my parents that they weren't so bad after all. I was driving way too fast in my desire to get home, and I got into a terrible car crash. I was to go on an interview the next day and luckily I didn't get hurt, but I demolished the car.

Though different in almost every way, Natalie and Margaret were, in the early fifties, both fascinated by a new kid on the block, an eccentric, troubled young actor from New York. James Dean, the symbol of rebellion to which many adolescents rallied, had completed *East of Eden,* a Kazan film not yet released, and would later co-star with Natalie (though neither of them knew it then) in *Rebel Without a Cause.*

One day when Natalie and Margaret were having lunch, they learned that Dean and his motorcycle were nearby on the Sunset Strip. Like fans, they rushed to see him. Margaret's mother happened by, grabbed her by the hair, and dragged her home.

Immediately thereafter, Natalie and James Dean did a TV show together. It was Natalie's first grown-up role, "with a kiss and all that stuff." She was thrilled. Almost thirty years later, she recounted to me her first meeting as a rebellious young girl with the young cult figure who became Hollywood's legendary misfit.

The TV show I did with Jimmy was a *GE Theatre*, broadcast live. An actor named John Smith was popular at the time. They wanted him to play my boyfriend, but my agent said if they couldn't get John Smith they would settle for some kid from New York, James Dean, who had done something for Kazan. The producers were very disappointed when they lost out on John Smith and were stuck with James Dean! They'd already heard that he was eccentric.

We rehearsed in an old warehouse downtown. Beside the regular entrance, there was a garage door, and if you entered that way you had to jump six feet to the floor because there were no steps. Except for Jimmy, we all arrived on time. Then he arrived by motorcycle through the garage door, peered down at all of us, parked his motorcycle, and leaped down. He had a safety pin holding his fly together, blue jeans, and an old tattered T-shirt. He was exactly what I expected, a junior version of Marlon Brando. He mumbled so you could hardly hear what he was saying, and he seemed very exotic and eccentric and attractive. When lunchtime came, everybody wandered off, and I was trying to figure out where I would eat. I happened to look back and Jimmy was following me. "Do you want to have lunch?" he asked. "Oh, sure," I said. So he said, "Hop on the motorcycle." I was thrilled.

We went speeding off to some greasy spoon. He had a little portable radio on which he played classical music. All during lunch in this tiny diner, his radio played beautiful classical music. I would have expected bongo drums.

At the time, Jimmy and Pier Angeli had just broken up. The diner was next to a little newsstand, and since Pier was a big star, her picture was on all the magazines, with articles about how her mother had broken up the romance between Pier and some eccentric kid from New York. Jimmy picked up a few magazines and read them. He was very upset, because he was obviously in love with her. He was fascinated by her stardom, and he was fascinated by the fact that he was becoming a celebrity—yet not wanting it, not wanting fame.

For Natalie, *Rebel Without a Cause,* which she did with James Dean, created problems at home. "That was the first time I got into an argument with my parents. They didn't want me to do it. They didn't like the script. They thought it presented parents in a very bad light," Natalie explained. But Natalie, though brought up in a "very strict European fashion," stuck to her guns. She wanted to change her image and raise the level of her work. And she did. With *Rebel* she became a full-fledged star, and an actress who was taken seriously.

In the process of changing her image, Jane Withers also met James Dean. Jane had longed to "do something other than old happy-face Jane." Even as a child, Jane felt that her pictures lacked quality. At seventeen, she left Fox because she "cared too much."

Sam Goldwyn asked Jane to play a serious role in *The North Star,* his film about the Russians during World War II. *Giant* gave Jane an opportunity to play another dramatic part as an adult, and to work with Elizabeth Taylor, Rock Hudson—and James Dean, by now a youthful legend still struggling to come to terms with life. As usual, Jane warmed to the challenge.

James Dean and I developed a marvelous friendship, but it didn't start out that way. He came over to me one day and said, "You don't like me, do you?"

"I've never said I didn't like you."

"Well, you never talk to me."

"You're pretty difficult to talk to, fella. Stop and think about it."

Then I walked away. He followed and he said, "Okay, okay, I'm hard to talk to."

I said, "Well, I think it could be arranged, but we've both got to want it. I'd love to talk to you. There are a lot of things I'd like to ask you."

He said, "Yeah?"

I said, "Yeah. Do I make an appointment? I don't go for all that. I've been around too long, Jimmy, for your nonsense."

He said, "Well, yeah."

He never missed one scene I was in. The director, George Stevens, told me, "You have mesmerized Jimmy Dean."

Stevens would say to me, "Jane, Jimmy's got to do so-and-so in this scene; can you talk to him about it?" I would say, "Mr. Stevens, you're the director. You tell him what to do."

"Jane, we have no communication." And they didn't. So I would talk to Jimmy and tell him how much it meant to me to be in this industry and how grateful I was for the opportunity to be in this picture, and how lucky he was too. I adored Jimmy after I got to know him. I called him my number three son.

"Why do you call me that?" he asked.

I said, "Look, I've got two boys, four and two. They're children. You act like a child, I treat you like one. You're number three son."

For some of us, escape from the Awkward Age came in the form of an invitation from the armed forces. I was in high school when mine came.

"If I give you a C-minus so that you can graduate, do you promise never to take chemistry again?" Mr. Green had kept me after class. A senior at Fairfax High School, I was scheduled to be drafted. World War II was under way and I was just eighteen. I promised, finished the picture I was working on *(The Eve of St. Mark)*, wore my ROTC uniform to the senior prom, got sweaty handprints all over the back of my date's white dress, and reported to Fort MacArthur, California, for induction into the army. Mother cried.

On the onion fields of Camp Sibert, Alabama, I went through basic training: long hikes, target practice with a rifle (I qualified as "Expert," thanks to Gary Cooper and the FBI), phys ed, the obstacle course, marching, KP, bivouacs, cleaning the latrine. To me, all tasks were uniformly joyous. Basic training lasted only six weeks, whereupon I was assigned to the 39th Special Service Company, formed earlier to entertain the troops. Our lieutenant was a nice young man named Allen Ludden, who became a talk show host.

Good soldiers though they were, my colleagues in Special Services did not share my affection for the army. Yet they were friendly souls, generous with opinions and advice, who never mocked my naiveté.

Knowing that to do otherwise would ostracize me from my chums, I disguised my boundless glee on learning that we were shipping overseas. As we packed to leave, a major sent for me.

"Good news, Private Moore: 20th Century–Fox needs you for retakes on your last picture, and the army has approved a temporary leave, so you're going back to Hollywood."

"But, sir, I don't want to go." I made no effort to conceal my disappointment. The major offered me a cigarette, lit his, and patiently explained why I should want to go: I'd be transferred out of the 39th Special Service Company, and after retakes at the studio I would be assigned to New York City to recruit volunteers for the Women's Army Corps.

"Sir, may I ask, can the army *order* me to go? I really like the company I'm in." The major snuffed his cigarette, stared at me for what seemed like an eternity, and told me to come back in an hour. When I got back, the major said that if I returned to Hollywood, the army would, when retakes were completed, transport me to Seattle to rejoin my unit at its point of embarkation. I thanked the major, saluted, clicked my heels, and left.

Mother hadn't expected to see me so soon. She was proud but worried. Proud because the major had written her that I was a fine young patriot; worried because she'd heard that Darryl F. Zanuck, on learning of my attitude, vowed that I would never set foot on the Fox lot again.

After forty-nine days at sea, our platoon dropped anchor at what was left of Garapan, capital of the island of Saipan. That night, the Japanese dropped bombs. Then we debarked and boarded trucks for the uphill trip.

My friend Arnold Stanley shouldered his saxophone, and examined his combat pack to be sure his piccolo was intact. Chuck McCrea, keeper of the records, checked the three dozen contraceptives he had optimistically tucked into his ammunition belt. Frenchy cradled his bass fiddle, Jack Teagarden, Jr., carried his trombone,

Pete Seeger had his ever-present banjo. Whitey, the driver, shared the cab with Captain Gray. The rest of the platoon followed in other trucks, no headlights.

Captain Gray was by now our only officer and we were his only troops. At several places on the narrow, winding road, the trucks slowed to a halt.

Jack Fletcher and Wendell Hulett had written a song, "Soldiers in Greasepaint," which we sang in our show. Wendell hummed it going up the hill.

A sudden shower of tracer bullets briefly lit the sky and vanished into a cluster of trees by our truck. People in the trees shot back. We were in the middle. Captain Gray called out, "Who's in charge?" A voice from the darkness shouted to "get the fuck out of the way."

"Who are you?" Captain Gray got out of our truck.

"Who the fuck are you?" the voice called back.

"I'm Captain Norman Gray and this is the 39th Special Service Company. We're looking for Island Command Headquarters."

"You're in the front lines, buddy," called the voice, as a line of marines appeared out of the night and took cover in a ditch beside our truck. Firing resumed, then stopped. The marines moved past us and vanished into darkness.

I spent two years on Saipan, during which I was transferred to the army newspaper, *Stars and Stripes.*

One of my articles, about "surplus" equipment dumped at sea while we faced shortages, aroused the curiosity of visiting senators and angered the island commander of the navy. When the article appeared, the base commander, an army brigadier general, summoned me to his headquarters.

"Sergeant," he said laconically—by this time I'd been promoted —"fly up to Iwo Jima today. You'll get word when it's time to come back."

On the day when I had enough points to be discharged, I was flown back to Honolulu. I loved it there, but regulations said soldiers had to be separated from the service at their point of induction, so, at twenty-one, I was discharged at Fort MacArthur, California. I moved back with my parents. It never occurred to me not to.

Mickey Rooney had gone through Camp Sibert before I got there. Four Watson boys served in the coast guard, Gene Reynolds spent four years on a navy destroyer. Donald O'Connor, a licensed pilot, wanted to fly, but was assigned to Special Services. Sidney Miller, rejected for poor eyesight, played hospitals with Peggy Ryan.

Jackie Cooper, who had taught himself to play the drums, enlisted in the navy, where he "cleaned every toilet in sight," became an ensign, and was invited to join Claude Thornhill's Navy Band. I met Jack when they stopped on Saipan. They played a lot of hospitals.

"We walked the wards," Jack told me later. "I signed an autograph for a boy who had been blind only ten hours, who was feeling all over his bed for a piece of paper and a pencil for an autograph he was never going to see. Things like that caused us to drink a lot while we were over there."

Jackie Coogan enlisted in the medics before World War II began. By then, he and Betty Grable were divorced. Grable was the military's favorite pinup girl. The first time someone made a smart remark about his former wife, Jack kicked him in the groin. He was transferred to another outfit, where it happened again. Jack hit one man with a mess kit, another with a rifle. Soon word spread that Jack was crazy, and no one bothered him.

When war broke out, Jack sought transfer to the air force, a wish fulfilled when, stopping over in Palm Springs, he intervened in a dispute at the hotel between "some elderly guy" in a bathing suit and actor Sonny Tufts. Tufts had "always bothered" Jackie, so he knocked him into the pool. The old guy in the bathing suit said, "Thank you very much. Would you have lunch with me tomorrow?"

To his surprise, Jack lunched next day with General Ralph P. Cousins, commander of the West Coast Army Air Force Training Command. A licensed pilot like his friend Donald O'Connor, Jack passed the flying tests and ended up in Burma, landing gliders and building airstrips behind Japanese lines. Jack also spent time in Karachi, Pakistan, where he achieved prominence unrelated to his fame in Hollywood. I first heard of his adventure when I was on Saipan. Almost forty years later, I got the story firsthand.

Chiang Kai-shek was in Karachi when we were assembling P-51s. Everybody had to stand behind a fence that perimetered the field. A big C-54 pulled up, then a dozen motorcycle MPs with the sirens going, then ten or twenty Cadillacs. In the lead Cadillac was the Generalissimo and Madame Chiang. Then came the rest of the boys—Chinese admirals and generals, all five foot four, with medals down to their ankles. They're bowing and scraping and Chiang Kai-shek is stoned on opium—he can't see anything—and Madame Chiang tells him when to bow. Finally, she heads him up the ramp onto the plane and she tells him to wave, so he raised his hand, and that's when I yelled, "And have that laundry by Tuesday."

One guy said, "You shouldn't have said that. Don't you know they're our allies?" Another guy was on the ground, throwing-up laughing. Later, when Chiang heard about it, he asked Roosevelt to have my head chopped off with a sword. But Madame Chiang thought it was funny. She was a pretty hip broad.

Spanky McFarland was sixteen when World War II ended.

I wasn't working much. I was going to school and one day I just said, "I don't want to be in pictures anymore." My father threw a fit. He wasn't working, either. My Dad wasn't the most energetic man in the world. He said, "But this is the only thing you know how to do. We can make a living out here."

We moved back to Lancaster, Texas, to a two-bedroom frame house without gas. My mother cooked on a kerosene stove and I chopped wood in the winter to warm the house, and went to school and worked after school to help out.

I found out that if I joined the air force, I could send more money home, and they'd save on food because I wouldn't be there to eat any. There was Mother and Dad, and Tommy—two years younger than myself

—and Amanda, my sister, twelve years younger, and my other brother, about twenty years younger. My mother and dad were working by then, but at menial jobs. They weren't trained people.

So I went in the air force for eight months, then I got a hardship discharge and went to work. I was chauffeur for a guy in Dallas. He got a kick out of his chauffeur being Spanky McFarland and he used that to his benefit. I went to work for Coca-Cola, and sold insurance for a while. I worked for an aircraft company. They transferred me to California. In the meanwhile I got married. My first marriage went sour and I came back to Texas and met my present wife.

Spanky decided to merchandise his name. Things looked promising. Armed with a $2,500 advance, he flew his new fiancé to Hollywood, where they were married. The merchandising deal blew up when it was learned that Hal Roach, too, had the right to exploit Spanky's name. One by one, the deals fell through. "But by this time I had a pretty good helpmate and she went to work until I could find something to do, which I think was pumping gas. I pumped a lot of gas."

When Dean Stockwell was subject to the draft, we were fighting in Korea, but from sixteen to twenty-one, Dean dropped out.

I shaved all my hair. I was bald. I just disappeared. First I went to college—Cal-Berk—for a semester and a half. I didn't want to join the army because I didn't believe in the war. I also knew that I couldn't possibly endure taking orders. So I dodged the draft. I took drugs, pretended I was a fag. I stayed up three days and nights before I went for my physical and I never looked anyone in the eye.

As a result, the psychiatrist wrote: "Shouldn't ever be in service."

Then I dropped out of Berkeley and traversed the country, worked on a railroad, drove spikes on an electric gang, picked fruit, worked in a cannery, then as a mailboy for Standard Plumbing in New York, got promoted to the export department and decided that was it. I called an agent in New York and said, "My name is Dean Stockwell. I did all this acting once and I think I want to do it again." Eventually, I got a TV part that paid my fare back to L.A.

During wartime, many of Hollywood's young ladies sold war bonds, worked with the USO, visited hospitals, or danced with servicemen at the Hollywood Canteen.

Partway through a worldwide personal appearance tour, Sybil Jason was stranded in South Africa, her native land, when war broke out. Unable to return, she eventually was dropped by Fox. Reading about her friends in *Modern Screen* and *Photoplay* "drove me crazy. But," Sybil speculated, "maybe I was better off not going through those teenage years, either making it or not making it, either part of the 'in' group, or left completely out. Who knows?"

Not until he was a mature adult did Mickey Rooney feel left out.

As a youngster, I was very fortunate that I never had to vie for roles. When they wanted Rooney, they wanted Rooney. It's like the old story —the *whole* story of a career: First a guy says, "Who is Mickey Rooney?" The next stage in the career is when he says, "Get me Mickey Rooney." The next phase is "Get me a fella *like* Mickey Rooney." Then, "Who is Mickey Rooney?" That's just the way it goes.

12. Living in the Real World

After the war, I didn't want to go back to acting. Mother decided I should work on a newspaper. She talked to Edie Lake. Edie called William Randolph Hearst at San Simeon. Hearst called the *Los Angeles Herald* and ordered the Editor in Charge to "put this kid on salary."

"Come on down and bring your stringbook," I was told. William Van Ettisch was not thrilled by the articles I had written for *Stars and Stripes,* especially the one about officers and nurses on Saipan using ambulances for recreation. I knew he wondered why the Chief (as Mr. Hearst was called) wanted to hire me, but a date was set for me to start working as a copyboy, until I learned the ropes.

I'd begin a week from Monday. That morning, on getting out of bed, I fell on my face and couldn't get up. Dr. Godshall came. He called a specialist. Many tests and phone calls. An ambulance took me to Sawtelle Veterans Hospital. There the doctors said I had been paralyzed by a rare virus (they said I got it overseas). Slowly, I recovered the use of my legs.

It was in all the papers: Dickie Moore, War Hero. In truth, I had not fired a gun since Camp Sibert, Alabama.

At first I slept the days away. As I dozed I fantasized: Ann Rutherford, Shirley Temple, the Chinese girl in Honolulu who took me home for dinner, played my romantic partners. June Haver, Gloria DeHaven, Linda Darnell were other favorite players.

June Haver was giving a superb performance in a dream when someone shook me awake. A lady sitting on my bed, a colonel out of focus in the background. Framed by soft blond hair, this gorgeous lady's perfumed face was eighteen inches from my barely opened eyes. She stroked me, saying, "Dickie, do you know me? Do you know who I am?"

Still lingering, my fantasy was verbalized: "June Haver!" I blurted.

The colonel coughed, the lady backed away. Marlene Dietrich had come back into my life for a brief moment.

By the time I learned to walk again, calls began to come from studios. One from RKO was irresistible: a six-week guarantee as Robert Mitchum's deaf-mute buddy in a mystery film called *Out of the Past.* Shooting on location near Lake Tahoe started in a month; until then, the studio would send a tutor to my home to instruct me in the deaf-mute sign language needed for my part.

I liked everything about Bob Mitchum. He reminded me of Gary Cooper. His talent as a poet was surprising, especially his seeming mastery—though I was not an expert—of all poetic forms. Bob's command of language transcended the subject matter of his poems. One pithy sonnet, in flawless rhyme and meter, was about a farting horse.

After *Out of the Past,* I bought a new Chevrolet ($1,600—they were hard to get, but Mother had a friend), paid Dad's insurance premium, opened a modest bank account, studied journalism at Los Angeles City College, followed Pat east, got married, and turned again to acting.

I liked New York. Even though I didn't see them often, it was good to know that Roddy and Peggy Ann and Edith Fellows were in town. My career was a mixed bag: some leading roles on television, starring in summer stock, back to Hollywood for a few films —no starring parts—a show on Broadway. Nothing to set the world on fire, but enough to earn a living. Sometimes.

One night, the producer of a TV series called me at home. Would I co-star with Edith Fellows "one week from tonight? I know it's short notice, but I'm calling from the station. We go on the air in ten minutes, and we want to announce your name tonight. It's a good part, an airline pilot, and you get co-star billing."

I said my agent would have to call him back.

"Have him call me fast."

"Are they crazy?" My agent was still in his office. "That's no way to do business. We haven't even seen a script." He'd talk to them and call me back.

"Dickie, baby, they're in trouble. They want to announce your name on the air after tonight's show and put it in *TV Guide.* The money's lousy, I think the deal is bad. I know how things are at home, but if you can turn it down, I'd rather." Turn it down, I said.

The phone rang again. It was the producer, saying it was a shame that Edith and I weren't going to be working together, because she was looking forward to it. Maybe he should talk to my agent; perhaps they could get closer on the money.

Three minutes passed. "Well, Dick, maybe we ought to do the show. I can get an extra hundred. You need the money anyway, and I'll waive my commission. It's a no-quote salary, nobody'll know we cut our price. Also, I got the impression they're trying to keep the show on the air, and they could make it pretty hard on us if we let them down, you know what I mean? What can you lose? Besides, you'll have a ball working with Edith again."

"Well, then," I said doubtfully, "tell them it's okay."

Oddly, no script was available until the first rehearsal. Edith dashed over, threw her arms around me. The actors were introduced. The cast list said I was "Clerk." We read the script aloud.

"Clerk" asked Edith her destination, reported that her luggage was eight pounds overweight, and said, "Thank you, ma'am."

I called the producer aside and said I wanted out. "I'm sorry you feel that way, since we announced your name. You know, there's no such thing as a small part, only small actors."

My agent was surprised. "I thought you said the part was good," he scolded. "Well, don't worry, Dick, baby. You stick with me, you'll sleep in silk."

Edith called when the show was over. She wanted to have lunch. I said I was busy.

Edith had married Freddie Fields, an MCA talent agent, while she was starring in *Marinka* on Broadway. She had a daughter, but even that could not save her marriage. Her husband, she recalls, "was very disappointed when I started mumbling about wanting to be just a wife and mother. I was lousy at both and he told me so. I started to think of Freddie as my grandmother, and it destroyed our marriage."

Edith and Freddie were divorced in 1955. He became one of Hollywood's most successful producers. Edith continued to act, appearing with Menasha Skulnik in Broadway's *Uncle Willie*, later touring the Orient with a revue based on TV's *Your Hit Parade*. Two months after returning to New York, Edith participated in a charity show for the deaf, and discovered that she was in trouble.

During a dramatic scene, my legs froze. The words came out, but I didn't know what was happening. I saw the spotlight on me, and I thought: "Oh, my God, why doesn't it go away?" I wanted to run away, but I couldn't move. Finally, the scene was over. I don't know how I got off the stage.

The next time my agent called me for an interview, I could still see that spotlight menacing me. I said, "I can't go, I have the flu."

Then I hid, went into a cocoon. I told myself, "There is no reason for this fright; you've been in front of audiences forever." But I realized I needed professional help. I sought out a psychiatrist—the wrong one, unfortunately.

He said, "If you were younger, I could help you. But you're thirty-four. It's too late. You'll have to learn another way to earn a living." I believed him.

Then I had a breakdown. I lost touch with everybody except my little daughter. I felt I had betrayed my friends. Maybe I thought I was only loved when I was performing. Whatever I was thinking, for twenty-one years I never went near a stage, I turned down work, gave all kinds of excuses.

I ran out of excuses in 1979, when a lovely girl I worked with at a nurses' telephone registry introduced me to a writer, who said, "I want to do a play for you."

I told him what happened to me when I was thirty-four.

He said, "I'll take a chance if you will."

We met every Saturday morning until I had to go to work. My shift was three P.M. to midnight. We'd improvise and do scenes. Slowly, he built a story. The character I played was very much like me. On the day we played it to an audience, I said, "I could still walk out on you."

He said, "But I don't think you will." I went out onto the stage and looked up at the spotlight and it was my warm and gentle friend—no longer menacing. I was home because one guy believed in me.

Marcia Mae Jones also experienced early signs of a breakdown. One day, in her twenties, she went on an interview. Her body shook; she couldn't hold the script. Although Marcia Mae didn't see this as a warning of serious trouble ahead, she wanted to see a psychiatrist. Her mother interfered to stop her.

After Marcia did *The Daughter of Rosie O'Grady* in 1950, a strike in the motion picture industry put everybody out of work.

I was divorced and had the full responsibility for my two kids, so I lied to get a job and said I could operate a switchboard. I worked for Greg Bautzer, a prominent Hollywood attorney, for six years. He let me come and go, so I did TV shows with Eddie Cantor, Joan Davis, Burns and Allen.

People in the industry came in and said, "How dare you work here?"

I asked if they had any suggestions for me on how to feed my kids, but I never got an answer. They really resented what I was doing, yet no one would give me a job as an actress.

Marcia Mae began to drink, and blamed her mother.

I didn't use liquor so that I could operate. I used it to escape, to kill that well of loneliness, that emptiness in your gut that you want to fill up. I didn't want to feel or think. I wanted out. I attempted to take my life and I was very angry that I was still alive when I came to. I hadn't called anybody for help, I didn't leave a note. I felt that my kids would be better off without me. I thought I was doing the right thing.

My mother saved me. I hadn't spoken to her in five weeks, but on this morning she must have known, because she came to the house.

At UCLA Medical Center, they told Marcia she had battle fatigue. Marcia protested that she had never been in the front lines. "Oh, yes you have," they told her.

This time Marcia's mother followed her to make sure she saw a psychiatrist.

I'm so grateful that God gave me another chance. It's a terrible thing to attempt to take your life.

I didn't see my mother for about two years, which was very hard for me. I had to close the door on her while I tried to get well. Eventually, we got together.

I did not have years of drinking, but I am an alcoholic who has not had a drink for fifteen years. I have the gift of surviving and I try to help others with the same disease. I was raised always to worry about the future. Now I've learned to live a day at a time.

When the subject of drinking came up at our meeting, Donald O'Connor sat forward in his chair. "Many interviewers have said, 'Donald, you escaped it. We never read about you being drunk or popping pills or having arguments at home.' They didn't hear about it because, one: I've always kept a low profile; and two: Many people who love me protected me. I went through the booze bit. I didn't escape it. Booze took over until I was given the gift of sobriety.

"With Judy, of course, it was booze and drug abuse—pills to keep her awake, to put her to sleep. A case of being patted on the head for all the wrong things. She never had a chance to grow."

Diana Cary, too, had emotional problems. She told me, "The Hollywood experience in childhood for many of us was devastating. I think it sprang from the upside-down world which our being the breadwinners created. The experience was also damaging because most child actors didn't make it as adults. They had the feeling that they had never really been given a chance." Diana paused and then went on:

> Most of the children who were well known had to either go to a psychiatrist or get some kind of help. A Franciscan priest took me on as a project. He let me come into the office and talk. I was thirty years old and about to go under because I couldn't handle the identity of Baby Peggy. I couldn't get rid of her, I couldn't absorb her into myself, I couldn't become *me.* People didn't see *me;* when they looked at me they saw *her,* and I had this feeling of wanting to murder my other self. I was very close to a schizophrenic situation.

Mother and Dad were upset when I started therapy. Every time we talked, they'd raise the subject. "What did we do wrong?" they asked. Or, "What do you *say* to your analyst?"

When he got out of the service, Gene Reynolds saw a psychiatrist, who suggested that he live alone. "The idea had never occurred to me. I found a furnished room, wrapped up my things one night, and stole out of the house like a thief, scared to death."

Darryl Hickman came to the point in his therapy "that I was able to confront my mother, and later I was able to go through her death with her in a wonderful way. Then I felt it was all done. She did the best she could, I think. She was a lovely, mixed-up woman."

Natalie Wood was in analysis for eight years, until age thirty, when she became pregnant with her first child.

A common thread for all of us is that we played many parts and had many different sets of parents. We were always charming and nice, we knew how to behave socially better than other little kids; but I, for one, really didn't know what I should be saying "yes" or "no" to.

What analysis did for me was to help me clarify what I wanted to do, and when I started figuring out what *I* wanted, it didn't make me more self-centered, it made me less self-centered.

Analysis made me look at things. When R.J. and I were first married, I started to decorate our house. I had never thought about furniture or things like that. All I'd thought about was acting, and whether I got the part or not. When the decorator said, "What about the coffee table?" I realized I'd never even noticed what goes on a coffee table. I'd never looked. I didn't have any opinion about the kind of furniture I wanted. I'd always been so worried about being shy, or what people were going to think of me, or what I was going to say, that I'd never notice *anything* when I entered a room. Later on, as I got a little inner security, I felt I was discovering windows everywhere. I could see *out.* I became aware of how *other* people lived and what their homes were like.

What analysis did for me was to put painful childhood memories in the past. Now, when I look back, I can still recall them, but they don't have the power to make me crazy.

Roddy McDowall never told his mother he was in analysis. "It wasn't out of fear," Rod emphasized, "it was out of common sense. I knew I'd have to go through all that moaning about 'Where did we go wrong?' "

Encouraged by his friend Jane Powell (who loved his mother but felt she was destroying him), Roddy went to New York, where he met Montgomery Clift. That friendship changed Rod's life. Before that, he had starred in summer stock, where he gave good performances but couldn't repeat them. He'd never learned the craft of acting because "I had been taught that I was a movie star and had nothing to learn."

"Fuckin' rubbish," Clift told him. "You've got to *learn* to act." He introduced Rod to Mira Rostova, Clift's acting coach and confidante.

For six months, Roddy sat in class, not knowing what the group was talking about. "I said absolutely nothing. I had no idea what this foreign language was all about. Then it began to click, and I began to respond. I worked very hard," Roddy recalls. "I was terribly angry, which I didn't yet realize; but my anger didn't show up in hostility, it showed up in productivity."

With three plays in 1955, the breakthrough came: *The Doctor's Dilemma* at New York's Phoenix Theatre; *The Tempest* at the Stratford, Connecticut, Shakespeare Festival; *No Time for Sergeants* on Broadway. *Life* magazine took note. In 1960, Rod co-starred with Dean Stockwell on Broadway in *Compulsion*, played in *Camelot* with Richard Burton; and in 1961, the movie *Cleopatra*, with Burton and Roddy's friend Elizabeth Taylor. No longer thought of as an ex–child star, Roddy had become an actor.

Peggy Ann Garner also spent most of the fifties in New York: TV, four Broadway shows, summer stock, some films.

Peggy and singer Richard Hayes were married and divorced in 1953. In 1956, Peggy married Albert Salmi, her leading man in the national company of *Bus Stop*. Their daughter is Cassandra (Cas). Peggy tried a third time, with Los Angeles realtor Kenyon Foster Brown.

Kenyon and I had four cars. When we were divorced, guess who got the two that didn't work?

We sold the big house and I called Barbara Whiting because I had to get a car. Barbara's husband was with General Motors and I thought maybe I could get a deal.

I made out like a bandit. I went to the Pontiac dealership in Santa Monica to sign the papers. Later, the dealer called and asked, "Would you be interested in fleet sales?" So they trained me and I became fleet manager. I was proud of my reputation in the car business. I moved to a Buick dealership, then to Chevrolet. Nothing was doing in acting. With each successive dealership, I made more money. I dealt with people and learned a lot about the car business. I can read a window sticker and tell you to the penny what the dealer paid for that car.

No one in Hollywood wanted Jackie Cooper after World War II, so he went to New York and knocked on doors. He thought of entering another profession, but "didn't have credentials. I couldn't practice law, I wasn't a plumber, I didn't really know how to act."

John Forsythe and Eli Wallach encouraged him to study acting and slowly Jack built a respected name on stage and in television.

Jack and Gene Reynolds had worked together as teenagers. After the war, Gene acted, sold suits, was a casting director at NBC. As a lark, Jack asked Gene to play a small part in the pilot for his TV series *Hennessey.* Gene did; then, when *Hennessey* was sold, Jack asked Gene to sign on as an observer—for practically no money. When Gene was ready, Jack would let him direct some shows. "Jesus, I've got to have a steady job," Gene fretted.

"This series is going to be a hit," Jack assured him. "The fact that you've done some shows for us will launch you as a director."

Gene Reynolds is today perhaps the most successful (and respected) producer-writer-director in television, responsible for such series as *Room 222*, *Lou Grant*, and *M*A*S*H.*

Gene Reynolds made an impact on Bobs Watson, who remembers his friendship.

Before Bobs graduated from seminary in 1968, doctors diagnosed his father's lung cancer. They gave Coy Watson twenty-one days to live. Bobs watched his dad fade, wondering if he would die with the same faith he'd lived with. On the twenty-first day, Coy died, "pure right to the end."

Bobs was associate minister of the Magnolia Park Church. In the minister's absence, it fell to Bobs to conduct his father's funeral. "My Dad and I were as close as any two people could be and this was the greatest challenge I'd ever had. Remember, I was the crybaby of Hollywood. I cried at card tricks. I'm still emotional."

Bobs didn't cry. The five hundred people in the church smiled as he talked about the humor of his dad; and about how he wore plaid shirts with striped ties, blue socks with green pants; about how Coy Watson didn't get through sixth grade but had more common sense than anyone Bobs knew. Mrs. Watson died at eighty-four and is buried next to Coy. Bobs conducted her service, as well.

A few years ago, Bobs was divorced. To be separated from his three boys "was very hard." Other ministers and his brothers and sisters were not as supportive as Bobs hoped they would be. He took a leave of absence from the church. Bobs sought counseling during his medical leave because "that divorce struck at the base of my very being."

He needed a job. Another minister worked as a family counselor at a mortuary.

He introduced me to the headman, who hired me. For six months, I worked on the other side of funerals. Often, ministers deal with the bereaved for a few minutes at a mortuary, at the graveside, or in church. But to counsel a lady who has lived with her husband for forty-five years, and then to go back to the prep room and see her loved one laid out on a slab after an autopsy, with his insides out—it was extremely difficult. I quit.

I'd heard that Gene Reynolds was the producer of the *Lou Grant Show*, so I wrote to him: "Gene, it's been a long time since we've seen each other and I don't know many people in the business anymore. But you're one who may remember and may be able to do something for me. There's no obligation, no load of guilt I'm putting on you, but I'm divorcing now. I have to support my wife and my two kids during this time. I'm finding it difficult, having been in the ministry, to get work. I feel that I can still perform and if something comes up, I'd appreciate it."

Gene came through for me and I worked the show twice. He put me in the kind of role—one of the editors in the conference room—that could have been a running part. And he treated me very well.

Soon after that, I came back to the ministry. I would do anything in the world for Gene Reynolds.

Delmar Watson, Bobs's brother, is now a professional photographer. His photo studio is a handsome building on Hawthorne Avenue in Hollywood, a few blocks from the studios where the Watson family worked. Without thought of payment, Delmar gave me access to his files.

The television series *Man Against Crime* was filmed in New York in the 1950s. I worked on it. The program starred Ralph Bellamy, then president of Actors' Equity, the stage actors' union. I'd last seen Ralph on the set of *Disorderly Conduct* when I was five.

Explaining that actors ran the union, Ralph encouraged me to take an interest in Equity's affairs. Divorced, lonely, often unemployed, I filled my life with meetings, was elected to the board, helped overhaul the union's magazine, and, when its editor for thirty years retired, agreed to publish it until they found someone full time.

"Someone" turned out to be me. New purpose and a salary to go with it. No more standing in the unemployment line, going to the movies, or turning on the television set and seeing other actors play the roles I wanted.

I'd been offered jobs, but the way I had arranged my life, as an actor I couldn't win. When I did act, the act was agony, plagued by my secret inability to smile within a hundred miles of an important director. In stock in Myrtle Beach, South Carolina, where no chance existed that important roles would come my way, I smiled like a Christmas tree. It was only in New York or Hollywood that I sabotaged myself. Yet I needed work and wanted to play more than second fiddle. Catch-22. Equity represented liberation.

While there, I met my second wife, Elly. Our marriage lasted twenty years. I'd been single for five years, Elly longer. Steve, her son, was seven. Friends had arranged a party to bring us together. Afterward, we stood in the rain, flagged a cab. Silhouetted against the night was this gentle lady in a trench coat, with big doe eyes; elegant and slender, quiet, mouth set in a way that comes from meeting large responsibilities alone, with no help from anyone. Pride, humor, a dichotomy of shyness and sensuality.

After her divorce, she'd packed her child, left Iowa, and come to New York, a talented aspiring painter, drawn by the desire to live near the finest galleries and museums. She found a job, scrimped to send her son to private school.

We were married in 1959. The unconscious bargain struck by me, which neither of us knew, was: I'll care for you *if* you make things right for me.

I adopted Steve, imposed my value system, and infuriated the tigress who had raised her cub alone. Bad times during those early summers when both boys were with us.

Years of modest acquisition obscured our problems: I changed jobs, then started my own business. My pride approached omnipotence when Elly no longer had to work. A cottage at the beach, a small farm in New York State, eating in good restaurants. Not opulent, but nice.

I assembled a structure of dependence in which Elly took up residence. It fell on both of us. For me, an out-of-town affair that ran its course. Four years of separation; attempted reconciliations, hurts that wouldn't heal, back to analysis. Finally, we let go.

Shirley Temple married her second husband, Charles Black, on December 16, 1950, the year they met in Hawaii. Charlie was not a movie fan. He'd never seen Shirley on the screen, "*really* never seen me, and he didn't know much about me at all." Shirley flashed her well-remembered smile.

He asked, "Are you a starlet?" I have nothing against starlets, but I wasn't one. I said, "No, I'm not a starlet."

I think the reason we fell in love was that Charlie hadn't seen any of my films. He had no preconceived notions of who or what I was. He's nine years older than I am and was on a different track the whole time. His work is aquaculture, food from the sea, and training people how to harvest it.

Shirley, a grandmother, and Charlie have two grown children. She has an older daughter by her marriage to John Agar.

In 1954, Shirley got her interior decorator's license from the State of California. Her interest in decorating was born on movie sets. She decorated several homes and took a job in a small local shop. Her card read: "Shirley T. Black, Interior Designer." Many calls came in.

One of them sounded like a promising job. I was asked to go to a woman's home at ten A.M. I arrived on time with my color kit and tape measure. To my surprise, she had ten women sitting in the living room having coffee. She said, "Oh, here's Shirley Temple now. Would you like to have some coffee?" The women all clustered around.

I said, "May I first find out what you need?" She needed quite a bit of help, but all she wanted was to know what kind of curtain she should put over the kitchen sink. I suggested that she go to Sears or Macy's.

I had a cup of coffee, but they only wanted to ask me about movie stars.

Interested in politics, Shirley ran for Congress and lost. "It was a good learning experience, a wild race. There were eleven men and me. It would have made a good Deanna Durbin movie."

President Richard Nixon gave Shirley a "crash course in international relations" in 1969 by naming her a U.S. representative to the United Nations.

Winding up her UN duties, Shirley worked in Washington for the Council on Environmental Quality. In 1974, President Gerald Ford named her ambassador to the Republic of Ghana. "That was the best job I ever had," she says with pride.

"What did you do as an ambassador?" I wondered.

Your job is to represent not only the U.S. people but U.S. business interests and to help relate those interests to the Ghanaian interests.

Equally important is to explain to the host government American foreign policy, which wasn't always easy.

The third part of the job is to try to create a better climate in the host country for our presence, and because I've done a lot of volunteer work in the health field, I was able to get large quantities of medical supplies, including measles vaccine, to inoculate the children. Measles is a killer in developing countries.

We developed teams to work with Ghanaian doctors and nurses so they could go into the forest—never call it jungle—and teach people how to sterilize water and make use of available natural foods that are high in protein but that people historically don't eat.

Shirley worked twelve-hour days, then donned long dresses for the endless rounds of diplomatic functions. Those were "the hard part of the job."

When I left, they gave me a silver box inscribed: "Ambassador Shirley Temple Black, Accra, Ghana, July, 1976."

I went back to Washington to be chief of protocol for Ford, and held that job for six months, until Jimmy Carter fired me. I worked for him for a couple of months, even planned his inauguration.

After her divorce from David May, Ann Rutherford eventually married producer William Dozier. Having taken to the "lovely life" of movie stardom "like a duck to water," Ann happily retired to spend her full time with her daughter and stepdaughter—Dozier's child by Joan Fontaine. Because of Bill's position, Ann maintained contact with the film community and didn't miss acting.

A few years ago, Ann acceded to a producer friend's request and returned to MGM for a picture called *They Only Kill Their Masters.* Movie making had changed during the years Ann stayed at home.

In my day, the women had to be in makeup no later than six forty-five. By the time we had our hair shampooed and set and sat under the dryer —we all had long hair then—had our makeup put on, reported to the set, waited while they finished setting up, and rehearsed the scene, nobody exposed a foot of film before ten A.M. So at least we had a chance to wake up and have a glass of orange juice and look alert.

Before I started shooting *They Only Kill Their Masters,* I went back to MGM to sign my contract. I checked the shooting log, and said, "What's with wardrobe?"

The man said, "Wardrobe? It's been vacant for years." I remembered standing inside this teeming building, staring up through the winding banister at four floors of costumes from every picture MGM ever made. Now it was kaput. So I said, "Well, I better go over and check with the makeup department."

The man said, "There is no makeup department. You get made up on the set."

An alarm went off in my brain. "You mean one of those tacky dressing tables with lights around it, right out in public on the set?" He said, sure, it would just take a minute to make me up. "What about my hair?" I asked.

"The makeup woman has a curling iron. She'll do your hair. If you can get here at seven-thirty, you can start shooting at eight."

"All this in half an hour? I don't even dress to go to the supermarket in half an hour. I'll tell you what: I will arrive at seven-thirty already made up, with my hair done. If they don't like what they see, let them change it a little, but I am not permitting a total stranger to draw funny eyebrows on me and a mouth like a cupid's bow."

I think I retired in time. I don't know how women today survive in motion pictures. Imagine exposing film at eight o'clock in the morning! It's so tacky.

"I'll work until I'm twenty-one," Jane Withers told her parents. "Then I will stop. I want five children. I want to raise them myself. I want to do whatever I can to help them until they're on their own. I plan to go back to work again when I'm fifty. Then I want to write my children and let them know how much I appreciate the incredibly interesting life I've had."

Jane has five children. In 1947, she married Texas oil millionaire William Moss, bore him two sons and a daughter, and lived with him in Big Springs, Texas, until her divorce in 1954.

"It used to upset me because my first husband only wanted to entertain what I call 'name people.' I said to him, "Some of the people you'd like to invite I wouldn't have in my home."

Jane blamed herself because the marriage wasn't working, and in 1953, developed rheumatoid arthritis. Paralyzed, hospitalized for months, she told herself one day: "You don't have time to be ill! Get yourself together!" Three months later, Jane walked out of the hospital. Devoutly religious, she says grace before each meal.

In 1955, Jane married lawyer Kenneth Erriar (a former member of the Four Freshmen singing group) and produced another daughter and son. Kenneth died in a plane crash in 1968. Jane hasn't remarried.

Jane Powell and Elizabeth Taylor (bridesmaids at each other's first wedding) enjoy a birthday party for Jane's baby. Children are Sissy Steffen and Michael Wilding, Jr.

While Jane feels that she has seldom had a chance "to do what I know I'm capable of doing," offers to do TV and movie roles are, in the main, declined because she feels that "good, positive thoughts are lacking. In our day, people got their money's worth, and our films had happy endings."

Like Ann Rutherford and Jane Withers, Jane Powell was more interested in her family than in her career. Jane, the mother of two daughters and a son, loved being pregnant—even loved throwing up. "It made me feel so normal." She ironed her son's baby socks.

Jane has been divorced four times. She is "not proud of that." And she remembers, too, the marriage that never happened.

George Brent was forty-three, Jane was seventeen, when she played his daughter in *Luxury Liner.* She had "such a crush on him I couldn't stand it, and we laughed ourselves to death. I couldn't wait until the days he worked." They didn't see each other off the set or after the film ended.

Thirty years later, Jane toured in *South Pacific.* Three dozen long-stem roses and a note from George Brent were delivered to her dressing room in San Diego, near Brent's home.

Brent had emphysema and seldom left his house. Jane phoned. They talked frequently. Eventually, he agreed to travel to Los Angeles to see the show. "But," Brent emphasized, "I will not come backstage, because every time I have seen you, there have been others around and we never had a chance to talk. You were a little girl and your mother was always there. When I see you again, I want to see you alone." Jane agreed.

He came to a Sunday matinee. Everybody in the cast peeked through the curtain to catch a glimpse of him. He looked like an El Greco, thin face, white hair; he had a little goatee. Very slender, straight as a ramrod. He saw the show and left.

I dined with him the next day. He'd taken a suite at the Beverly Wilshire Hotel. I got all dressed up. I couldn't wait to see him, and obviously he felt the same way.

In *Luxury Liner,* leading man George Brent was the father of teenager Jane Powell. Thirty-three years later he proposed marriage to Jane.

He opened the door, put his finger to his lips, and said, "Shh." I thought somebody was sleeping in the room, but he led me to a couch and on it was a robe with his monogram. He lifted the robe; under it was a framed picture of us, laughing. I had autographed it to him years before. The glass was broken.

He said he had always loved me but could not pursue me because he was too old, that he had kept this picture with him always.

I went on tour again, but we talked often, and in every town I played, he sent me flowers. Because he was too thin, I sent him vitamins and got him to gain weight. He seemed so happy.

Around Christmas, I flew down to see him for the day. I went to his house and met his dog, a small, too-fat part German shepherd, really ugly, but so sweet. They lived by themselves. He loved that dog.

George had said, "We won't give Christmas presents." So we didn't, but I brought the dog a silver bowl.

Out of the blue, George asked me to marry him. He said we could live separate lives if I wished.

I said, "George, I can't do that." I loved George, but I wasn't *in* love with him. He was very upset.

Later, when I married my last husband, I called George. I didn't tell him about my marriage, but he'd read it in the paper. He was very angry with me. After that, he didn't want to talk to me. He lost fourteen pounds.

Then, three weeks later, *he* got married, to a lady in Hawaii he'd known for thirty years.

One day, I was going through my telephone book and I saw his name and thought: "I must call George." But I didn't. I wish I had. He died that night.

There was a glow of well-earned satisfaction on Mickey Rooney's face as he accepted a special Academy Award in 1982 for his lifelong contribution to the motion picture industry. Mickey, then the star of the smash Broadway hit *Sugar Babies,* had won television's Emmy Award and was an Oscar nominee for his work in *The Black Stallion.* His comeback was complete.

Quietly, modestly, Mickey expressed his gratitude to Hollywood, but recalled that although he had been its biggest star at fifteen, no one would give him a job at forty. In the interim, Mickey married many times, sired nine children, promoted resort hotels and hot dogs, and opened his mail order acting school, called ACT by Mickey Rooney. (ACT stands for Associated Creative Theatre. Its motto: Success is how you act.)

Despite the runaway success of *Sugar Babies*, it was "not the epitome" of what Mickey wants to do on Broadway. He wants to remind people that "Mickey Rooney is a tragedian as well as a comedian." He wants to play Little Caesar. "It's a dynamite idea." Mickey described the final scene of the play he has in mind.

> Instead of dying in the alley, we'll electrocute him on stage. Rico [Little Caesar] goes completely bananas before he dies. He leaves, and just before the curtain, as the houselights dim three times, this guy is describing Rico's death. He says, "I hope to God I never have to see anything like that again."
>
> Then the other guy lights a cigarette and says, "Fuck him."

Spanky (they call him George in the business world) McFarland, executive of a furniture buying company in Dallas, lives near Fort Worth with Doris, his wife since 1955. Their large yard—a small farm, actually—is shared by goats, some ducks, chickens, four dogs, five cats, a peacock, and a guinea hen. Spanky's mother, eighty, lives nearby. So do his three grown children.

The McFarland home boasts mementos of Spanky's role as leader of "Our Gang": the hat he wore, scrapbooks, photos on the wall.

Every year, on the first weekend in May, George travels to Marion, Indiana, for its Celebrity Golf Classic. He is honorary chairman. Proceeds go to the local boys' club. He shoots in the eighties. George makes other appearances and says his life is "richer than three feet up a bull's ass."

Organization of a celebrity fishing tournament is next on his agenda. I'm invited and I'll go.

After making her fifty-fifth picture, *Guilty of Treason*, in 1949, Bonita Granville stopped acting. Two years before, she had married young oil millionaire–producer Jack Wrather, and she wanted to rear a family. The mother of a son and a daughter, Bunny, a grandmother, is an officer of the Wrather Corporation, actively participating in its worldwide business interests. One of these was the TV series *Lassie*, for which Bunny served as executive producer.

Close friends include Nancy and Ronald Reagan, with whom the Wrathers have a long association. Jack was a member of President Reagan's "Kitchen Cabinet."

Dad retired at sixty-eight (not sixty-five—he'd lied about his age), and he and Mother sold their duplex and moved to Laguna's Leisure World.

One day, Mother called my sister Pat and told her that she and Dad were going to be cremated. Dad hated the idea, she said, because he always wanted to be buried in his family's plot in Canada. But Mother wasn't going to let Dad leave her alone in California, so she made arrangements with the Hollywood Cemetery, where many stars are buried, to buy a niche for both of them next to where Rudolph Valentino's ashes are. Mother was elated and Dad finally conceded that they had gotten a bargain.

When Mother and Dad celebrated their fiftieth wedding anniversary, my sister and her husband, Jack (who met Pat when she was six), gave a party for them. Guests included Aunty Jo, Aunt Ruth, and Dr. Godshall.

"Isn't this a lovely party?" Mother said cutting the cake. "What did I ever do to deserve this?"

"Nothing, dear." Pat smiled.

Sipping bourbon, Dad confessed that he was not born in Bordeaux, France. I asked why he had lied for fifty years. "Because if the bank knew I was born in the West Indies, they'd think I was a Negro and fire me."

Business often took me to Los Angeles. I'd drive down to see Mother and Dad, and we always stocked the larder.

"I don't know why your sister can't be here. She's not very considerate." Dad took a canned ham from the supermarket shelf and placed it in the shopping cart.

"She's working, Dad. Besides, you saw her yesterday. She can't spend every day with you. She has a family and a job."

"Not very attentive to your mother!" Dad turned up another aisle, pushing the loaded shopping cart.

"Pat's *very* attentive to Mother. She takes her shopping, buys her clothes, has you over for dinner every week."

"Not last week! Last week they were in Mexico!"

"You know, Dad"—I felt my irritation grow—"you're a very selfish man. You think of no one but yourself. You never have!" Oh, God, I thought, that's done it: Dead for sure! In dread, I awaited Dad's reaction.

"The hell with that!" Dad grabbed a jar of macadamia nuts. "You never invite me to New York! I want to come to New York! I want to go fishing!"

The man is indestructible! I need not have waited fifty years to tell him how I felt. He doesn't care! He never did!

"Come to New York if you want to. I'll meet the plane. But people don't go there to fish."

"Well, we'll see." Dad put a fruitcake in his basket. "I don't feel up to traveling."

As Dad and I unloaded the groceries, Mother carefully folded the paper bags and insisted that I take them home. She offered me a piece of candy, a magazine, an ashtray, lunch. Suddenly, she asked, "What time is it?"

"It's early, darling, two o'clock. We'd better wind your watch."

"What watch?"

"Remember where you got it, Mother? Remember Barbara Stanwyck?"

"I think so. What does she do?"

The last time Dad (now ninety-three) and I visited Mother in the nursing home, she didn't know us. Happily she exclaimed, as she squeezed our hands in welcome, "You know, I've lost my mind. It was the only way I could get rid of it."

The reuniting of Natalie Wood and Robert Wagner was a storybook romance. Married young; divorced from each other for ten years; both married to other people, then to each other for a second time—it resembled the plot of a Noel Coward play. The tale of how she and R.J. were reconciled delighted Natalie, who told it to me.

Even though R.J. and I were divorced, I had stayed close to his parents and his sister, and he had done the same with my parents and my older sister. We exchanged letters and occasionally we'd bump into each other.

We were both invited to a party when I was pregnant with Natasha, and were seated next to each other. We spent the whole evening together and reminisced about our love for our boat and the sea. Neither of us had owned a boat since our marriage, but we both spent a great deal of time on chartered boats.

We recalled all the good things, but it never occurred to us that we would get back together. It was just a bittersweet interlude. Each of us realized that we were married to other people. Actually, R.J. was separated, but nobody knew that.

When we said goodbye, he asked me, "Are you happy?" and I asked him if he was. He answered indirectly by saying he was happy that I was pregnant, because he knew how much I wanted a baby.

I came home from the party and I cried and thought about him, and he did the same.

A year or so later, my marriage broke up and it was in the newspapers. He called and said he was sorry and that he understood what an unhappy time it was for me. He asked if there was anything he could do. I assumed he was just being friendly. He's very thoughtful and it was the kind of thing he would do, without romantic motives.

But then he called often, and I thought maybe he did feel something besides friendship. He asked if I was dating someone important to me and

I said, "No, no, there's nobody." Then I said, "I understand you're seriously dating someone—how is that going?"

"Oh, no," he said, "that's nothing!"

That was it. We lived together for six months before we got married again.

Reunited, Natalie and R.J. acquired a yacht, a possession dear to both of them. They could not know that the sea they loved so well would shortly claim Natalie's life.

13. Fade Out

Another trip to Hollywood. Dean Stockwell's interview completed, I drove my rented car toward the hotel, up Melrose past Fairfax High School—the sweeping lawn is now a parking lot—past Genesee Avenue. On impulse, I drove around the block, stopping across the street from 721 North Genesee: where we lived when Pat was born; when I got scarlet fever; when we built the Fifth Street house. On the lot where Iris Herndon and I collected caterpillars, a commercial building stands.

I crossed the street and rang the bell. No answer. Tentatively I walked up the driveway to the backyard.

A ghost of its former self, its fecund days long gone, the old apricot tree bravely, wearily lifted its tarred, truncated arms. No trace of the treehouse where Stymie and I played.

A curtain moved. Would police come and haul me off? I rang the back doorbell. Minutes passed. I rang again. A frail old man peered through the glass. Slowly, the door opened. My words gushed forth:

"I'm sorry to be standing in your yard, but I rang the bell and no one answered and I'm visiting from New York and I lived in this house when I was five years old and was driving by and wanted to stop and see if the old apricot tree was still in the backyard. . . ." He stared. "We sold this house almost fifty years ago. I haven't seen it since. . . ." Long pause. "My name is Moore, Dick Moore. . . . I'm . . . from New York. . . ."

At last, he spoke: "Are you Dickie Moore's father?"

"No, I'm Dickie Moore."

Silence. A polite stare. Wonderment? Finally, "Would you like to come in?"

The vast living room, where Rags chased the cat; my room, where I lay ill with scarlet fever and Dad held a pillow over my head during an earthquake, in case the ceiling fell; the dining room, where we heard the radio announce that Roosevelt beat Hoover; the bathroom, where the boat—the gift from Marlene Dietrich—sank. This colosseum of my childhood was now a postage stamp. Was it always this small? They'd added another room. No wonder.

"When you are little, things look very big," Jane Powell told me the night we met, the night she and Roddy and I had dinner, drank some wine, and talked about the "Rosebuds" I was looking for.

One, I found, was that most of us tried unconsciously to stay the way we were, because that's what people wanted us to do. Most of us never completely outgrew the unique, highly public childhood that we shared.

When Darryl Hickman first went into therapy, his doctor asked him when Darryl thought he had reached his maximum potential. Without thinking, Darryl said, "Seven." Then, appalled, he clutched at the word in a vain, belated effort to retract it. "My God," he wondered, "is it all downhill from seven?"

One night, Darryl told me, he watched a television talk show with his ex-wife Pam. Richard Burton was a guest. Elizabeth Taylor, married to Burton at the time, joined him on camera and Darryl noticed that "she used her body in a certain way." He said to Pam, "Don't think about it—just tell me how old that woman is?"

"Eleven," Pam said immediately, and Darryl agreed. "That beautiful lady was absolutely, in a strange way, *National Velvet*, pre-puberty eleven."

Darryl raised a finger, pointing at me. "You're stopped too, and so am I. I hear it in our voices. They are not fully developed, resonant voices. They haven't been brought forward in time. Listen to Jane Withers's voice. The mental, spiritual Jane is a thousand years old, but Jane is a 'gee-whiz' fifteen. Her spiritual insight is incredible, but part of Jane is stopped at 'gee-whiz.'

"Take Roddy," Darryl went on. "He's still trying to be the dutiful son to a lot of famous people who are images of what he tries to live up to. Yet he is way beyond most of them.

"The problem is that all of us played roles. Dean Stockwell, for instance, didn't do what was natural to him. He did what he thought he was supposed to do.

"When we were children, Elizabeth Taylor was not clever in a calculating way. She didn't think out what was good for her career. Other people did that for her. When she was fifteen, she was the most beautiful young woman that ever existed, but her career determined who she should be with, who she should marry, who she should do this and that with. That manipulation distorted and fucked up her natural development." Darryl's voice grew intense.

"It's the same with Peggy Ann and me. The feelings that were starting to develop between us at fourteen were healthy. But for her mother, they got connected with whether I was good for her career."

Gene Reynolds agrees that we all had trouble growing up. I asked him why. He conjured up the memory of being driven to work in the morning as a child, feeling the kind of apprehension a man of forty would feel when he's on the Long Island Railroad to

New York City, preparing to convince a meeting of the board that his next project is feasible. Every time he went on an interview, or every six months at option time, he felt "this big sense of responsibility."

Gene spoke precisely, weighing his words. "This business of premature responsibility makes later responsibility distasteful. People said to us, 'It's wonderful to be a child actor. You grow up fast, and that's a big advantage over other kids. You become an adult earlier than most.' As though this strengthened us. It did not. Actually, it weakened us, because those adult experiences which normally are welcome at the *right* time of your development become burdensome and loathsome if encountered too early. That's why often we don't mature, or why we have a harder time maturing than others.

"Also, we were always at the other end of a teeter-totter. We were not working with peers but with directors, teachers, executives, agents, parents. As children, we were always the slaves. All these people had this goddamn age and experience over us and a certain ruthlessness that children do not have."

Diana Cary, now a settled wife and mother, feels that she experienced real childhood for the first time through watching her son playing in his sandbox. "That's what I should have been doing as a child—meeting little problems geared to my age. He was on top of his environment, and I never was. Watching Mark at play was a truly healing experience for me," Diana recalled.

Diana took Mark to visit her parents when he was nine months old. Her father, then on his deathbed, said, "Look at that kid's eyes. He's a natural."

Diana's mother came out of the kitchen. "That's right. Peg, you should put him on television. Think of the money, the residuals. Why, he could have a college education!"

"I can't do that!" Diana almost screamed.

"You're crazy," her mother countered. "Just because you don't like acting, for some dumb reason, are you going to deny your son all the advantages you had?"

My sister Pat has a daughter, Kathy. When she was six, my mother encouraged her to be an actress. Kathy didn't want to.

"But you would make a lot of money to give to your mother," Mother told her.

"Grandma, if I made a lot of money I would keep it for myself," Kathy said. Mother, aghast, reported to us that Kathy was "very mercenary." As the years passed, Mother never doubted the validity of her perception. "Rosebud."

Will the child star era ever return? I asked Roddy McDowall. He believes that the child star era resulted from a social need, as trends in entertainment always have. Gloria Swanson, for instance, epitomized a certain sort of luxury in society. Her career was killed not by talking pictures—she managed that transition well—but by the Great Depression, the very thing that made film stars out of Marie Dressler, Will Rogers, and Shirley Temple. There was a social need for homey, simple people at that time.

Most ex–child stars agree that the era as we knew it will never return, even though there will always be children in pictures. "The kids may talk dirty," Donald O'Connor said, smiling, "but there'll always be kid pictures."

Maybe. But never real, long-lasting movie stars. "I don't think that a child is going to come along that can hold a picture together," Jack Coogan declared.

There's more to it than that. Television does not furnish lasting, lifelong recognition. Kathleen Nolan's theory is that television audiences feel less loyalty toward their stars because they live with the illusion that television is free. TV viewers control the environment in which they see their entertainment. They can turn the actors on or off. They are larger than the people they are watching.

In movies, the audience pays to be admitted and sits without distraction, conforming to the rules of those who run the theater; and the viewer is smaller than the actors (even children) on the screen.

Margaret O'Brien, wife, mother, and, occasionally, actress, is glad she no longer has to rely on acting to earn a living. "Pretty soon after a child star's TV series ends, you don't know who he or she is. But you always know us, even if we don't work anymore. Studios built up names we'll never lose. That's the difference between Hollywood today and Hollywood then."

Gary Coleman is a huge success, but there is no studio behind him. Tatum O'Neal, an authentic star, has had a minimum of output because there is no studio system to expose the stable, indeed no stable to expose. Now it takes so long to conceive and create a movie project that by the time a child finishes three films, the child has grown up. In 1941, when Roddy McDowall made *How Green Was My Valley,* he appeared in five successive films in that same year. Over forty of my pictures were released between 1931 and 1935 (not including the "Our Gang" comedies).

In a short span of time, Gene Reynolds played Don Ameche as a boy in *Sins of Man;* Tyrone Power as a boy in *In Old Chicago;* James Stewart in *Of Human Hearts;* Robert Taylor in *The Crowd Roars;* John Beal in *Madame X;* Ricardo Cortez in *The Californian.* Gene feels that had there been no Shirley Temple, the child star phenomenon would probably not have evolved as it did. This has always been a business that follows trends. Gene agrees that the child star era will never come again. It was an age of naiveté.

"Audiences had no idea," Gene said, "of what the children were being put through. The business was very exploitative, which was kind of denied by everybody."

The use of child actors persists today, in different forms. Director Jackie Cooper sees it firsthand in the circle of "not well known but very well paid kids in commercials. Ricky Schroder was making $300,000 a year before they found him for *The Champ.* Franco Zeffirelli had no idea this kid was making so much. He thought he had discovered somebody."

One agent (without a New York office) makes $200,000 a year just handling children for commercials. "These are kids nobody ever heard of," Jack told me. "But they're suffering through all the same problems that we did: They get taken out of school, stick out like sore thumbs in their neighborhoods, and very few are having their money saved for them."

Was there a common denominator, I asked Jack, in terms of family history or attitude that impelled our parents to seek that life for us? "Money," he answered. "The Depression. Wasn't your family poor?" A "Rosebud."

As a director, Jack Cooper hates to work with kids. Gene Reynolds tries hard to take pressure off the child, to make the child feel loved, to make the work a game.

Gene hated the recent remake of *The Champ*, which he felt was "old-fashioned and ridiculous." But watching it, Gene was detached. "I kept counting how many times they were cranking up that kid to cry, because in the master shot he'd be crying. Then I'd see the over-the-shoulder shot and he'd be crying. Then I'd see a close-up and he'd be crying. And I know how long it takes to go from setup to setup. So this kid had to stop crying, dry up, and then start again. The poor kid never stopped crying."

Although the era of the child star may not be seen again, the "child star problem will continue as long as there is entertainment," Diana Cary says, "because when you put a small child on the tube, even eating cornflakes, he's in a strange environment, with different responsibilities. He has a responsibility to his parents, to the producer, the director, to the rest of the cast. He is out of context with his normal time and place. Some children are exceptional and can cope. We did. We were asked to stimulate feelings we'd never experienced: what it's like to drown, to see your house on fire, to see your parents dead. A child's emotions are not equipped to handle that. Something has to give. It's like a hernia. It doesn't show at first. You don't go lame. You don't go blind. But years later, down the road, it shows up."

George (Spanky) McFarland briefly pondered my question about "Rosebuds": "Everybody's story more or less has the same grain running through it. The studios took advantage of the ignorance of the parents. The parents took advantage of the children. But I am glad that I had the experience, regardless of whether it was good or bad—even if there was no money. I am proud to say, 'Look what I did at one time,' even though I don't remember nine-tenths of it."

Some remember their early lives with pleasure. Bobs Watson considered that "working in films was a beautiful, revered occupation. I enjoyed all aspects of it. But," Bob feels, "there is a price to be paid, because the publicity that builds you up also leaves you stranded. Then what do you do? What happens to your ego? Unless you have someone who loves you and will help you to get through it, you've got a serious problem."

Sybil Jason, who loved her life as a child star, doesn't understand why some of us felt bitterness. That bitterness, I think, stems as much from aching for a life that's gone as from reacting to a life that was.

Sybil has formed a club for ex–child stars. She calls it The Survivors. "Do you think there is a jinx on ex–child stars trying to make a comeback?" Sybil asked me.

Of course there is. One almost never equals one's first impact. "You can't," reflected Roddy McDowall, "unless you arrive a decade later at something that appeals to a whole new generation."

"Many people strive for a lifetime to achieve something," Gloria Jean stated. "I have already achieved. I go through the old trunks of souvenirs in my garage. Hours pass. My sisters and my mother come out and we look at these fantastic things, and I think, 'Gloria, you made it.' "

At the cosmetics company, Redken Laboratories, where Gloria

has worked for years as spokesperson and chief receptionist, Roddy was shooting on location. On discovering each other, he and Gloria hugged and posed for pictures.

"Roddy, how good it is to see you," Gloria greeted him. "How I miss the industry."

Rod lit into her: "Gloria, listen to an old-timer. Kiss the ground that you're not in the business."

"Why?" she asked, bewildered.

"Because you have to deal with such rejection. There's so much bitterness. Look at me. I'm an old man," Roddy joked.

"Roddy, you look fantastic."

"I don't mean my outward appearance. . . . But you have a good life here. Acting is such a hard, hard row to hoe."

Ann Rutherford recommends the experience to anybody. "But you have to know when to quit."

One day, Ann got off early from the studio. Her daughter, Gloria, was four and Ann told the nurse, "I'll take her this afternoon." But Gloria was playing with the nurse and didn't want to go with Ann. Ann sat on the stairs and asked herself, "What am I doing, letting a strange woman raise my daughter?" So she quit acting.

Then, when Gloria was nine, she came home from school one day, depressed. "What's your problem?" Ann asked.

"Everybody in my room's somebody, and I'm nobody," Gloria told her mother.

"What are you talking about?" Ann asked.

"Tish's mother is Ann Sothern. She's on television." Gloria reeled off the names of others who were "somebody."

"I used to be a somebody," Ann said.

"You never were," her daughter admonished her.

"Yes I was," Ann insisted.

She started doing quiz shows. Her daughter "became a midget Mrs. Temple," Ann reported. "I'd come home and this little thing in her nightgown would be sitting on the stairs with her arms folded and she'd say, 'Don't you ever wear that blouse again. You looked like you were in the bathtub. The camera just got your shoulders. I'm very embarrassed.' " Still, Ann recalled, her appearing on those TV quiz shows enabled Gloria to hold her head up in school. She was somebody again.

Toward the end of an interview taped recently for radio, Edith Fellows was asked, "If you had to do it all over again, would you do it?"

Edith asked if she could revise the script a bit. No, the interviewer answered, nothing could be changed. Edith wanted to shout "No!" but murmured, "Yes, I guess so." The words were out and Edith was so angry with herself she couldn't sleep that night. Given a choice, Edith would not relive her life up to the present. But the script is not complete. Edith wants to see the ending before she edits herself out of it.

"I think being a child in show business is one of the most delightful things that can happen to a youngster," Mickey Rooney exclaimed.

Darryl Hickman, teacher, author, actor, producer, and director, thinks that being a child actor "is an abnormal thing to have to struggle with. I don't see how it can be healthy."

Natalie Wood didn't think the work was difficult. Rather, she thought it "wonderful because it is creative and can be helpful even as a growing process. The constant attention is what is so difficult. People say, 'Come here, do this, do that, let me take your picture, get up early, go on this tour, go out with that person, don't go there, do that, wear that dress.' That's where all the confusion sets in.

"If there were no publicity and acting was your only job, I don't think anybody would get into very much emotional trouble."

Natalie continued: "That's why I feel sorry for Brooke Shields. Not because she is acting—great, if she's enjoying it—but because of all this other superfocus, not on work but on the superficial aspects—the trappings. The stress of a relentless career where she's being photographed every day, playing the sex symbol, doing commercials, posing for the cover of *Vogue*—being so visible, such a *star!* That's difficult."

If someone asked Natalie for her advice on becoming an actor, I inquired, what would she say? "I would ask, 'What about it is going to give you pleasure? The trappings? Stardom? The money? Clothes? The billing or to see your picture in the newspaper? If so, forget it! It'll be a disaster. You'll get into horrible emotional trouble because you can't get any nourishment out of that end. But if you want to act, fine. You endure the trappings in order to be able to enjoy the creative experience."

When parents approach producer Gene Reynolds for advice, he tells them, "Keep the kid in school. Keep him in a natural environment. Get off his back." Gene strongly suggests postponing the professional experience. "Let him go to college for four years; there's plenty of time." Still, if Gene had a child who "really wanted to act, who really enjoyed it, who was struck with that terrible notion," he would try to be a source of encouragement.

One of the big problems with child actors, Gene believes, "aside from being born into the wrong family, is that for every child that succeeds, hundreds don't But those hundreds are still the products of and living with these driven parents. They are still their victims." Gene thinks that "people who push their kids like that are a little crazy."

My son, Kevin, in his thirties, is a banker in Atlanta. Occasionally, he flirted with the idea of acting as a sideline, but I haven't been much help. When I suggested that if he was really serious he ought to study acting, the subject died. My stepson, Steve, is a musician, an ambition developed on his own, and at which he works obsessively. It's not an easy life.

History can't be renegotiated. It's not your fault if you're handed a bad script. It is your fault if you live your whole life never doing anything about it.

Bonita Granville Wrather had told me that our perceptions of the past, our feelings about having been child stars, are necessarily colored by what has become of us since then. Surely that is true.

What, then, does Bunny feel? Bunny, who started later than most of us, who saved her money, got a decent education, and achieved professional success and recognition—and even was nominated for an Academy Award: not a "special" child's Oscar, but a big one, for her work in a specific film. Bunny, who quit acting voluntarily, who married well and only once; who today enjoys a life envied even by those who now own the studios we worked for; who flies to England to shoot grouse, and enjoys the close friendship of the President of the United States.

Far from being a pawn in someone else's game, Bunny moves the pieces on life's chessboard. Would Bunny, then, uncover an unexpected "Rosebud," give me an added insight unperceived by others of us?

I asked my final question. Bunny repeated it aloud, as if to lock it in her mind: "What would I say to parents who have aspirations for their children as actors? As little as possible."

One night not long ago, I sat in Sardi's in New York with Jane Powell, Donald O'Connor, and Donald's wife, Gloria. People stopped to chat with Donald and Jane, expressing admiration, colored at times with a tinge of envy. How wonderful to be them, to be recognized, to have headwaiters thrilled whenever you arrive, their attitude suggested.

What no one knew was that Donald and Jane were comparing notes about how insecure they often felt. I thought: "Thank God, it's not just me."

Donald had recently entertained at the White House. He was

one of the last acts on the bill, and his rehearsal was scheduled late. When it ended, the refreshments were all gone. Then, by the time Donald appeared after his performance, the receiving line to meet the President and Mrs. Reagan had already passed by and guests were heading out the door to their cars. Donald stood at loose ends as the First Lady sailed toward the stairs leading to their living quarters, with the President striding determinedly behind her. Donald backed quickly out of the way.

Gloria O'Connor is not a pushy lady, but on impulse, she rushed up to President Reagan and grabbed his arm.

"Don't you want to say hello to Donald, President Reagan?" she said urgently.

"What . . . who?" President Reagan looked distracted.

"You didn't get to say hello to Donald." Gloria pulled the President toward him, whereupon the President called to Nancy and they greeted Donald warmly, thanking him for his appearance.

"I don't ordinarily do that, and I wouldn't have if I'd had time to think about it, but it just made me mad," Gloria explained. "Donald's always in the background. We don't know how to push."

"I know just how you feel." Jane nodded sympathetically. "All my life, I've felt like a fly on the wall. Like I never belonged, even at MGM when they told me I was a big star. One day in the commissary, Clark Gable came over to my table to say hello and I was so frightened I forgot his name."

Jane continued: "I always felt I had to explain why I was driving my car through the studio gate. Every day I would say to the guard, 'They told me I can drive through. Is that okay?' "

"When I was at Universal, making millions of dollars for the studio—the Elvis Presley of my day—the guards at the gate never knew who I was." Donald emptied a packet of Sweet'n Low into his iced tea. "I still won't go backstage to visit friends if they're in a show," he said. "I'll meet them someplace afterward. Stage doormen never know me. I feel like a process server."

I recalled an incident that happened when Jane and I saw Elizabeth Taylor perform on Broadway the year before. We had a pair of Elizabeth's house seats and found ourselves seated next to Natalie and R.J. Wagner. Elizabeth expected us, so we all went backstage together after the performance.

During the conversation, Natalie turned to me and whispered, "Isn't it wonderful that Elizabeth let us in her dressing room! When R.J. and I visited Marsha Mason backstage in Los Angeles, we had to wait in the hall."

Silence for several seconds.

"The last time we went to an opening night party," Gloria recalled, "the TV cameras were there, along with the press. Someone was interviewing Donald on TV, when right in the middle of his answer to a question, the TV camera and the lights suddenly turned away and focused on Richard Burton, who had just walked in. Suddenly, Donald was in the dark and talking to the air. They didn't even wait to hear his answer."

"That's such a terrible feeling," Jane said. "You don't know what to do, you don't know where to look. It's so embarrassing, being out there and suddenly you're all alone. There's always someone more important."

As Jane, Donald, and Gloria talked, I had an overwhelming urge to cry. Life on the fast track is the seven o'clock news. When you're the topic of discussion, no one else exists. But when another story breaks, you might as well be dead.

And it doesn't have a thing to do with you.

Why did I want to cry? Was it the pressure of unbearable, still buried feelings, feelings of being nobody now because I was somebody once? Was it a montage from the past, of cameras, people, lights, a buzzing noise all focusing on me, the center of attention; so important, so indispensable, until the director yells, "Cut!" and I am whisked into a blackout while someone else moves into camera range?

Even on the set when two or three years old, I must somehow have been aware that this shattering contrast between darkness and spotlights was unnatural. But you can't handle such emotions at so early an age. So, belatedly, I found myself fighting back the tears.

We emerged from Sardi's and several people asked Jane and Donald for their autographs. One person asked for mine. We got into the waiting limousine.

INDEX

Academy Awards, 77–78, 273
ACT (Associated Creative Theatre), 274
Actors Studio, 173
Adler, Larry, 231
Agar, Charles, 266
Ameche, Don, 19, 142, 284
Anchors Aweigh, 216
"Andy Hardy" series, 63, 125, 218, 219, 239
Angeli, Pier, 245
Angels with Dirty Faces, 220
Any Number Can Play, 169
Arkansas Traveler, The, 150
Arzner, Dorothy, 145
Astaire, Fred, 240
Autry, Gene, 176–178

Babes in Toyland, 71
"Baby Burlesk" short subjects, 19, 62
Baby LeRoy, 8, 151–152
Baby Lillian, 23
Baby Peggy, *see* Cary, Diana
Baby Peggy Corporation, 200, 201
Baby Rose Marie, 231
Bainter, Fay, 150
Bankhead, Tallulah, 213, 214, 215
Bank of America, 203, 204
Barrymore, John, 1, 4
Barrymore, Lionel, 77, 151, 160–161
Bartholomew, Freddie, 73, 84, 96, 120, 121, 122, 133
Bartley, Lillian, 86–87, 136–137, 216, 243
Barton, Charlie, 86
Bautzer, Greg, 258
Beal, John, 284
Beatty, Warren, 228
Beery, Noah, 156
Beery, Noah, Jr., 156
Beery, Wallace, 92, 151, 154–157, 159
Bellamy, Ralph, 9, 161
Beloved Rogue, The, 4
Benny, Jack, 123
Berlin, Irving, 175
Bernstein, Arthur L., 193, 194, 195–198, 200
Beverly Hills Hotel, 122
Big Little Books, 102
Birth of a Nation, 192
Black, Charles, 266
Black, Shirley Temple, *see* Temple, Shirley
Black Fox Military Academy, 128

Index

Black Stallion, The, 273
Blondell, Joan, 172
Blonde Venus, 138, 139
Blue Bird, The, 89–91, 118
Bogart, Humphrey, 62, 110–111, 167–169
Booth, Edwin, 48
Boys Town, 70, 72, 73, 95, 131, 161, 218
Boy with the Green Hair, The, 85, 115
Brando, Marlon, 245
Brennan, Walter, 147, 148
Brent, George, 271–273
Bride Wore Red, The, 145–147
Bright Eyes, 9–12, 61, 75, 87–89
British Equity, 103
Broadway Gondolier, 220
Brown, Bonnie, 124
Brown, Clarence, 171
Brown, Kenyon Foster, 262
Brown Derby, 125
Buckwheat, 86
Bullock's Wilshire, 35
Burns, Bob, 150–151
Burns, Lillian, 93, 242
Burns and Allen, 258
John Burroughs Junior High School, 130, 134
Burton, Richard, 262, 281, 292
Bus Stop, 199, 262
Butler, David, 11, 39, 88

Cagney, James, 7, 8
Californian, The, 284
Camelot, 262
Camp Sibert, Ala., 247, 250
Canterville Ghost, The, 69, 70
Cantor, Eddie, 258
Capra, Frank, 171
Captain Blood, 160
Carillo, Leo, 122, 215–216
Carmen, Jr., 114
Carolina Pines, 102, 103
Carter, Jimmy, 268
Carter, Mrs., 54, 127, 131
Cary, Diana (Baby Peggy), 67, 92–93, 105–106, 108, 110, 111–113, 114, 126, 130, 200–201, 202, 216, 217, 223–224, 227, 260, 282, 285
Cathay Circle Grammar School, 130
Central Casting, 11, 15
Champ, The, 46, 182, 284, 285
Chaney, Lon, 176
Chaplin, Charlie, 23–25, 167, 175–176, 195
Chase, Charlie, 15
Chiang Kai-shek, 23, 251
Children's Casting Directory, 12
Children's Hour, The (Hellman), 78
child stars:
- adolescence of, 59, 237–253
- adult stars and, 138–184
- ambition of, 67–68, 77–78, 84–85, 282, 285
- in armed forces, 247–253
- childhood friends of, 79–84, 95, 217
- contract vs. free-lance, 58, 108, 131, 133, 178, 198, 203, 208
- crying on cue by, 39, 53, 68–74, 172
- in Depression, 28, 185–186, 202, 283, 285
- directors and, 76, 171–174
- early romances of, 210–226
- earnings of, 5, 185–209
- education of, 124, 127–137, 204–205
- exploitation of, 111–115, 192–209, 282–293
- families of, 22–23, 27–39, 192–209, 242–244, 275–277, 289
- isolation of, 82–84, 113–115, 217
- later careers of, 254–278
- lies about age of, 105–108
- lines memorized by, 74–77
- marriages of, 226–229
- maturing of, 44, 46, 115–116, 227–229, 237–253, 280–283
- merchandising of, 192–193, 200–201, 206, 252
- mothers of, 19, 42, 43, 45–46, 47, 49, 74–76, 92–94
- parties given by, 40–41, 117–127
- as part of bygone era, 283–293
- personal appearances by, 203, 204, 230–237
- psychotherapy needed by, 226, 228, 257–261, 280
- "rosebuds" about, 85, 279–293
- scene-stealing by, 90–91, 154, 175–176
- screen personalities of, 61, 239–241, 246
- sexual ignorance of, 210–229, 237–238
- siblings of, 39–40
- in vaudeville, 23, 47, 192, 206, 230–231, 234
- work schedule of, 37–38, 58, 61–63, 106–108, 115, 124
- *see also individual child stars*

Cleopatra, 205, 262
Clift, Montgomery, 261–262
Cobb, Irvin S., 150, 151
Cochran, Steve, 170–171
Cohn, Harry, 178–179
Colbert, Claudette, 61, 137, 174, 179
Coleman, Gary, 284
Collins, Cora Sue, 15, 120–122, 133–134, 161, 167, 177, 217, 224, 227
Columbia Pictures, 47, 86, 137
Comet Over Broadway, 175

commercials, television, 284–285
Compulsion, 262
Coogan, Jack, Sr., 23, 25, 153, 156, 170, 193–194, 236
Coogan, Jackie, 8, 11, 51, 63, 91, 95, 133, 144, 152–153, 155, 156, 159, 178–179, 223–224, 236, 250–251, 283
  Chaplin and, 23–25, 167, 175–176, 195
  fame and stardom of, 23–25, 67, 82–83, 126, 192–193, 202, 206, 235
  lost fortune of, 25–27, 192–199
Coogan, Lillian, 194, 195–198
"Coogan Law," 198–200
Jackie Coogan Productions, Inc., 193, 200
Coolidge, Calvin, 235
Cooper, Gary, 147, 148, 149, 157, 247, 255
Cooper, Jackie, 46–48, 68, 71, 73, 76, 85, 95, 96, 108, 115, 122, 133, 154, 155, 172, 182–183, 206–207, 223, 250, 263, 284–285
Cooper, John, 47–48
Copacabana, 170–171
Cortez, Ricardo, 284
Cousins, Ralph P., 250
Crawford, Joan, 145–147, 167, 170, 241
Crosby, Bing, 12, 151, 163–166, 203
Crowd Roars, The, 284
Curtiz, Michael, 171

Dante's Inferno, 162–163
Darnell, Linda, 255
Daughter of Rosie O'Grady, The, 258
David Copperfield, 84, 103
Davies, Marion, 32
Davis, Joan, 258
Davis, Sammy, Jr., 237
Dawn, Jack, 110
Day, Doris, 39
Dead End, 221
"Dead End Kids," 123, 220
Dean, James, 20, 240, 244–247
Death of a Salesman, 46
DeBorba, Dorothy, 56
Dee, Frances, 19
DeHaven, Gloria, 255
De Havilland, Olivia, 160
De Mille, Cecil B., 143–144, 151
Devil Is Driving, The, 6
"Dickie Moore's Women," 213
Dieterle, William, 142–143, 169
Dietrich, Marlene, 138–140, 141, 213, 215, 255, 280
"Dietrich's New Romance Has Hollywood Agog," 215
Dillinger, John, 233
Disorderly Conduct, 161
Dispatch from Reuters, 142–143
Doctor's Dilemma, The, 262
Douglas, Melvyn, 137, 179
Dozier, William, 268
Dressler, Marie, 283
Dunn, Jimmie, 172
Durbin, Deanna, 63, 73, 78, 98–99, 227, 241, 267
Durkin, Junior, 194

East of Eden, 244
Eddy, Mary Baker, 31
Edwards, Cliff, 126–127
Eisenhower, Dwight D., 234
Erriar, Kenneth, 269
Eve of St. Mark, 247
Expert, The, 53–54, 74

Fairfax High School, 130, 247
Fargo, Ray, 28, 186
Farina, 86
Farmer Takes a Wife, The, 169
Farrow, John, 38–39
Fay, Alfred, 33, 187
Fay, Frank, 145
Fellows, Edith, 12–15, 61, 86–87, 100, 123, 126–127, 136–137, 152, 164–166, 176, 178, 179, 203–204, 215–216, 221, 224, 243, 256, 257–258, 288
Fenneman, George, 171
Ferber, Edna, 144–145
Fields, Freddie, 257
Fields, Ron, 153
Fields, W. C., 8, 151–154, 155, 192
film industry:
  exploitation in, 111–115, 192–209, 282–293
  make-believe vs. reality in, 59–61, 218
Fink, Hymie, 117, 118, 119, 120, 124, 125, 136, 210
Five Little Peppers, 12
Fletcher, Jack, 249
Flynn, Errol, 151, 157–160
Fonda, Henry, 84, 160, 167, 169
Fontaine, Joan, 268
Ford, Gerald R., 267, 268
Ford, John, 171
Forsythe, John, 263
Foy, Brian, 6
Francis, Kay, 134, 168, 175
"Francis" series, 241
Free Wheeling, 18, 55

Gable, Clark, 167, 169–170, 216, 291
Gallant Lady, 102
Garbo, Greta, 15, 167, 174–175

Gardner, Ava, 110, 229
Garland, Judy, 96, 106, 109–110, 122, 134, 223, 227, 239–241, 260
Garner, Peggy Ann, 24, 44–46, 63, 78, 131–133, 172, 199, 217, 218–220, 221–222, 224, 243, 256, 262–263, 281
Gentleman's Agreement, 85
George, Uncle, 32, 33
Germain, George, 189
GE Theatre, 245
Giant, 246
Gish, Dorothy, 190–192, 202
Gish, Lillian, 190–192, 202, 229
Gladys, Aunt, 33
Goddess, The, 242
Godshall, Leon, 103, 104, 254, 275
Goldwyn, Sam, 193, 246
Good Fairy, The, 92
Grable, Betty, 172, 195, 196, 197, 224, 250
Grainley, Mrs., 128
Grant, Cary, 138
Granville, Bonita, 15, 16, 70, 78, 134, 160, 208, 220, 223, 274–275, 290
Grapes of Wrath, The, 84, 171
Grauman, Sid, 23
Grauman's Chinese Theater, 23
Gray, Norman, 249
Grayson, Kathryn, 216–217
Great O'Malley, The, 62
Great Ziegfeld, The, 15
Green, Mitzi, 231
Griffin, Merv, 44
Griffith, D. W., 192
Guess Who's Coming to Dinner?, 162
Guilty of Treason, 274
Gwenn, Edmund, 60

Haley, Alex, 10–11
Hallelujah!, 17
Hamman, Alphonse, 211
Hamman, Joan, 211–213
Handle with Care, 11
Happy Land, 19, 21
Harding, Ann, 15, 16, 102
Harlow, Jean, 216
Hauptmann, Bruno Richard, 233
Haver, June, 255
Hawks, Howard, 147
Hayes, Richard, 262
Hearst, William Randolph, 254
Heaven Can Wait, 142
Heidi, 91
Hellman, Lillian, 78, 226
Henderson, Skitch, 127
Henderson School of Dance, 14
Henie, Sonja, 204
Hennessey, 263
Henry, Charlotte, 75
Hepburn, Katharine, 84, 162
Her First Beau, 86
Herndon, Iris, 79–80, 215, 279
Hickman, Darryl, 84–85, 94, 96, 120, 122, 135, 156, 167, 169–170, 179–180, 217–218, 219, 221–222, 260, 280–281, 288
Hill, Howard, 160
Holiday in Mexico, 96, 97
Hollywood, *see* film industry
Hollywood Canteen, 253
Hollywood Cemetery, 275
Hollywood Professional School, 136–137
Hollywood Reporter, 6
Holy Terror, The, 177
Hoover, J. Edgar, 233–234
Hopper, De Wolf, 184
Hopper, Hedda, 90, 183, 184
Horne, Lois, 134
Horner, Bob, 194
How Green Was My Valley, 40, 96, 284
Huckleberry Finn, 12
Hudson, Rochelle, 93
Hudson, Rock, 246
Hulett, Wendell, 249
Human Side, The, 75
Huston, Walter, 8, 107

If I Had My Way, 163–164
Imitation of Life, 15
In Love with Life, 15
"In My Arms," 21
In Name Only, 44
In Old Chicago, 71, 73, 284

Jane Eyre, 12, 44
Jarman, Claude, Jr., 136
Jason, Sybil, 62, 63, 90–91, 109, 110–111, 113, 125, 133, 169, 171, 175, 199–200, 220–221, 224, 253, 286
Jean, Gloria, 63, 96, 106, 131, 153, 155, 163–164, 167, 202–203, 213, 216, 221, 222, 235–237, 286–287
Jim Jeffrey's Barn, 122
Jo, Aunt, 101, 103, 104, 189, 212, 275
Johnson, Erskine, 211
Jolson, Al, 150
Jones, Marcia Mae, 61, 70, 76, 77, 120, 121, 122, 202, 214, 226–227, 235, 258–259
Jordan, Bobby, 123, 221, 243
Journey for Margaret, 109
Junior Miss, 44, 199, 217

Kahanamoku, Duke, 83
Kazan, Elia, 46, 172–174, 244, 245

Keats, Patricia, 215
Keeper of the Flame, 84
Kelly, Gene, 49
Keys of the Kingdom, The, 44
Kid, The, 23–25
Kid from Borneo, The, 57
Killer Shark, 40
Kim, 85, 157–160
Kipling, Rudyard, 157
Kiss and Tell, 84
Kitty, Aunt, 224, 225
Koverman, Ida, 183
Kruger, Otto, 102

La Cava, Gregory, 179
Lake, Arthur, 32, 230
Lake, Edie, 32, 189, 254
Landau, Arthur, 197
Lang, Walter, 90
Lasky, Bill, 148
Lasky, Jesse, 148
Lassie, 275
Laughton, Charles, 69, 70
Laurel, Stan, 17
Laurel and Hardy, 17
Lawford, Peter, 218–220
Lear, Norman, 11
Leave Her to Heaven, 84, 219
Lesser, Sol, 126
Lewis, Jerry, 237
Liberty, 187
Life, 262
Lifebuoy soap, 150
Life of Emile Zola, The, 77
Lindbergh, Charles A., 233
Little Big Shot, 220
Little Miss Roughneck, 216
Little Princess, The, 90
Little Rascals, *see* "Our Gang" comedies
Little Red Schoolhouse, 134–136
"loanout," 55
Loeb & Loeb, 30
Lombard, Carole, 44
Looney Tunes, 11
Los Angeles City College, 255
Los Angeles Herald, 254
Lou Grant, 263
Louise, Anita, 93
Lubitsch, Ernst, 141–142
Ludden, Allen, 247
Lukas, Paul, 158
Lux Radio Theatre, 144
Luxury Liner, 271, 272

McCrea, Chuck, 248
McCrea, Joel, 123, 156, 220
McDonald, Mary, 135, 136
McDowall, Roddy, 20, 40–42, 44, 68, 85, 95–96, 97, 98, 133, 204–205, 242, 256, 261–262, 280, 281, 283, 284, 286, 287
McDowall, Tom, 40
McDowall, Virginia, 40, 41–42
McDowall, Winifriede, 40, 41, 42
Macfadden Publications, 187
McGuire, Dorothy, 172
MacRae, Gordon, 39
Madame X, 284
Magnolia Park Church, 263
Maher, Peter, 49
Main, Marjorie, 174, 175
Malibu Lodge, 115
Man Against Crime, 265
Man Hunt, 40
Mannequin, 61
Man's Castle, A, 165
March, Frederic, 226
Marco Juvenile Revue, 94
Marin, Edwin, 211
Marinka, 164–166, 257
Marshall, Herbert, 138
Marx, Groucho, 167, 170–171
Mascot, 106
*M*A*S*H,* 263
Mason, Marsha, 292
May, David, 268
Mayer, Louis B., 26, 93, 125, 126, 133–134, 178, 182–183, 197, 208
Meek, Donald, 165
Meet Me in St. Louis, 206
Meglin Kiddies, 19
Menjou, Adolphe, 32, 74, 75, 188
Men of Boys Town, 85, 161, 162
MGM, 40, 55, 84, 85, 93–94, 96, 108, 110, 124, 125, 131, 134–136, 145, 182, 183, 184, 204, 206, 218, 235, 238, 241, 242, 268, 291
"Mickey McGuire" series, 19
Miller, Arthur, 46
Miller, Sidney, 61, 72, 122, 123, 161–162, 175, 241, 250
Miracle on 34th Street, 60, 235
Miss Annie Rooney, 63–64, 65, 89, 210–211
Mitchell, Cameron, 46
Mitchum, Robert, 255
Modern Screen, 117, 253
Monogram, 19
Monroe, Marilyn, 216
Moore, Dickie (John Richard, Jr.):
  adolescence of, 241–242
  in armed forces, 247–250
  childhood friends of, 79–82
  decline in career of, 84, 85, 101–105, 118, 292–293

Moore *(cont.)*
directors who worked with, 138–144
early romances of, 210–215
earnings of, 185–190
education of, 127–130, 134, 204
fame and stardom of, 1–9, 27–38, 51–59, 84, 101–105, 213–215
female stars who worked with, 138–141, 144–147
as journalist, 249, 254, 255
later acting career of, 238, 245, 254–257, 265
male stars who worked with, 147–151
marriages of, 224–226, 265–266
in "Our Gang" comedies, 17, 18, 54–55, 127–128
parents of, 27–39, 80–82, 94, 101–105, 127–128, 185–190, 231–232, 275–277
personal appearances by, 230–234
photographs of, 2, 7, 36, 52, 56, 65, 75, 81, 129, 139, 146, 149, 165, 168, 214
scarlet fever contracted by, 84, 85, 103–105, 280
shyness of, 5–6, 10, 123–124
in television shows, 238, 245, 256–257, 265
Temple kissed by, 63–64, 65, 89, 210–211
Moore, Elly (second wife), 265–266
Moore, John (father), 27–31, 36, 82, 102–103, 186, 275–277
Moore, Kevin (son), 226, 289
Moore, Nora (mother), 28, 29, 30, 32, 36, 40, 53, 231–232, 275–277, 283
Moore, Pat (first wife), 224–226, 255
Moore, Patricia (sister), 34–35, 36, 38–39, 103, 104, 187, 189, 275, 283
Moore, Steve (stepson), 265, 266, 289
Moorhouse, Frank, 102
Morris, William, 200
Moss, William, 269
Motion Picture Academy Players Directory, 215
Mr. Smith Goes to Washington, 171
Muni, Paul, 8, 77, 142
Mussolini, Benito, 235
My Bill, 134, 168

National Velvet, 15, 238, 281
"Nature Boy," 115
Nelson, Gene, 241
Newsweek, 196
New York Times, 201
Nixon, Marian, 7
Nixon, Richard M., 267
Nob Hill, 199
Nolan, Kathleen, 23, 131, 132, 283
North Star, The, 246
No Time for Sergeants, 262

Oakie, Jack, 151
O'Brien, Margaret, 69, 70, 76, 78, 93, 96, 109, 124, 126, 134, 136, 154–156, 161, 175, 206, 224, 235, 244, 284
O'Brien, Pat, 8
O'Connor, Donald, 12, 99, 122, 123, 175, 216, 221, 222, 250, 283, 293
career as viewed by, 59–61, 113, 124, 241, 259–260
fame and stardom of, 98, 290–291, 292
family of, 23, 48–50, 208–209, 239
O'Connor, Gloria, 50, 290, 291, 292
O'Connor, Gwen, 48
Of Human Hearts, 284
Old-Fashioned Way, The, 153
Oliver Twist, 51–53, 123, 176, 189
On Borrowed Time, 76, 77, 160
O'Neal, Tatum, 284
O'Sullivan, Maureen, 38
"Our Gang" comedies, 8, 15–17, 18–19, 46, 54–55, 56, 57, 81, 85–86, 106, 111, 127–128, 129, 143, 180–181, 185, 274, 284
Out of the Past, 255

Paramount, 55, 153
Parker, Jean, 151
Parsons, Louella, 90, 183–184
Pasternak, Joe, 237, 242
Paul, Vaughn, 98
Pennies from Heaven, 12, 164, 165, 203
"Pennsylvania Polka," 216
Pete ("Our Gang" dog), 55, 56
Photoplay, 117, 241, 253
Pichel, Irving, 21, 53, 174
Pius XI, Pope, 235
Players, The, 48
"poverty row" pictures, 111
Powell, Dick, 220–221, 237
Powell, Jane, 22, 42–44, 67, 85, 96–98, 124, 125, 133, 134, 135, 136, 148, 156, 182, 184, 204, 205, 224, 234, 240, 241, 261, 270, 271–273, 280, 290, 291, 292, 293
Power, Tyrone, 284
Proctor's Stock Company, 190
Ptomaine Tommy's, 102–103

Queen Christina, 15, 177
Quigley, Juanita, 15, 98, 133, 206, 238

Rank, J. Arthur, 209
Ray, Leah, 218
Ray, Nicholas, 172–173

Reagan, Nancy, 275, 291
Reagan, Ronald, 220, 275, 291
Real McCoys, The, 148
Rebecca of Sunnybrook Farm, 67
Rebel Without a Cause, 173, 240, 244, 246
Redken Laboratories, 286–287
Republic Pictures, 176–178
Reynolds, Gene, 71–73, 118, 120, 122, 130, 161, 171, 218, 250, 260, 263, 281–282, 284, 285
Rin Tin Tin, 83
RKO, 255
Roach, Hal, 14, 18–19, 54, 143, 160, 180–181, 207, 252
Hal Roach Studios, 15, 17, 18, 33, 55, 56, 85, 127–128
Robinson, Bill, 64, 67, 235
Robinson, Edward G., 142, 160
Rocamora, Wynn, 242
Rogers, Will, 283
Room 222, 263
Rooney, Mickey, 19, 23, 61, 68, 78, 96, 108, 122, 123, 229, 250, 288
  in "Andy Hardy" series, 63, 125, 218, 219, 319
  personality of, 85, 94, 134, 239
  stardom of, 72, 73, 94–95, 107, 160, 218, 253, 273–274
Roosevelt, Eleanor, 235
Roosevelt, Franklin D., 27, 112, 150, 189, 233, 235, 251, 280
Roosevelt, Theodore, 190
Rossi, Alfred, 80
Rostova, Mira, 262
Royal Wedding, 240
Ruth, Aunt, 3–4, 101, 189, 275
Rutherford, Ann, 19–20, 21, 92, 96, 106–108, 110, 124–125, 160, 208, 218, 219, 235, 239, 255, 268–269, 271, 287–288
Ryan, Peggy, 49, 64, 123, 250

Sale, Chic, 53–54
Salmi, Albert, 262
Sammy's Steak House, 186–187
Santa Anita Racetrack, 207
Sawtelle Veterans Hospital, 254–255
Schary, Dore, 182
Schenck, Joseph, 3
Schildkraut, Joseph, 77
Schlesinger theaters, 209
Schoonover, Gloria Jean, *see* Jean, Gloria
Schroder, Ricky, 284
Screen Actors Guild, 39, 131
Screen Gems, 47
Secret Garden, 96
Seeger, Pete, 249
Sennett, Mack, 71
Mack Sennett studio, 72
Sergeant York, 147–148, 149
She Married Her Boss, 137, 179
Sheridan, Ann, 62
Shields, Brooke, 288–289
Shirley Temple's Storybook, 238
Shreves, Art, 195
Silver Screen, 213, 215
Singin' in the Rain, 49
Sins of Man, 284
Skelton, Red, 123, 178–179
Skippy, 46
Skulnik, Menasha, 257
Small Town Deb, 106
Smiling Through, 161
Smith, John, 245
So Big, 144–145, 146
"Soldiers in Greasepaint," 249
Something in the Wind, 99
So Red the Rose, 7
Sothern, Ann, 287
South Pacific, 271
Spanky McFarland, 8, 54, 55, 56, 57, 86, 109, 127, 129, 131, 180–181, 251–252, 274, 285–286
Special Services, 247–249
Spirit of Culver, 71–73
Splendor in the Grass, 173, 228
Squaw Man, The, 143–144
Stanley, Arnold, 248
Stanley, Kim, 242
Stanwyck, Barbara, 8, 9, 144–145, 146, 213, 215, 276
Star Overnight, 38
Stars and Stripes, 249
Steffen, Geary, 204
Steffen, Sissy, 270
Stevens, George, 246–247
Stewart, James, 107, 284
Stockwell, Dean, 85, 96, 115, 134, 136, 157–160, 216–217, 238, 252, 262
Story of Louis Pasteur, The, 142
Stymie (Matthew Beard), 8, 15–19, 54, 55, 56, 57, 81, 82, 110, 113–115, 127, 129, 160, 180, 185, 279
Sugar Babies, 273, 274
Sullavan, Margaret, 7, 92, 93
Sullivan, Betty, 243
Sullivan, Ed, 243
Survivors, The, 286
Swanson, Gloria, 283

Tamblyn, Rusty, 136
Taurog, Norman, 73, 95

Taylor, Elizabeth, 22, 40, 96, 98, 108, 134, 135, 136, 182, 221, 238, 246, 262, 270, 281, 292
Taylor, Robert, 284
Tea for Two, 39
Teagarden, Jack, Jr., 248
Technicolor, 141–142
Tempest, The, 262
Temple, George, 28–29
Temple, Gertrude, 19, 35, 67, 84, 87, 91, 94, 118, 179
Temple, Shirley, 12, 108, 133, 179, 220
  fame and stardom of, 8, 19, 28–29, 62, 63–67, 74–76, 78, 83–84, 87–91, 118–120, 206, 233, 255, 283, 284
  later careers of, 115–116, 238, 266–268
  marriages of, 227, 266–267
  Moore's kissing of, 63–64, 65, 89, 210–211
  Withers as rival of, 9, 61, 75, 87–89, 120, 180
That Certain Age, 98
There's No Business Like Show Business, 175
These Three, 15, 70, 78
They Only Kill Their Masters, 268–269
39th Special Service Company, 247–249
Thomas, Frankie, 72
Thornhill, Claude, 250
Thrifty Drug Store, 37
Tierney, Gene, 142, 219
Time, 67, 196–197
Tomorrow Is Forever, 174
Tom Sawyer, 130
Tone, Franchot, 145–147
Tracy, Spencer, 9, 70, 73, 84, 151, 161–163, 165
Treasure Island, 46
Tree Grows in Brooklyn, A, 24, 44, 63, 78, 172, 199
Trotti, Lamar, 69
True Story, 187
Tufts, Sonny, 23, 250
Tuna Clipper, 40
Turpin, Ben, 8, 151
TV Guide, 256
20th Century-Fox, 41, 87, 89–90, 118–119, 120, 176–178, 199, 220, 242, 246, 248, 253
Two Sailors and a Girl, 241

Uncle Willie, 257
Under-Pup, The, 213
United Artists, 6
Universal, 49, 63, 98–99, 129, 209, 222, 235, 237, 241, 291
University High, 131–133

Valentino, Rudolph, 275
Vallee, Rudy, 46
Van Ettisch, William, 254
Variety, 6
Violinski, Sully, 195
von Sternberg, Josef, 138–140, 141

Wagner, Robert, 20, 207, 228, 261, 277–278, 292
Wallach, Eli, 263
Wallis, Hal, 55–58
Wallis, Minna, 55–58
Warner, Jack, 173, 175, 200
Warner Brothers, 58, 62, 110, 134, 142, 168, 186, 199
Watson, Bobs, 70, 71, 72, 76, 77, 84, 91–92, 95, 121, 123, 142, 143, 156–157, 162, 188, 263–264, 286
Watson, Coy, 70, 71, 72, 76, 91–92, 108–109, 156–157, 263–264
Watson, Delmar, 71, 72, 91, 108–109, 123, 171, 264–265
Welles, Orson, 174
West, Mrs., 129, 144, 151–152, 153
West India and Panama Telegraph Company, 29
Westlake School for Girls, 89
Westward Passage, 15, 16
Whiting, Barbara, 220, 262
Wilde, Cornel, 219
Wilding, Michael, Jr., 270
Willard, Jess, 193
Wilson, Carey, 125
Wilson, Lois, 87
Winchell, Walter, 196
Winner Take All, 7
Withering Heights (Withers residence), 206
Withers, Jane, 85, 167, 169, 176–178, 224, 246–247, 281
  fame and stardom of, 86–87, 154, 162–163, 269–271
  family of, 68, 100, 205–206, 269–271
  as independent-minded child, 68, 69, 94, 106, 113
  parties given by, 10, 48, 120–124
  Temple as rival of, 9, 61, 75, 87–89, 120, 180
Wizard of Oz, The, 106
Women's Army Corps, 248
Wood, Lana, 39–40, 235
Wood, Natalie, 19–22, 39–40, 59, 60, 67–68, 73–74, 77, 96, 109, 124, 130–131, 133, 174, 207, 235, 238, 240, 244–246, 261, 277–278, 288–289, 292

Wrather, Jack, 208, 275
Wrather Corporation, 275
Wyler, William, 70
Wyman, Jane, 220
Wyoming, 92, 156–157, 175

Yates, Herbert, 176
Yearling, The, 40
Young, Loretta, 160, 161
Young, Robert, 69
Young People, 120
Your Hit Parade, 257
Yule, Joe, 95

Zanuck, Darryl F., 23, 89–90, 172, 178, 179–180, 248
Zeffirelli, Franco, 284

PHOTO CREDITS

The Eric Benson Collection, New York: 24 (bottom), 69 (top and bottom), 159 (bottom), 177 (bottom) and 272.

Larry Edmonds, Hollywood: 240 (bottom).

Gene Feldman and Suzette Winter, Wombat Productions, New York: 13, 24 (top), 60, 75 (bottom), 129 (top and bottom), 155 (top and bottom), 159 (top), 165 (bottom), 236 (top and bottom).

Marvin Parge's Motion Picture and TV Research Service, Los Angeles: 16, 62 (top), 65 (bottom), 72 (top and bottom), 107, 132, 177 (top), 181, 191, 214 (top), 219 (top and bottom) and 222.

Delmar Watson Photography, Los Angeles: 121.